LOST'S

BURIED TREASURES

3RD EDITION

THE UNOFFICIAL GUIDE TO EVERYTHING
LOST FANS NEED TO KNOW

LYNNETTE PORTER & DAVID LAVERY

D0034367

Published by Sourcebooks, Inc.
P.O. Box 4410, Naperville, Illinois 60567-4410
(630) 961-3900
Fax: (630) 961-2168
www.sourcebooks.com

Library of Congress Cataloging-in-Publication data

Porter, Lynnette R.
  Lost's buried treasures: the unofficial guide to everything Lost fans need to know / Lynnette Porter and David Lavery
      p. cm.
  Includes bibliographical references and index.
  1. Lost (Television program) I. Lavery, David
Title.
  PN1992.77.L67P66 2010
  791.45'72—dc22
                            2009042090

Printed and bound in the United States of America.
VP 10 9 8 7 6 5 4 3 2 1

ACKNOWLEDGMENTS

We both want to thank Hillary Robson for her earlier contributions to this book. We are also in the debt to those who contributed individual entries to "*Lost* Reading and Viewing": Tyler Hall, Lisa Williams, David Gill, Sarah Bryant, Janice Lupo, Sean O'Sullivan, Caty Chapman, and Sarah Caitlin Lavery. Thanks, too, to Uwe Stender for his continuing guidance and, at Sourcebooks, Peter Lynch, our excellent and supportive editor.

—David and Lynnette

Thanks to my friends in Hawaii who "found" me and taught me about aloha spirit. Leilani, Malia, Pat, Jean, Jill, and Maile—thank you for sharing your insights and being such excellent tour guides during the past few years! Thank you, too, to everyone in Tol Andûne for your friendship and support.

A special thanks to Ed Kos and Kos Hummer Tours' guides for their photographic assistance in the preparation of this edition. Thank you, too, for an enjoyable locations tour.

As always, my thanks to David, a good friend and gracious collaborator. Deepest thanks to my Constants, Bart, Nancy, and Heather.

—Lynnette Porter

Thanks, of course, to Lynnette, a most excellent friend and collaborator. I am indebted as well to all those students who have listened to me go on about *Lost*, especially those in my Spring 2009 graduate course on *Lost*.

Most of all I want to express my gratitude to my amazing family, Sarah, Rachel, and Joyce, all of whom watch *Lost* avidly (wish we could visit the Island together more often). When my life "flashes before my eyes," it is their achievements I see.

—David Lavery

Contents

Is There an (Ancestor) Text on This Island?
Books in the Narrative: *Are You There God? It's Me,
Margaret* | *Bad Twin* | The Bible | Book of Law | *A Brief
History of Time* | *The Brothers Karamazov* | *Carrie* | *Catch-22* |
Everything That Rises Must Converge | *The Fountainhead* |
The Gunslinger | *The Invention of Morel* | *Lancelot* | *Laughter
in the Dark* | "An Occurrence at Owl Creek Bridge" | *Our
Mutual Friend* | *A Separate Reality* | *The Third Policeman* |
The Turn of the Screw | *Ulysses* | *VALIS* | *Watership Down* |
A Wrinkle in Time | *Y: The Last Man*
Ancestor Texts: *Alice in Wonderland* | "The Damned Thing"
| *Gilgamesh* | *The Little Prince* | *Lord of the Flies* | *Moby-Dick*
| *The Mysterious Island* | *The Odyssey* | *Of Mice and Men* | "A
Psychological Shipwreck" | *Robinson Crusoe* | *Solaris* | *The Stand*
| *Stranger in a Strange Land* | *Walden Two*
Must-See TV and Essential Movies: *The Adventures of Brisco
County, Jr.* | *Alias* | *Back to the Future* | *Buffy the Vampire Slayer,
Angel, Firefly* | *Cast Away* | *Crossing Jordan* | Disaster Movies
| *Fantasy Island* | *Forbidden Planet* | *Fringe* | *Gilligan's Island* |
Jurassic Park | *Lost Horizon* | *Nash Bridges* | *The Prisoner* | *Star

A Note About Documentation

All the documentation for this book, the endnotes, the bibliography, and the filmography, are available at http://davidlavery.net/LBT.

INTRODUCTION

Flash to summer 2004. I eagerly anticipate the debut of a new show, *Lost*. After reports surfaced in March about a polar bear on Oahu, I surf the net every day to find out more about the pilot episode. Unfortunately, I'm not in an area that receives a "surprise" broadcast of the pilot late at night, but I read all about the sightings.

Flash to summer 2009. I eagerly anticipate the arrival of *Lost*'s Season Six, even if it also heralds the series' impending death. Like many of its characters, however, *Lost* likely will turn up in surprising ways and have a post-death life longer than anything I might envision. I surf the net every day to find out more about plot threads and casting rumors. Unfortunately, I'm not going to be at Comic-Con to hear the latest, but I read all about the panels and theories.

Flash to September 22, 2004. Sitting in my New Orleans hotel room, I hide out from other attendees at a popular culture conference so that I can watch the first episode of *Lost*. By the time Charlie utters that prophetic line, "Guys, where are we?" I'm as much an addict as the has-been rocker. When I sheepishly confess to my friends what I was doing instead of having dinner, several admit they were doing the same. We begin a discussion that lasts for many years.

Flash to June 2005. In Burbank, California, *Lost* fans gather for an official convention. Not only do actors Emilie DeRavin (Claire), Jorge Garcia (Hurley), John Terry (Christian Shephard), Mira Furlan (Rousseau), William Mapother (Ethan), and Daniel Roebuck (Arzt) mingle with fans, but Damon Lindelof, Bryan Burk, Michael Giacchino, and Javier Grillo-Marxuach answer lots of questions about how the series is made and what is in store for Season Two. It's very cool, and, as fans would come to appreciate over the years, the actors and creative team behind the cameras are just as interested as we are in where the story is going and how it can surprise us.

Flash to January 2009. Back in Hawaii, I enjoy a KOS Hummer Tour of the Kualoa Ranch, where many of *Lost's* scenes have been filmed during the past five years. This is my third trip to Oahu in as many years; like hundreds of other tourists each year, I look forward to getting *Lost*, but I'm still surprised how many locations I immediately recognize from episodes. A few weeks later I watch the episode "Jughead," noting that Ellie and I have trod the same path past that landmark framework where the bomb was precariously perched.

Flash to January 2011. Back in Hawaii for a *Lost* convention, I join colleagues discussing the series' lasting contribution to television. Once more I visit Papa'iloa Beach (castaways' camp) and the Kualoa Ranch. Like the 2007 castaways hearing the echoes of the 1977 DHARMA Initiative, I know what happened here, to them and me. I'm *Lost* in memories.

Flash to January 2031. At a Los Angeles retrospective of groundbreaking series in TV history, the *LOST* title sequence again floats eerily across the screen. Most people there have never seen black-and-white TV, or even TV as we knew it back in '04, so the harsh opening is a bit of a shock. They sit mesmerized as Jack Shephard once again opens his eyes to a whole new way of serialized storytelling.

Farfetched? Not really. Just as *Lost's* Season Five presented adventures in time and space, the series also has leaped around the ratings and global popularity, likely landing at some future fond and critically exalted place in TV history. *Lost* has flashed back and forward between the highs of its early success to the depths of Nikki's and Paolo's graves, from their (and our) past lives and into an unknown future. By summer 2010, *Lost* will be over, but I doubt it will ever be "finished." We've had to fasten our seatbelts for more than one bumpy ride, but the journey has well been worth the plane crashes, exploding freighters, and nosebleeds. Six years of being *Lost* in an intriguing, innovative story is time well spent.

While filming a documentary about *Lost* and its fandom, Los Angeles-Catchphrase Entertainment's Dean Shull noted "The fans have helped this show to be like no other. The ways we interact with the show have been groundbreaking and the passion can be seen in the frustration and celebration after each show, especially if you peek into the world of *Lost* Internet postings and podcasts."[1] *Lost* fans are intelligent, vocal critics who help change the face of network television by forcing television producers and network executives to look at the many ways people "watch television" online, via mobile phones, on DVD, and during weekly TV broadcasts. They interact with other fans and the creative talent behind *Lost*, and they spend valuable time dissecting the series and putting it back together in personally meaningful ways.

My coauthor and I are long-time *Lost* fans. Individually and together, we have spoken at conferences and taught classes about what *Lost* means and how and why its popularity says a lot about television and fandom; academics, fans at public presentations, students learning more about television, and the media capturing the *Lost* phenomenon are among those seriously studying *Lost* and recognizing it as more than just a fad. We expect that trend to continue far beyond May 2010's series' finale.

Lost fandom is large and inclusive; fans come from diverse backgrounds and have different reasons for watching the series, but they are united in their continuing interest. They revel in their ownership of the series and its fandom. They often like insider information (but sometimes protest the ways spoilers are leaked, as occurred in May 2007 when details of the "snake in the mailbox" ending to Season Three somehow wriggled onto fan sites; a similar problem occurred in May 2008 when Lostfan108 struck again with detailed information about the Season Four finale, dubbed "Frozen Donkey Wheel" by series' creators/writers Damon Lindelof and Carlton Cuse). Fans share just about everything they know about the show, debate it, and want to know more. They gather to watch episodes and immediately post online their kudos and criticisms of each episode. They develop websites—a June 2009 search of "*Lost* fan sites" pulls more than 102 million English-language sites dealing with the series, including videos, reviews, actor or character sites, blogs, and wikis. Fans buy *Lost* merchandise and become immersed in ARGs that unravel clues to international conspiracies. This isn't your parents' fandom—*Lost* creates a global community whose diverse members express their interest in hundreds of different ways but are linked by their interest in and evaluation of the series.

What do *Lost* fans need to know *beyond* the facts of the series to enhance their viewing pleasure? Which songs, books, TV programs, movies, or even places should be understood and, we hope, (re)visited and enjoyed to attain even greater ownership of their series? That's where this book comes in—a guide to the buried treasure only glimpsed in episodes, the gems just waiting to be picked up and admired. New fans needing to catch up with the best of *Lost* or long-time fans looking for more ways to "get *Lost*" can find where to go and what to read, watch, or listen to as part of the complete *Lost* experience. Keeping track of the Island, its many part-time or permanent residents, its statuesque landmarks and security devices across space and time often requires more than a pendulum or coordinates for the next available window for a visit. In the following chapters, we highlight past characters and mysteries that continue to haunt us and unravel Jacob's carefully woven pasts and the futures of those who first boarded Oceanic 815 and Ajira 316, as well as the many Others who find themselves cast away on the mysterious island.

*Lost*lore is steeped in published works, and during the first five seasons, the creative staff and characters lead us into the world of literary masterpieces, some well-known, some more obscure. The first chapter, *Lost* Reading and Viewing, leads us into the *Lost* library to uncover literary clues to the Island's mysteries. Like any good popular culture icon, *Lost* offers much more than the traditional library; after all, the Hatch enticed us not only with its bookshelf but an eclectic collection of videos and vinyl, and the DHARMA Initiative left a musical and photographic legacy that can't be purged. "Must-See" TV and Movies brings us up to date on the essentials from television and film history.

Music deserves special attention, and the *Lost* Playlist features the greatest hits of Geronimo Jackson and DriveShaft, hits from the past forty years, as well as a guide to composer Michael Giacchino's soundtrack for the series.

"Sawyerisms" have become a mainstay on the Island and in TV culture, and Between the Lines: *Lost* and Popular Culture not only lists what Sawyer/LaFleur says but discusses our favorite con man's knowledge of television, film, and literature. What makes *Lost* an important part of our popular culture? This chapter also explains how being *Lost* has changed the nature of television and become part of global culture.

Season Six has jokingly been anticipated as the "Zombie Season" because so many dead, formerly dead, possibly shapeshifted, or otherwise "undead" have been unearthed. We offer a scorecard for who's currently "undead," who's likely to return during Season Six, and who may finally be laid to rest by the end of the story. Chapter Four explores the living and the living dead and the reason why we (and *Lost*'s writers) just can't let go of our favorite characters.

A tropical island, even a surprisingly well-populated, creepy, deadly one, reminds us that we might someday want to be *Lost* on Oahu. After all, if Rose and Bernard can happily retire there, why shouldn't we? The Significance of Place offers a global triptik to places important to characters, and a special section at the end of the chapter highlights where fans might go to relive their favorite *Lost* moments.

Season Six presents the daunting final challenge of completing the story in a satisfying way while keeping us on the edge of our seats until the final credits roll. Although Season Five's episodes answer lots of questions, from "Where is Vincent?" to "Who or what is Smoky?" to "What does Jacob look like?" the series' creators and writers still have a lot of explaining to do.

Behind the Scenes provides a Who's Who of the talented individuals in front of and behind the cameras. Finally, a series of new Top Ten lists provides checklists of the best of the best—what every fan should read, watch, listen to, or do for the definitive *Lost* experience. We also added a list of the episodes that, at least in hindsight, are "missable," with plot points or characters who should've been detonated long before the Incident.

Once again, for this edition, we've revised each chapter to provide insights and investigations into each episode through the Season Five finale and analyzed fan speculation leading into Season Six. *Lost* offers us a wealth of treasures, but we have to dig into the story to find them. In the following pages, we go treasure hunting once more to help you understand *Lost* a little better and enjoy some unexplored facets of the *Lost*verse.

—Lynnette Porter

CHAPTER ONE

LOST READING AND VIEWING

IS THERE AN (ANCESTOR) TEXT ON THIS ISLAND?

Even before the library in the Swan Hatch, entered for the first time in "Man of Science, Man of Faith" (2.1, the initial episode of Season Two), and that Bible Mr. Eko finds in the Arrow Hatch, the one the Tailies stumble upon in "...and Found" (2.5) made Mystery Island more bookish, tomes were common enough on *Lost*—not as common as miniature liquor bottles, but not exactly rare either.

Throughout Season One, we find the unlikely avid reader Sawyer page-turning a variety of books, from Richard Adams' *Watership Down* (a book he rereads in "Left Behind," 3.15) to Madeline L'Engle's *A Wrinkle in Time*. In Season Two, he continues to read from his word horde: Judy Blume's *Are You There, God? It's Me, Margaret* and Walker Percy's *Lancelot*. In The Swan even more books have screen time: James' *The Turn of the Screw*, Bierce's "An Occurrence at Owl Creek Bridge," and, most notoriously, O'Brien's *The Third Policeman*, an obscure Irish novel that became a surprise bestseller due to its unintentional product placement cameo. And speaking of product placement, in "The Long Con" we find Hurley reading the manuscript of *Bad Twin*, a *Lost* tie-in novel written by the late Oceanic 815 passenger Gary Troup, later released by Hyperion, the publisher of official *Lost* books. Season

Three continued to be bookish. The opening scene of the first episode ("A Tale of Two Cities," 3.1) shows a book club—the assigned book Stephen King's *Carrie*. Later, in "Every Man for Himself" (3.4), Ben evokes Steinbeck's *Of Mice and Men* in his humbling of Sawyer, and in "Not in Portland" (3.7), Aldo is seen reading Stephen Hawking's *A Brief History of Time*. In Seasons Four and Five the books kept appearing: Philip K. Dick's *VALIS* and Casares' *The Invention of Morel* in "Eggtown" (4.4); Joyce's *Ulysses* in "316" (5.6); Castaneda's *A Separate Reality* in "He's Our You" (5.10); and Flannery O'Connor's *Everything That Rises Must Converge* in "The Incident" (5.17).

To paraphrase a question literary critic Stanley Fish once famously asked in the title of a book: "Is there a text on this island?" Many, many texts is the answer. On the official website a *Lost* book club has been established, and though it's not likely to rival Oprah in sales, it is impressive nonetheless. Astonishingly, given that *Lost* is the story of the aftermath of a plane crash, not a single John Grisham novel has been found.

Not all the "texts" are literary, of course. Cinema ancestors—disaster films, *Cast Away*, *Jurassic Park*—and television series—*The Adventures of Brisco County, Jr.*, *Buffy the Vampire Slayer*, *Gilligan's Island*, *Survivor*, *The Twilight Zone*, *Twin Peaks*, *The X-Files*—have all influenced *Lost's* themes, its mise-en-scéne, its characterization, its narrative style. The postmodern, as Umberto Eco has noted, is the age of the "already said." Books, films, and television have all had their say on *Lost*.

Each time a new *Lost* text opens for perusal, the fans go wild and speculation runs rampant as the *Lost*-fixated begin to read, backward and forward, an extraordinarily complex, still unfolding, still entangling narrative. The threads of a text, a "kind of halfway house between past and future," the critic Wolfgang Iser would write, always exist in "a state of suspended validity" (370), and such threads are particularly well-suited for today's avidly conjecturing, anxious to conspire "fan-scholar."

"Quality" television series, according to Robert Thompson's authoritative delineation, are "literary and writer-based" (15), and most readily, proudly acknowledge their ancestors and their influences. When *Twin Peaks'* Black Lodge turned out to be in Glastonbury Grove and Windom Earle and Leo Johnson cozied up in their Verdant

Bower, the Arthurian legends and Spenser's *Faerie Queene* were born again in a new medium. When Tony Soprano sobbed uncontrollably at the ministrations of Tom Powers' loving mother in *Public Enemy* (as seen on TV), televised and filmic mobsters became brothers in the same gang—and genre.

Books, film, music, television, as well as other manifestations of both low and high culture—to borrow the witty formulation of film scholar Robert Stam—are governed by the same principle as sexually transmitted diseases. To have sex with another is to have had sex with all of his or her other sexual partners, and every "text"—every new novel or short story, song, or movie, or television series—is far from innocent; each potentially carries the "contagion" of every other text it and its creators have "slept with."

Lost is highly promiscuous, sleeping around with a wide variety of textual "partners." We divide these partners, one form of buried treasures, into three sections: Books in the Narrative considers texts that have actually put in a physical appearance on *Lost*. Ancestor Texts[2] offers accounts of *Lost*'s literary predecessors. Must See TV and Movies provides a guide to the series' film and television predecessors.

BOOKS IN THE NARRATIVE

Are You There God? It's Me, Margaret—When caught reading Judy Blume's novel *Are You There God? It's Me, Margaret* ("The Whole Truth," 2.16), Sawyer downplays his interest in the preteen drama by calling it "predictable" and with "not nearly enough sex." (Though Sawyer belittles the book for its lack of sex, *Margaret* is, according to the American Library Association, among the top 100 frequently challenged books in libraries because of its frank treatment of sexuality and religion. Needless to say, it is certainly more than a simple, preteen drama.)

With its focus on the title character's experiences with menstruation and buying her first bra, *Margaret* is often referred to as the quintessential teen novel, but it is just as much about struggling with spiritual development. Margaret grows up with a mixed religious heritage—one Christian and one Jewish parent—and the novel follows her efforts to come to grips with her own beliefs. Menstruation and training bras aside, it is a story of religious quest.

Lost often delves into the importance of faith, of good vs. evil, of scientific vs. spiritual. Like Margaret, the *Lost*ies have trouble deciding if they buy into spiritual mumbo jumbo, and, like *Margaret*, they receive many mixed messages about faith—at once bringing people back from the dead and pitilessly killing off members of the group.

Perhaps it would seem more fitting for a character like Locke, who frequently stresses the importance of faith and, even more frequently as of late, battles with his own ability to believe in the Island's spiritual properties, to be seeking answers in Judy Blume. Perhaps Margaret would have taught him that it's okay to not be sure about every facet of spiritual experience—that it's okay to question a higher power.

Instead, it is the Island's resident literati and bad boy who finds himself reading the coming-of-age novel. Sawyer has not yet had much affiliation with the Island's spiritual properties, though he often struggles to find a balance between what is right and wrong. Even more, his proclamation that the novel doesn't have enough sex further brands him as the most hormonally driven of the *Lost* clan. He is the one, after all, who regularly engages in sexual activity—with Ana Lucia and Kate—on the Island.

When Margaret and her friends are desperate to increase their bra size, they chant, "I must, I must, I must increase my bust," a catch phrase that has surely raised the eyebrows of overprotective mothers across the world. But to Sawyer, of all people, Margaret's spiritual journey is predictable and the book's lust-factor dismal.—**Sarah Caitlin Lavery**

Bad Twin—Hurley introduces the audience to the "original" *Bad Twin* manuscript in "The Long Con" (2.13) before it later ends up in Sawyer's hands. Sawyer's reading is spoiled when Jack burns the manuscript in "Two for the Road" (2.20)—before Sawyer can finish the final ten pages. Damon Lindelof and Carlton Cuse affirm that within the series, author "Gary Troup" (an anagram for "purgatory" and pseudonym for ghostwriter Laurence Shames) survived the crash but was the first to die when sucked into the turbine engine. *Bad Twin*'s storyline focuses on small-time P.I. Paul Artisan's investigation of Clifford Widmore's missing twin, Alexander ("Zander"). The book is largely standard detective-fiction fare, with a storyline that peripherally mentions some minor characters and entities that are part of the

Lost universe, mainly those that involve the wealthy Widmore family and their corporation, the Hanso Foundation, Paik Industries, Oceanic Airlines, and Mr. Cluck's Chicken Shack.

For all intents and purposes, *Bad Twin* is a tie-in text that throws *Lost* fans a few familiar nibbles in its pages, primarily involving the numbers (for example, Cliff Widmore was born on 8/15). Other references include literary texts like *Gilgamesh*, *Lord of the Flies*, the *Odyssey*, and *The Turn of the Screw*. The most important component of *Bad Twin* is its significance in the 2006 *Lost* Alternate Reality Game (ARG) launched near the end of Season Two. Print ads for the ARG included a "Don't Believe *Bad Twin*" ad campaign hosted on the Hanso Foundation website (hansofoundation.org) that accused the book of committing libel, with threats to sue publisher Hyperion.

Fans and Lindelof and Cuse alike were largely disappointed with the bestselling text, perhaps because the creative team had given Shames a wealth of elements to include in the text and the author instead picked and chose only those he wished to include.—**Hillary Robson**

The Bible—Within the first three episodes a character with a prophetic name—Christian Shephard—had been introduced. Since then, *Lost*'s ever-interlocking characters and multiple-meaninged events have created a mythology of biblical proportions. How appropriate, then, that the Bible is one of, if not *the* most important ancestor text for this evolving series.

Popular names with biblical origins abound in the *Lost*verse: Aaron, Adam, Benjamin, Daniel, David, Elizabeth, Isaac, Jacob, James, John, Mark, Mary, Naomi, Ruth, Samuel, Sarah, Stephen, Thomas. Some names or their variants, such as Daniel/Dan/Danny/Danielle and Thomas/Tom/Tommy, are repeated frequently.

Both Old and New Testament references have made their way into *Lost*. Series' creators and frequent episode writers Damon Lindelof (a Jew) and Carlton Cuse (a Catholic) have said that they sometimes infuse their philosophical and religious perspectives and questions into the story. "The 23rd Psalm" (2.10) and "Exodus" (1.23–24) are biblically inspired episode titles, only two of the many references worked into the series. To illustrate the number and variety of biblical references, here are only a few:

- Novice monk Desmond has difficulty understanding why God would test Abraham by requiring him to sacrifice his son, Isaac, a story recorded in Genesis ("Catch-22," 3.17). Although Brother Campbell explains the nature of sacrifice, Desmond still questions God's act. On the Island, however, Desmond finds himself in a similar predicament; he, like Abraham, lures the unaware potential sacrifice (Charlie) into the wilderness (jungle). When the time comes to sacrifice Charlie, Desmond can't stand idly by; he saves Charlie and thus sacrifices a future in which he will be reunited with Penelope. Desmond may well feel, as Abraham did, that God tested him by asking him to sacrifice his greatest love (Penny). Of course, Desmond eventually receives his "reward" by being reunited with Penny, after Charlie's self-sacrifice in the Looking Glass station.

- The life of John the Baptist, as described in the Gospels, plays prominent visual and symbolic roles in "Fire + Water" (2.12). In flashback, a portrait of John the Baptist hangs in young Charlie Pace's home; adult Charlie dreams of his mother, Claire, and Hurley dressed and placed similarly to the background figures in the painting. This dream motivates Charlie to have Aaron baptized at whatever cost. By the episode's end, Mr. Eko baptizes both Claire and her baby.

- Ben points out the painting "The Incredulity of Saint Thomas" to "doubting Thomas" Jack; the painting hangs in the church where, in the basement, Mrs. Hawking maintains the Lamp Post station. Jack doubts whether the Oceanic Six can or should return to the Island, a train of thought that Ben wants to derail ("316," 5.6).

- Perhaps the most widely discussed *Lost* biblical name is Jacob. The mysterious leader of the Others, a (mostly) unseen but powerful leader, becomes the foundation of cult-like devotion by many on the Island. (Jacob is "revealed" to Locke as a shadowy image and disembodied voice during "The Man Behind the Curtain" [3.20], but we first see him on and off the Island during "The Incident" [5.16–17].) The Others often ask WWJD (What Would Jacob

Do?), and Jacob's teaching becomes a key part of the brainwashing film to which Karl is subjected ("Not in Portland," 3.7). Jacob seems to control the fate of the Oceanic Six, and he obviously has been aware of everyone on the Island. Biblically, Jacob is important because he is Isaac's son and Abraham's grandson, which peripherally ties him to the previously mentioned story of sacrifice, a theme prominent in Christian Shephard's interaction with Locke before he leaves the Island ("The Life and Death of Jeremy Bentham," 5.7). Furthermore, Jacob is a deceiver; he disguises himself as his slightly older twin brother Esau in order to gain his father's blessing and inheritance as firstborn son. This story forms the basis of fan speculation about the relationship between Jacob and his unnamed Island nemesis, who is intent upon killing Jacob and gaining control of his destiny. The biblical Jacob becomes father to Benjamin (and the ephemeral Jacob at first seems to be a father figure to Ben Linus), a favored son used to test his older brothers' loyalty. Like the biblical Benjamin, for most of his adulthood, Ben wants to stay in Jacob's good graces and acts jealous when Locke hears what Jacob says. When Locke seems to have won Jacob's favor and replaced him, Ben turns over the job of running the Island—and doing Jacob's bidding—to Locke. However, at the end of Season Five, Ben agrees to do "Locke's" (or Jacob's nemesis') bidding by stabbing Jacob and apparently killing him.

Lost's writers add weight to their story when they invoke biblical precedents, whether through plot details or character names. *Lost* provides a modern context for biblical themes and spiritual dilemmas important in human development throughout history.

Book of Law—Mr. Eko uses this name for the Bible's Old Testament as he tells Locke the story of Josiah ("What Kate Did," 2.9). He then explains the parallel between the story of Josiah and the castaways' recent experiences.

A Brief History of Time—Stephen Hawking's bestselling *A Brief History of Time* shows up twice in Season Three of *Lost*. In "Not in Portland" (3.7), Aldo is reading it while standing guard at the Hydra during Karl's brainwashing in Room 23. Later, in "The Man from Tallahassee" (3.13), the book can be glimpsed in Ben's house. First published in 1988, *BHT* was intended to be the famous astrophysicist's explanation of everything "From the Big Bang to Black Holes" (the book's subtitle) for the layman. Writing in an accessible prose style, almost devoid of mathematical formula, about the nature of space and time, the expansion of the universe, the uncertainty principle, elementary particles, the fate of the universe, and the hope for a unification of physics, as well as providing brief capsule biographies of Einstein, Galileo, and Newton, Hawking largely succeeds at his goal.

Given that *Lost*'s creative team has indicated that they have been reading books on physics and string theory, fans found it significant that Hawking's *BHT* would appear on the Island. Its Season Three cameos, not to mention the first appearance in "Flashes Before Your Eyes" (3.8) of a mysterious woman who shares a surname with the famed physicist (Eloise Hawking), seem now to be foreshadowing of Season Five's time traveling.

BHT also makes pop culture appearances in such films as *Harry Potter and the Sorcerer's Stone*, *Harry Potter and the Prisoner of Azkaban*, *Donnie Darko*, and *Legally Blonde*.

The Brothers Karamazov—In a Season Two episode of *Lost*, "Maternity Leave" (2.15), a new character, Henry Gale (later revealed to be Benjamin Linus), suspected of being one of the infamous "Others" and bearing the surname name of Dorothy from *The Wizard of Oz*, is given a copy of Dostoevsky's *The Brothers Karamazov* to entertain him during his captivity in the Swan's armory. This leads to Locke's comments to Jack about Ernest Hemingway's inferiority complex about his Russian literary predecessor, a bookish digression seemingly inconsequential until the episode's end, when a clearly scheming Ben uses it to provoke Locke's second-banana anger against Jack.

Brothers is often considered to be the finest novel of the Russian writer Fyodor Dostoevsky (1821–1881), author as well of such important books as *Notes from Underground* (1864), *Crime and Punishment* (1866), *The Possessed* (1866), and *The Idiot* (1869), who died only months after its publication. The influential critic Mikhail Bakhtin (not to be confused with *Lost*'s Mikhail "Patchy" Bakunin) once praised Dostoevsky as superior to his contemporary literary titan Leo Tolstoy because of his ability to give expression—in a process Bakhtin deemed "dialogism"—to a wide variety of voices in the culture of the day without "authorizing" a single point of view as the "Truth" (in Bakhtin's terminology "monologism"). *Brothers* is a near-perfect example of Dostoevsky's art. Primarily concerned with the murder of the patriarch of the Karamazov family, the novel never fully establishes the culprit, but along the way it does explore, in depth, the psyches of the major characters:

- Fyodor Pavlovich Karamazov, the father;

- Dmitri Fyodorovich Karamazov, the spendthrift and hedonistic oldest son, who is ultimately tried for parricide;

- Ivan Fyodorovich Karamazov, a rationalist and atheist, obsessed by the world's suffering (his poem "The Grand Inquisitor" is one of the book's most famous sections);

- Alexei (Alyosha) Fyodorovich Karamazov, the hero (or so the narrator claims), a deeply religious visionary.

Profound questions of faith, reason, redemption, guilt, justice, suffering, and happiness are plumbed as well.

Lost shares *Brothers'* (and Dostoevsky's) dialogism. No one voice, no single point of view, no solitary backstory to date can be established as authoritative. *Lost* is fascinated, too, with many of the same themes and shares an interest in the figure of the patriarch: Mr. Paik (Sun's ruthless father), Christian Shephard (Jack's alcoholic, womanizing fellow surgeon), Charles Widmore (Penny's tyrant of a dad), Wayne (Kate's loathsome stepdad), and Anthony Cooper (Locke's cruelly manipulative con-man parent). Wayne is already dead when our story begins, and Cooper is murdered, at Locke's behest, by Sawyer in "The Brig" (3.19). That Season Five ended with Ben's manipulated murder of the Island's ur-patriarch Jacob suggests that *Brothers'* appearance in Season Two may well have been something more than window dressing.

Carrie—In the opening scene of Season Three ("A Tale of Two Cities," 3.1), Juliet hosts a book club meeting in her cottage. Being the host, it's her turn to pick the book, and she chooses *Carrie* by Stephen King. It's a curious choice—not typical book club material. It was King's first published novel (1974) and tells the story of Carrie White, a 16-year-old girl with telekinetic powers raised by a fanatical, fundamentalist, Christian mother, who is teased and humiliated incessantly at school. The climax of the story is a cruel plan hatched by one of Carrie's classmates to rig the vote and have Carrie crowned queen of the prom. Then, when she is on stage, a bucket of pig's blood can be dumped on her head. The plan succeeds and pushes Carrie over the edge. Rage fills her, and she uses her powers to set fire to the dance, burning nearly everyone alive.

During the book club meeting, Juliet tells the other members that *Carrie* is her "favorite book." While a horrific story, it's not an unsurprising choice. Juliet can identify with Carrie. Both consider themselves outsiders living in an isolated, self-sustaining environment full of social and political tension. Juliet is a prisoner on the Island, unable to return home. She lacks the unquestioning faith in the Island Ben and the Others possess. Carrie is trapped in high school. She's naïve, unsophisticated, and the constant butt of jokes.

Lost viewers familiar with King's novel might notice additional similarities between the two women. While ultimately strong, female characters, our first impressions find both in vulnerable situations at the mercy of their peers. In the opening scene of *Carrie*, she is naked, showering after gym class when she begins to menstruate for the first time. She panics. The other girls realize what's going on and chant "Plug it up!" while pelting her with tampons and sanitary napkins. Juliet is caught off-guard when her doorbell rings and burns her hand in the oven. Injured but looking forward to the book club, she's accosted by other members for choosing *Carrie*. One man says, "It's not even literature. It's popcorn," and alludes to Ben's disapproval, too. If not for Oceanic 815's catastrophe overhead, the argument would have continued.

As Juliet's character moves into Seasons Four and Five, she sheds her former Carrie-like skin and finds something Carrie White never could—love. Carrie is cruelly tricked into going to the prom with Tommy Ross, who pretends to have feelings for her. Carrie's initial apprehension is similar to how viewers of *Lost* felt upon learning of Juliet and Sawyer's committed relationship during their stay with the DHARMA Initiative. Sawyer, an untrustworthy con man, defies expectations when he settles down into domesticity. While that decision might have initially been out of necessity, their relationship does turn into real love by the end of Season Five. Both Juliet and Sawyer confess their love for one another as she falls down the mine shaft ("The Incident," 5.16).

Taking a step back and looking at the structure of *Carrie*, we see that it's broken up into a third-person narrative mixed with newspaper articles, eyewitness accounts, and letters detailing the events unfolding within the story. Nearly 50 percent of the novel is written this way. King uses these pieces to add additional details that might not have fit naturally in the narrative. They help solidify Carrie's story by providing multiple points of view. This technique works well for *Lost*'s producers as well. While each episode furthers the overall story line, there is typically a backstory told through flashbacks, and more recently, flash-forwards. These extra scenes create a complex web of coincidence and crossed paths in the lives of the castaways. —**Tyler Hall** and **Hillary Robson**

Catch-22—The seventeenth episode of *Lost*'s third season, offering the second Desmond backstory in less than two months, owes its title to Joseph Heller's 1961 book, one of the greatest antiwar novels ever written, a novel so influential its title has become part of the language.

Set, like *Lost*, on an island (off the west coast of Italy), *Catch-22* tells with the blackest of humor the story of an American bomber squadron toward the end of World War II. Paranoically but accurately convinced that the enemy is trying to kill him, Heller's hero, Captain John Yossarian, wants out of the war and hopes to do so by having himself declared insane, but his path to freedom is blocked by "Catch-22." The desire to get out of war—to no longer, in Yossarian's case, insanely pilot a flimsy B-24 bomber through the flak and fighter interceptor–filled skies over enemy cities—is, of course, perfect proof of his sanity. Hence, by the strictures imposed by the impossible, absurd Catch-22, he cannot escape by reason of insanity.

The mysterious, Portuguese-speaking parachutist, Naomi Dorritt (a strangely Dickensian name), who arrives in "Catch-22" (she will later be knifed in the back by Locke in the Season Three finale) is carrying with her a copy of a Portuguese translation (*Ardil-22*) of *Catch-22* (a copy of the photo of Penny and Desmond is found therein). Soon after finding the book, Desmond opts to save Charlie's life by pulling him out of the way of a Rousseau arrow that had proved fatal in his earlier vision of the incident, leaving both Desmond and the audience to wonder if in so doing he had altered the course of events—in his vision, after all, the parachutist appears to have been Penny herself. That question became somewhat moot in light of all of Season Five's time-warping fiddling with destiny.

Director Mike Nichols completed an all-star cast film version of *Catch-22* in 1970.

Everything That Rises Must Converge—In 2000, John Locke confronts his horrid father concerning his involvement in the death of Peter Talbot ("The Man from Tallahassee," 3.13) in a hotel room high over Los Angeles, an encounter that prompts Anthony Cooper to push his son out the window. Down below, ensconced on a bench, Jacob waits patiently, reading a book, evidently well aware that the very man his nemesis will, in 2008, make use of in order to enact at last his murderous plans is about to plummet to his death. Locke, however does not die. The touch of Jacob, administered at various times in the past in Season Five's two-part finale "The Incident" to Kate, Jack, Sun and Jin, and Sawyer, brings Locke back to life—making it possible for him to die again years later, murdered by the very man, Ben, who had foiled his suicide attempt, the very man who would, in turn, knife Jacob at the end of Season Five.

We cannot help but take note of Jacob's reading material—for a moment the front and back covers of Flannery O'Connor's *Everything That Rises Must Converge*, held open in Jacob's right hand, fill the frame until the camera pulls back to reveal a wider view and a body falls from above. Jacob gets up, bookmarks his page, and goes to the side of the apparently dead John Locke. After his touch rejuvenates, he tells the fallen, with a soft, calming voice, "Don't worry. Everything is going to be alright. Sorry this happened to you."

Everything That Rises Must Converge is a collection of short stories by Flannery O'Connor (1925–1964), a Georgia writer who produced some of the finest short fiction of the twentieth century prior to her untimely death to Lupus. An exemplary practitioner of the literary mode known as a grotesque and a distinctly southern writer, she was also a staunch Catholic—"For me," she would write, "the meaning of life is centered in our Redemption by Christ and what I see in the world I see in relation to that"—whose recurrent themes are, as *Lost*'s have always been, distinctly religious.

In one story Jacob might have read—the tale that gave the book its name—an arrogant, self-important young college graduate, embarrassed to be riding the bus in Atlanta with his uneducated, racist mother, condescendingly seeks to expose her for what she is and ends up destroying her instead. In another, "Revelation," a self-satisfied hog farmer has her illusions about her own status as a member of God's elect few destroyed by a college girl in a doctor's waiting room who throws a text books at her head and deems her a "warthog from hell." Later, in an apocalyptic, distinctly Catholic vision while she is slopping the hogs, she realizes that all of creation is capable of salvation, not just a chosen few.

As he so often does, *Entertainment Weekly*'s ever-stimulating Jeff Jensen offered a fascinating explanation of the significance of Jacob's choice of reading material:

As it happens, Flannery O'Connor's…book takes its title…from a phrase coined by an egghead and fellow Catholic provocateur named Pierre Teilhard de Chardin [1881–1955], who concocted a theory of evolution called [the] "Omega Point." Basically, it's the idea that there is some kind of transcendent entity or consciousness that is guiding everyone and everything toward greater complexity and enlightenment, until everyone and everything becomes transcendent, too.

Based on what we know of Jacob from "The Incident," in particular the following exchange with his nemesis—

Nemesis: I don't have to ask. You brought [the Black Rock*] here. Still trying to prove me wrong, aren't you?*
Jacob: You are wrong.
Nemesis: Am I? They come. They fight. They destroy. They corrupt. It always ends the same.
Jacob: It only ends once. Anything that happens before that is just progress.

—Jensen thinks Teilhard's ideas would appeal to the Island's patriarch:

Chardin believed his Omega entity was basically Jesus Christ himself. His phrase, "everything that rises must converge," is a poetical expression of a key Christian idea known in the Greek apokatastasis. *It's like the opposite of apocalypse, or rather, what comes after apocalypse...* apokatastasis *is the idea that in the end, Satan will be defeated and that all of creation will be redeemed and unified under Christ. "Now is the judgment of the world: now shall the prince of this world be cast out. And I, if I be lifted up from the earth, will draw all things to myself." (John 12:31–32) Or, again, to use a line from the show: "He who will save us all." That, my friends, is the answer, translated from Richard Alpert's Latin, to Ilana's riddle: "What lies in the shadow of the statue?"*

No wonder Jacob would find O'Connor a kindred soul. Still, we have to wonder: Did he order *Everything That Rises Must Converge* on Amazon? Do they deliver to the Island? Or did he pick up the book on one of his many visits to the larger world?

Authors' Note: The character referred to in this entry as "Nemesis" will be called by various names in these pages: Nemesis, Esau, Non-Locke, Man in the Black Shirt, Loophole Man. In each instance, we are talking, as the context will make clear, about the same "man," played by Titus Welliver, who appears for the first and only time in the teaser of "The Incident." So far, he has not been named.

The Fountainhead—In Season Three's "Par Avion" (3.12), Sawyer is seen on the beach reading Ayn Rand's novel *The Fountainhead*. First published in 1943, Rand's story of a New York architect, Howard Roark, who refuses to compromise his principles for mere monetary gain, stands as a manifesto of its notorious author's philosophy of "objectivism," her absolute faith in what she would call "the virtue of selfishness." The title refers to the Russian émigré Rand's bedrock principle that "man's ego is the fountainhead of human progress." Although Rand struggled for some time to find a publisher, the book became a bestseller and was made into a movie in 1949, with Gary Cooper playing Rand's mouthpiece hero Roark.

Throughout the novel, Roark must do battle—often in court, where he has plenty of opportunities to spout his creator's philosophy—with those who would, through their sinister machinations, bring him down to their lower level. His genius triumphs, of course, and at the book's end, he is building the world's tallest skyscraper as a symbol of his triumph over lesser souls.

Other than Sawyer's unphilosophical selfishness, no close connection between Rand's novel and the world of *Lost* immediately presents itself, and Sawyer's egocentricity has its limits. Does he not ask that his reward in "Every Man for Himself" (3.4)—a Randish title, undercut by the end of the episode—be put in trust for his daughter to be? Do not Kate and later Juliet bring out the willing-to-sacrifice hero in him?

The article on *The Fountainhead* in Wikipedia[3] details numerous other appearances the novel has made in popular culture, including the films *Dirty Dancing* and *Heaven Can Wait* and the television shows *Barney Miller*, *Desperate Housewives*, and *Gilmore Girls*.

The Gunslinger—When Locke confronts Ben in "The Man From Tallahassee" (3.13), a copy of Stephen King's *The Gunslinger* is sitting on Ben's bookshelf. While not the first King novel featured in *Lost* (*Carrie* and *Hearts in Atlantis* in "A Tale of Two Cities" [3.1]), this is the first connection to his *Dark Tower* series. Spanning seven volumes, *The Dark Tower* is King's magnum opus—a sprawling epic that connects all of King's other novels together into a common plotline. It is the story of Roland, the last gunslinger, and his quest to save the Dark Tower. The Tower is said to stand at the center of all worlds—a place where all of space and time converge at a single point. If the Tower should fall, then all of existence will fall with it. It's fortunate that *The Gunslinger* remains tucked away safely on Ben's bookshelf rather than in the eager hands of Sawyer. If the castaways on *Lost* were to learn about Roland's world, they might notice eerie similarities with their own.

King tells us that Roland and his companions are traveling through a world that has "moved on." The disease spreading through the Tower has caused the fabric between worlds to grow thin, allowing artifacts from one world to pass through to another. They pass ancient, half-working machines created by a lost race simply referred to as the "old people." The lush prosperous world that Roland remembers from his youth has worn down and dried up. As he searches for the Dark Tower, he sees the same rot and deterioration present in every world he visits. It's a symptom the castaways would find familiar. As they trek across the Island, they come across the technological leavings of the DHARMA Initiative. They know very little about who these people were or the purpose of the things they left behind.

As the mystery unfolds, Locke becomes the group's chief inquisitor—communing with the Island and divining its secrets. When the lights go out in the Hatch in "Lockdown" (2.17), Locke sees a mural drawn on the blast door. It depicts each DHARMA station on the Island arranged in a circle around a question mark. In "The Cost of Living" (3.05) we find out that the question mark location is a Hatch called "The Pearl," which is connected to every other station by video cameras. In *The Dark Tower* Roland often talks of how the Tower is circled by twelve portals like the numbers on a clock. Each portal is said to be a gateway between worlds and connected to the Tower by six beams—one portal at the end of each. As a child, Roland was taught the names of each portal in his nursery rhymes: Bear, Turtle, Eagle, Lion, etc. It's a naming scheme similar to that picked by DHARMA for its stations: Pearl, Swan, Arrow, Flame, etc. Each is a simple, singular noun.

Physical similarities aside, perhaps the most striking connection between *Lost* and *The Dark Tower* is the driving presence of fate throughout their storylines. Roland believes wholeheartedly in fate—a force King calls Ka. No matter how much one may rail against it, Roland says time and time again that there is no escaping the life Ka has planned. It's such a strong factor in the Tower that the ultimate conflict becomes Roland fighting against a destiny he knows he cannot escape. In *Lost*, Locke places a similar faith in the Island itself. He sees events on the Island happening for a reason.

Daniel Faraday would disagree. As Season Five unfolds, we learn that there is no sure thing in *Lost*. When he returns from doing research at DHARMA headquarters in Michigan, Daniel tells us that people are variables ("The Variable," 5.14). Their decisions in the past can change the events of the future. His plan to prevent the crash of Oceanic 815 by detonating Jughead positions him uniquely within the world of *Lost*—he's the one character who understands the rules governing the world they inhabit. He's a wild card, much like Stephen King in the Tower series, when King (the author) inserts himself into the storyline in order to alter the outcome of events that the characters could not escape on their own. It's a bizarre metafictional ploy by King but one only available to characters like himself and Faraday who understand the rules.—**Tyler Hall**

The Invention of Morel—In "Eggtown" (4.4), Sawyer is immersed in Adolfo Bioy Casares' 1940 novella during his time in the Barracks, an exceedingly strange Argentinean fiction by a countryman, close friend, and frequent collaborator of the polymathic genius Jorge Luis Borges, that would seem to be the product of a very *Lost*-like epistemological mind-set. On an uncharted Polynesian island, a fugitive, a Venezuelan writer condemned to life in prison apparently for political crimes that he did not commit, attempts to survive despite the rumor that anyone who has encountered the island developed a strange, fatal disease. Although a group of "white men" built a museum, swimming pool, and chapel on the island, they did not stay. The unnamed narrator takes up residence in the museum and keeps a diary that records his experiences, most significantly the sudden arrival of a group of tourists. Initially certain the group arrived to seize him and turn him in to the authorities, the fugitive/diarist soon realizes that they know nothing about him and are uninterested in anything other than listening to their music and enjoying their stay.

While he is terrified at being caught, he cannot contain his curiosity, especially toward a beautiful woman who frequently watches the sunset near his hiding place. As he battles the urge to make himself known to her, he is disappointed to find that the group of tourists has left as suddenly as they arrived. After a short interval, however, they return, and soon the unnamed narrator realizes he is in love with a beautiful tourist, a woman called Faustine, who may or may not be in love with another tourist, a tennis player named Morel. The few times the fugitive stands before Faustine, she does not respond to him.

In addition, weird anomalies begin to take place. For example, the sky now has two suns and two moons which eventually vanish entirely, only to reappear soon after. The fugitive/diarist's speculation about the island's riddles fills many pages, as do his feelings for Faustine, which range from desperate love to vile hatred. Eventually, the fugitive ventures into the museum late one night to settle his questions about Faustine's feelings for Morel and discovers that Morel is calling a meeting to order. Morel explains that he is in possession of a device of his own invention that reproduces reality, captures souls, and makes possible a repetition of time in an endless loop. He excitedly reports his accomplishment to his group of friends, but one of them quickly rebukes Morel, claiming his invention, when used at a Swiss business, had cost many employees their lives. Morel exits abruptly, leaving his friends confused and disbelieving. The narrator also leaves, unwilling to accept that the tourists—including the woman he loves—are merely illusions, "a new kind of photograph." After reading Morel's speech (which the fugitive swiped), the fugitive/diarist, overcome with emotion, realizes that Morel is not only telling the truth, but so is the outspoken friend who claims that his invention kills those it records. Desperate to be free of the intolerable island and its ghostly inhabitants, the fugitive contemplates suicide several times before using Morel's device to reconstruct reality with Faustine, now his love. His diary essentially becomes his eulogy as well.

Like Bierce's "A Psychological Shipwreck" and O'Brien's *The Last Policemen* (both available on the Island), *The Invention of Morel* offers no simple resolution and no real closure. Although each phenomenon is explained in "reasonable" detail, we are as confused—and mesmerized—at its end as we have been throughout. Like *Lost*, it interweaves profound questions about time, space, and reality with themes of love and loss in a science fiction narrative. Some of the more compelling similarities include the issue of suicide; the presence of a leader who believes his ends justify his means (how many episodes of *Lost* feature Benjamin Linus dryly justifying even the most brutal acts?); "innocent" characters in trouble with the law; and a general haziness as to the reliability of a character (is John Locke right or is he having daddy issues again?). And do the similarities end there? If *Lost* ends as inconclusively in May 2010 as *Morel* does at the end of its barely one hundred pages of rich text, millions of fans may well be gravely disappointed.—**Janice Lupo**

Lancelot—In "Maternity Leave" (2.15), the always-reading Sawyer has his head buried in (for him) a new book, Walker Percy's 1977 novel

Lancelot. When he opened it to the title page he would have found the following epigraph:

> *He sank so low that all means*
> *for his salvation were gone,*
> *except showing him the lost people.*
> *For this I visited the region of the dead…*

If Sawyer had been a fan of *Lost* rather than himself a *Lost*away, he might well have taken this epigraph to be yet another invitation to read the series, contrary to the repeated denials of Carlton Cuse and Damon Lindelof, as a story of a kind of purgatory, for the words are from Dante's *Purgatorio*, the second book of *The Divine Comedy*.

The fourth of only six novels by the Louisiana-born physician (trained as a brain surgeon) Percy (1916–1990), *Lancelot* is the story, related in a series of monologues, of lawyer Lance Lamar, told in a mental hospital where he has come for a rest cure, to his childhood friend Percival, now a minister. His wife has been burned alive in their palatial home, and his daughter, he discovers, is not his. Obsessed with the nature of evil, he seeks to indulge in it, blowing up his house and killing his unfaithful wife.

We don't know, of course, if Sawyer ever finished *Lancelot*, but if he did, the man who had half-heard Kate's incoherent soliloquy beside his sick bed (in "What Kate Did") that she had murdered her stepfather, who had twice encountered Claire's real but secret father in Sydney, and whose friend Hurley had spent a good amount of time in an institution, might well have found *Lancelot* a relevant book to be stuck with on this particular desert island. Why, had he not himself fathered a child without being at first aware of it? And surely its investigation into the nature of evil would have kept a man whose parents had died violently and who had himself committed two murders while seeking revenge turning the pages.

Laughter in the Dark—In "Flashes Before Your Eyes" (3.8), we see Hurley on the beach reading Vladimir Nabokov's 1932 *Laughter in the Dark*. (When first translated into English in 1936, its title was *Camera Obscura*.) Not the most famous book by the great Russian-American writer (1899–1977)—his notorious *Lolita* (1955) and the brilliant *Pale Fire* (1962) are better known—*Laughter* seems unlikely reading material for Hurley, but then again, the selection of books on the Island is fairly limited.

Like *Lolita*, *Laughter* is the darkly humorous story of a middle-aged man (Albinus), an art critic in Berlin, seduced by a very young woman (Margot), who aspires to be a movie star. With an old lover, Margot betrays Albinus, attempting to rob him of his wealth. Over the course of the novel, Albinus degenerates into a blind shell of his former self.

In Nikki's seduction (and eventual murder) of Howard Zuckerman in "Exposé" (3.14), we can detect an echo, conscious or not, of Margot and Albinus's relationship in *Laughter*.

Reportedly, *Laughter* was a major influence on American writer Joseph Heller, author of the book that supplied the title Season Three's seventeenth episode, "Catch-22," and was made into a film by British director Tony Richardson in 1969 starring Nicol Williamson and Anna Karina.

"An Occurrence at Owl Creek Bridge"—In "The Long Con" (2.13), Locke discovers and briefly handles a copy of "An Occurrence at Owl Creek Bridge" by Ambrose Bierce (1842–1914?). This collection of stories by the notorious nineteenth century American cynic and man of mystery (he disappeared in Mexico, never to be seen again), best known for his wonderfully dark *The Devil's Dictionary*, immediately fed fan interest, and why not?

Although at least two other stories in the collection ("A Psychological Shipwreck" and "The Damned Thing"—both discussed in these pages) are worth reading by *Lost* fans, the titular tale, an account of the hanging of a Southern plantation owner by Union soldiers during the Civil War, seems the most relevant. Though the victim escapes the noose and flees, we learn in the end, having fallen for Bierce's mislead, that his reprieve is all in his mind and his getaway transpires in the split second before the rope snaps his neck. The story's famous ending:

Doubtless, despite his suffering, he had fallen asleep while walking, for now he sees another scene—perhaps he has merely recovered from a delirium. He stands at the gate of his own home. All is as he left it, and all bright and beautiful in the morning sunshine. He must have traveled the entire night. As he pushes open the gate and passes up the wide white walk, he sees a flutter of female garments; his wife, looking fresh and cool and sweet, steps down from the veranda to meet him. At the bottom of the steps she stands waiting, with a smile of ineffable joy, an attitude of matchless grace and dignity. Ah, how beautiful she is! He springs forwards with extended arms. As he is about to clasp her he feels a stunning blow upon the back of the neck; a blinding white light blazes all about him with a sound like the shock of a cannon—then all is darkness and silence!

Peyton Farquhar was dead; his body, with a broken neck, swung gently from side to side beneath the timbers of the Owl Creek bridge.

For *Lost* fans already wondering if the frequently proffered conjecture that all the *Lost*aways are in fact dead and that the Island is a kind of purgatory—a supposition repeatedly, ardently denied by *Lost*'s creative team (despite their obvious shout outs in that *Purgatorio/Lancelot* epigraph [see *Lancelot*] and in the anagrammed name of *Bad Twin* author Gary Troup), the occurrence of *Occurrence* seemed irresistible evidence.

Several film adaptations of "Occurrence" exist, including a 1962 movie by Robert Enrico—available for viewing online—as well as *Alfred Hitchcock Presents* (1959), *Twilight Zone* (1964) and *Masters of Horror* (2005) versions.

Our Mutual Friend—Charles Dickens' 1864–65 novel, his last twenty-part monthly narrative, appears unexpectedly in the final episode of the second season, as Desmond Hume collects his effects at the conclusion of his term in military prison. When the guard asks Desmond about this Penguin paperback, he replies that he's read "everything Mr. Charles Dickens has ever written," and that he's been saving *Our Mutual Friend*, as "the last thing I ever read before I die." (Cuse and Lindelof acknowledge that this specific conceit was lifted from novelist John Irving, who claims to have a similar plan in mind.) The guard's reply to Desmond—"Nice idea, as long as you know when you're going to die"—aptly points to the tension between characters, who usually operate under the illusion of free will, and authors, who make dispassionate plot decisions over which the characters have no control. Given the number of plotters in the show—Benjamin Linus, Charles

Widmore, and Jacob, among others—the guard's reminder about the conflicting forces of design and accident is certainly fitting.

Desmond's story in particular illustrates the tension between plans (such as the round-the-world boat race that will supposedly win the heart of his beloved Penelope, or the protocol of entering the famous numbers into the Swan's computer) and accidents (storms at sea, releases of electromagnetic energy, Desmond and Jack meeting again). That recipe applies equally to the nominal hero of *Our Mutual Friend*, John Harmon, who returns to London to receive his considerable inheritance, only to be drowned, apparently, on the homeward journey; in fact, he survives and invents the fictional identity of John Rokesmith for himself. (Eerily appropriate for our purposes: Harmon's first words in the novel are "I am lost!")

Desmond's adventure explicitly echoes that lost-at-sea scenario, as does his perpetual self-doubt; likewise, the possibility of renewal and resurrection embodied in Desmond's tale mirrors not only a multitude of other characters on *Lost*—most prominently, Locke, Kate, Sawyer, and Sun and Jin—but also *Our Mutual Friend*'s focus on renewal and resurrection, principally through the river Thames and the dust mounds (garbage heaps) that are the source of Harmon's family wealth.

Desmond's love story offers another parallel between the narratives—accentuated in *Lost* by the tender note that Penelope inserts into Desmond's book before his prison term, a note that he does not discover until long after he is marooned. Harmon's inheritance is contingent on his marrying Bella Wilfer, a difficult young woman whose childish vanity makes her the precise opposite of the true-hearted Penny. When Harmon is presumed dead, Bella stands a good chance of being the beneficiary of the fortune; and when Rokesmith, employed as her father's secretary, asks to marry her, she initially spurns his advances, confirming her preference for surface over depth. Bella and Penny are both connected to money and power; but while Penny is one of *Lost*'s plotters—hiring a research team to track down the vanished Desmond—Bella is the subject of *Our Mutual Friend*'s most notorious plot, one cooked up by Rokesmith/Harmon himself.

That plot leads us to the richest of the connections between this novel and *Lost*, even more than individual characters or themes: namely, the style and influence of the novel's author. In a postscript to *Our Mutual Friend*, Dickens acknowledges the book's two signature plot strands, or secrets, both of them devised by Harmon. The first has to do with Harmon's reappearance as Rokesmith; while the narrator never explicitly tells us that they are one and the same person until very late in the book, it is blindingly obvious from the start and therefore barely qualifies as a secret at all. The second has to do with the Bella marriage plot, wherein Mr. Boffin—who now stands to inherit the fortune and to serve as Bella's benefactor—gradually devolves from kindly gent to cruel miser, a transformation that leads Bella to see the errors of her avaricious ways and to find her way back to Harmon/Rokesmith's arms. If the first secret was no secret at all, the second secret comes completely out of the blue, because the reader is given no hints whatsoever that Boffin has simply acted this new role, in collaboration with Harmon/Rokesmith, for a considerable portion of the novel. That double vision—the secrets that we know for a very long time (such as the fact that Claire is Jack's half-sister) and the secrets that arrive unannounced (such as the fact that Jacob has been present at many key events in the Losties' pre-Island lives)—speaks to the two extremes of authors' manipulation of audiences: on the one hand, making them feel very smart, and on the other hand, making them feel very stupid, or worse, duped. Dickens' posture in the postscript exactly anticipates Cuse and Lindelof's situation. In reference to the Harmon/Rokesmith angle, he announces, "I foresaw the likelihood that a class of readers and commentators would suppose that I was at great pains to conceal exactly what I was at great pains to suggest"; a more recent "class of readers and commentators"—bloggers and forum posters—have had similar responses to supposedly obvious twists in *Lost*'s development.

In reference to the infamous and somewhat implausible Boffin about-face, Dickens imperiously announces that "it would be very difficult to expect that many readers, pursuing a story in portions from month to month through nineteen months will, until they have it before them complete, perceive the relations of its finer threads to the whole pattern which is always before the eyes of the story-weaver at his loom." Just as Cuse and Lindelof continually play the high-stakes game of insisting that they know exactly where *Lost* is headed, despite the angry chorus of doubters, Dickens told his readers to get out of his face and to accept his authority over the narrative. His curiously antique image of a serial plotter—"the story-weaver at his loom"— presents Dickens as a pre-industrial artist, free of a huge public's accusations of disingenuous "retcon," and uncannily anticipates the picture we get of arch-schemer Jacob, in the Season Five finale, weaving inside the four-toed statue. The punishment inflicted on Jacob was one that Dickens managed to avoid from his agitated but always rapt audience.—**Sean O'Sullivan**

A Separate Reality—Next to Sawyer, Benjamin Linus is *Lost*'s most avid reader: *Brothers Karamazov* and *VALIS*—books given to him by Locke while in captivity; *The Gunslinger*—a King novel seen in his house in New Otherton; James Joyce's *Ulysses*—his plane book on Ajira 316. We also know, by hearsay, something about his dislikes: Adam opines (in "A Tale of Two Cities" [2.1]) that Ben would not read *Carrie*—despite his ownership of another Stephen King novel.

So it should not surprise us that young Ben is already bookish. In 1977, in "He's Our You" (5.10), teen Linus brings the captured Sayid a copy of Carlos Castaneda's *A Separate Reality: Further Conversations with Don Juan*, a book published earlier in the decade (1971), and recommends it highly (he has himself read it twice). The second volume in a controversial series that would eventually include nine books, *A Separate Reality* continues Castaneda's account of his difficult, mind-boggling apprenticeship to a Yaqui Indian medicine man, in which an anthropology graduate student is gradually weaned from his dependence on Western logic and rationality into the ways of a Native American sorcerer. (Castaneda would receive his PhD at UCLA for the third volume in the series, *A Journey to Ixtlan* [1972].) Books like Richard De Mille's *Castaneda's Journey: The Power and the Allegory* (1976), published the year before "He's Our You" takes place, had already begun to raise serious questions about the book's authenticity, and by the time Castaneda would die in obscurity in 1998 (his passing was not revealed until months later), the fictional nature of his work was widely acknowledged.

For many of us in the 1970s, Castaneda's Don Juan books were our introduction to the world of hallucinogenic drugs, and so it is only fitting that, later in the episode, DHARMA interrogator Oldham administers (with an eye dropper and a sugar cube) what appears to be a psychedelic to Sayid in order to get him to tell the truth. And where better for *A Separate Reality* to put in its cameo than Season Five, by far *Lost*'s tripiest?

The Third Policeman—When Desmond hurriedly packs a few belongings before he bolts from his underground home ("Orientation," 2.3), the camera briefly shows a copy of Flann O'Brien's novel *The Third Policeman*. Prior to this episode, rumors circulated that the book is important to understanding what is happening on *Lost*. Fans rushed to order the novel, a good read on its own, to discern any similarities between O'Brien's dark tale of life after death and the castaways' fate. The sudden increase in the book's popularity surprised publisher Dalkey Archive Press, which had to publish more copies, and illustrated the buying power of *Lost* fandom.

In O'Brien's novel, the narrator's journey involves a strange visit with two policemen at their station and on their rounds. Along the way, the student-turned-writer-turned-thief-turned-murder-victim learns about the absurd nature of the world he now inhabits. Bicycles, for example, not only meld with their owners physically and emotionally after they spend so much time riding together, but they also have a mind of their own. (A penny-farthing bicycle is the Village's logo in *The Prisoner*, forming yet another link among *Lost* and several ancestor "texts." See *The Prisoner* in the film and TV section.) Bicycles are an excellent example of the way "atomic theory" works; the atoms of humans and machines interact and eventually merge. Even more interesting, a mysterious vault contains whatever riches the policemen and the narrator can imagine; whatever they desire is provided. However, there is one catch: the goods cannot be taken above ground.

By the end of O'Brien's novel, the narrator finally meets the third policeman, who reveals to him the strange nature of time and space. They are not what living people presume, and the narrator discovers that what seems to have taken place only moments or hours before actually occurred in "real time" several years ago. He now can travel through walls or even back to his old home to visit with the partner who did him in for his share of pilfered wealth. O'Brien does more than create a good ghost story; he develops a "real" surreal world that plays with readers' notions of space and time, life and death.

Lost, however, may not imitate an important part of the book. O'Brien's main character, the story's narrator, is dead, although he fails to understand that for most of the novel. *Lost*'s creators persistently deny this is true of the castaways. Nevertheless, Claire's "transformation" that leads her to abandon her baby and join her dead father, Christian Shephard, in Jacob's cabin ("Cabin Fever," 4.11) makes us question whether she is alive or dead. The dead, like Charlie and Christian, seem to lead active lives, just as O'Brien's characters do.

What is a more direct link to the novel is the mysterious "box" Ben Linus introduces during Locke's second Season Three backstory ("The Man from Tallahassee," 3.13). To keep Locke in line, Ben tells Tom Friendly to bring the man from Tallahassee to the Barracks. Ben explains to Locke that whatever he wants can be provided by the "box." At the end of the episode, Locke discovers that the box has produced, to his shock and horror, the one person who could turn his island paradise into hell—his father. Although Ben insists that Locke is the one who has brought Anthony Cooper to the Island to work out their unresolved issues, Locke denies ever wanting to see his father again ("The Brig," 3.19). Apparently, whatever Ben desires, such as a way to motivate Locke to share his inside connection with the Island and to keep control of his followers, is manifested in the "magic box," just as it is in *The Third Policeman*.

The Turn of the Screw—As Locke looks for the DHARMA Initiative "Orientation" video just where Desmond told him it would be—"top shelf, right behind *The Turn of the Screw*," for just a moment the Dover edition of the classic Henry James' ghost story fills the left half of the screen. Set in a country house called Bly, not on a desert island, James' story is really the diary of a young governess who has become convinced the two small children she cares for, Miles and Flora, are demonically controlled by their former governess, Miss Jessel, and her lover, a servant named Peter Quint. The book has inspired a variety of readings since its publication in 1898, with some critics taking it to be a true tale of the supernatural and others convinced everything is in the mind of the young governess, who has "projected" the haunting out of her own repressed sexuality.

Other than serving (like *The Third Policeman*) as Desmond's reading material, is *Turn of the Screw* a *Lost* ancestor text? Mysterious children under the thrall of "Others"; the presence of ghosts—or are they?; an indecipherable text, capable of multiple interpretations. These factors make *Turn of the Screw* a must for the Hatch bookshelf, but it is clearly not a major source.

Ulysses—"How can you read?" a nervous-wreck Jack asks a battered-but-calm Ben onboard their Ajira Airlines flight back to the Island in "316" (5.6), and the episode owes its title to both the flight number and a particular page in the former leader of the Others' book, James Joyce's *Ulysses*. Ben's answer? Yet another prevarication from the prince of lies: "My mother taught me." (Mrs. Linus, of course, died in childbirth.)

More than 260,000 words in length, *Ulysses* (1922) offers enough reading material for the longest flight, even one like Ajira 316 that begins in 2008 and ends, for some of its passengers, in 1977. Ranked (by the Modern Library) as the most important English language novel of the twentieth century, *Ulysses* is a modernist version, rich in parallels to *The Odyssey*, of Homer's epic poem about Greek hero Odysseus' (in Latin "Ulysses") return from the Trojan War, and, as we establish elsewhere in these pages, is itself an important *Lost* ancestor text.

Set in Joyce's native Dublin, *Ulysses* focuses on three main characters: Stephen Dedalus (roughly the equivalent of Odysseus' son Telemachus), a writer Joyce had introduced in *Portrait of the Artist as a Young Man* (1916); Leopold Bloom (Odysseus/Ulysses), an advertising "canvasser"; and his wife Molly (a stand-in for the hero's long-suffering wife Penelope). The events of Joyce's novel take place on a single day, June 16, 1904—now celebrated in Dublin as Bloomsday.

In a promotion that aired before Season Five for "The *Lost* Book Club" on the official *Lost* website, Darlton spoiled *Ulysses*'s appearance, showing the cover of Ben's paperback edition, and even reading from the passage—on page 316—that had caught their attention and inspired their title:

*So off they started about Irish sport and shoneen games the like of the lawn tennis and about **hurley** and putting the stone and racy of the soil and building up a nation once again and all of that. And of course Bloom had to have his say too about if a fellow had a rower's heart violent exercise was bad. I declare* *to my antimacassar if you took up a straw from the bloody floor and if you said to Bloom: Look at, Bloom. Do you see that straw? That's a straw. Declare to my aunt he'd talk about it for an hour so he would and talk steady.*

No crystal ball nor Frozen Donkey Wheel enabled Joyce to foresee the coming of Hugo Reyes. The *Oxford English Dictionary* provides the following relevant meanings of the word as used in *Ulysses*:

1. The Irish game of "hurling"; hockey.
2. The stick or club used in this game; a hockey-stick; a club or cudgel of the same shape.
3. The ball used in "hurling."

Joyce's work has of course been brought to the big screen, though not always successfully. Perhaps the most ingenious of all the attempts is *James Joyce's Women* (Michael Pearce, 1985), which tells the story of six different real and imaginary Joycian females, including *Ulysses'* Molly Bloom. Molly's famous masturbation soliloquy is no doubt the most memorable (and longest) scene in the film. In a tour de force performance, one actress plays all six women, including Molly: Fionnula Flanigan—the woman who was responsible, in the guise of Mrs. Hawking, for identifying Ajira 316 as the vehicle for a return to the Island.

VALIS—In the first scene of "Eggtown" (4.4), Locke brings Ben some reading material, *VALIS* by Philip K. Dick (1928–1982). Ben, slightly offended that the book comes from his own collection, explains he's already read it. Locke suggests his nemesis read it again, saying, "You might catch something you missed the second time around." Ben apparently takes Locke up on the suggestion. He's seen reading the book two episodes later in "The Other Woman" (4.6). Given the novel's references to obscure Greek philosophers, Wagner's Parsifal, metaphysical philosophy, and the Dead Sea Scrolls, Locke's suggestion that Ben give the book another read is not unreasonable, nor is the book's appearance mere coincidence. The similarities between the novel and life on the Island should certainly strike Ben upon rereading the book.

The 1981 semiautobiographical novel is a complicated and dense metafictional exploration of what Dick termed his "mystical experiences," which began in March 1974. Impossible to summarize briefly, these involved communication with a higher intelligence that Dick termed VALIS, an acronym for Vast Active Living Intelligence System. He grappled with the nature of these experiences for the rest of his life, wondering if they constituted a legitimate divine experience or were perhaps a product of the same overactive imagination that made him such a respected and prolific science fiction writer.

In *æ*, Dick literalizes this duality by splitting his personality into two separate characters, Horselover Fat and Philip K. Dick. What follows is nothing less than an ontological whodunit that pits faith against reason as Horselover Fat, Philip K. Dick, and a small group of friends search for the latest incarnation of the Messiah. *VALIS'* presence as a *Lost* text of course fueled already-in-progress speculation about the Island as a living entity and enriched the popular hypothesis that the series' narrative might be some kind of Dickian simulation or illusion. But the similarities don't end there.

Both *VALIS* and *Lost* examine characters battling cancer (on *Lost*, Rose), and often use the illness as a way of questioning the morality of the universe. The pink, "information-rich" beam VALIS uses to communicate in the novel seems to have the ability to both cure and cause cancer. *VALIS*, like *Lost*, also features time travel. One aspect of Dick's mystical experience was that he believed he saw first century Rome superimposed over everything he saw and that an early Christian named Thomas occupied a place in his psyche. Dick felt that he was seeing what he called "partially actualized" realities that run parallel with our own. The laser Daniel Faraday uses to shoot the consciousness of Eloise the rat forward in time (in "The Constant" [4.5]) has many similarities to the pink light Dick describes in the novel.

In *VALIS*, Dick repeatedly quotes the Greek philosopher Heraclitus who proclaimed, "The nature of things is in the habit of concealing itself," and this theme may be its greatest connection to *Lost*. If the show's writers really want to mess with the minds of their most obsessive fans, *VALIS* is the perfect literary allusion, because the novel ultimately raises more questions than it answers. —**David Gill**

Watership Down—As Sawyer puts it in "Confidence Man" (1.8), Richard Adams' *Watership Down* is a nice little story about bunnies.

Just like *Lost*, the story isn't quite that simple or benign. Beneath the "nice bunny story" or "crash survivor story" lurk dangers and monsters in a world neither story's characters could have anticipated.

Lost fans quickly picked up on *Watership Down* as a possible ancestor text that could provide clues about the series' subplots. The rabbits face danger in their familiar world and escape toward what they hope will be a safer place. Although *Lost*'s castaways are forced to live on the Island instead of choosing to leave their homes, their encounters with dangerous monsters, human and otherworldly, and shifting timelines (at least during Season Five) force them to find new homes from time to time.

Throughout the series, the castaways' journeys require them to follow different leaders, depending upon the situation, but Jack and Locke lead them most often. *Watership Down*'s Hazel, the rabbit leader, finds a "paradise" with plenty of food, friendly rabbits, and few predators. Just as the Oceanic 815 and Ajira 316 survivors find threats within their Eden, such as Rousseau's, the DHARMA Initiative's, and the Others' deadly traps, snares, stations, and fences, Hazel discovers that his paradise hides wire snares. Cowslip, a spokesrabbit for the group already ensnared in this environment, knows about the deadly traps. He not only fails to share this information with the newcomers but refuses to help free a trapped rabbit. It seems that a few casualties are expected as a fair trade for food and relative safety from birds and dogs. Some *Lost* characters may be "Cowslips": Rousseau knows enough about the Others to fear them, but she doesn't share information easily. Kelvin saves Desmond from his wrecked boat and introduces him to the joys of underground living—with a price tag of personal freedom. Desmond has plenty of food and a relatively comfortable shelter, but as soon as he can escape, he imposes this fate on Locke and other castaways, leaving them to push the button. Ben knows how to leave and return to the Island, but he keeps this information to himself. Jacob apparently knows all about the Island, but he shares only cryptic messages with his faithful followers.

Watership Down's rabbits band together during their journey and develop a new society, with leaders and visionaries. The castaways do the same, as have other island societies before them. Season Five illustrates a long history of island inhabitants, from Jacob and his nemesis to the *Black Rock*'s castaways to the more recent Hostiles, DHARMA Initiative, and Others.

Watership Down's Fiver seems to have a sixth sense; his dreams often provide knowledge of current or future events. Several *Lost* characters act like Fiver at times: Locke follows his visions, which lead him to the Hatch and, after its destruction, to his captured friends living in the Others' camp; Charlie becomes motivated by his dreams to "save" other castaways; Eko acts in accordance with visions of his deceased brother Yemi. Desmond, however, becomes a true "Fiver" when he glimpses the future and modifies his actions either to prevent or ensure predicted events. He continues to have visionary dreams off the Island, when he receives a message "planted" during his stay on the Island; as a result, Desmond changes course to travel to the United Kingdom and United States, even though the journey endangers his family.

Part of the enjoyment of reading *Watership Down* is understanding the larger world from a rabbit's eye view. When Bigwig is nearly run down by a car one afternoon, he glories in the feel of wind rushing through his fur. He isn't afraid of the monster when it drives past. Bigwig believes the car can't hurt him during daylight. When the other rabbits point out road kill, Bigwig explains that the monster only kills at night. Then its large, bright eyes lure animals into its path of destruction. In a similar way, the Island's inhabitants (and the audience) only gradually become aware of *Lost*'s much bigger picture than the Island. The dangers, such as the Smoke Monster, look very different the more we learn about them. Only by the end of Season Six will we understand the complete story, which undoubtedly will present a very different perspective than the "rabbit's eye" views we've had for so many years.

In a similar way, Locke tempts fate by allowing the Monster to drag him toward and down a hole ("Exodus," 1.24). Locke tells Jack that he'll be alright, but Jack insists that Kate blow up the Monster in order to free Locke. As Locke regains his faith in the Island during Season Three, he seems to develop a divinely inspired understanding of the way some things work on the Island. Ben Linus, however, tells Locke that his understanding is limited, a problem that Ben begins to remedy in "The Man Behind the Curtain" (3.22). Locke may have limited knowledge, based only on his experiences with the Island; Ben is more like *Watership Down* readers, who understand how the greater world operates and might chuckle at Bigwig's interpretation. As Locke's and the Oceanic Six's understanding of the Island and its importance to men like Ben Linus and Charles Widmore increases, their (and our) initial ideas about the Island seem humorously naïve.

A Wrinkle in Time—Madeline L'Engle's Newberry Award–winning young adult science fiction action-adventure was published in 1962 and is widely considered a classic. The book focuses on the Murry family, primarily Meg, who goes on a journey with her younger brother, Charles Wallace, and her friend, Calvin, across space and time to find her missing physicist father. Mr. Murry, who had been working on a theory involving a tesseract as a way to travel through time, had mysteriously disappeared one day, effectively abandoning his family.

Late in Season One ("Deus Ex Machina," 1.19), Sawyer is seen reading L'Engle's book on the beach, and indeed *Wrinkle*, with its interesting parallel connections between central characters and themes, seems perfect reading material for *Lost* characters and viewers.

The strongest and most important of these parallels is the shared theme of space and time travel. The ability of the three children in L'Engle's novel to "wrinkle" is comparable to the Island's movement through space and time in *Lost*. Whereas the children are able to use this ability to find Mr. Murry, the Island is uncontrollable. Characters in *Lost* are forced to go whenever the Island's sporadic (not to mention potentially deadly) jumps through time take them.

In both *Wrinkle* and *Lost* many characters have troubled relationships with their parents, especially their fathers. In *Lost*, most major characters have a problem with one or more of their parents. In *Wrinkle*, Calvin suffers from neglect, while Meg and Charles Wallace's relationship with their father is strained due to his long (albeit forced) absence.

Charles Wallace and *Lost*'s Walt are two young "special" boys with extremely perceptive, if not psychic, abilities that allow them to know things before they happen. Presented as the "golden child" of their respective stories, they even share similar experiences, including being kidnapped.

Yet another point of comparison, both in appearance and purpose, is *Lost*'s "security system" and *Wrinkle*'s "the black thing." Both entities take on the shape of dark clouds, and their roles, at least initially, are as the monsters of their respective stories. The "black thing," however, remains a force of evil, while the true nature of Smokezilla remains unclear.

Settings in both stories mirror each other as well, especially *Lost*'s DHARMAville and *Wrinkle*'s Camazotz. In both places everything, from the clothes residents wear to the homes they live in, are uniform, and both appear to be utopian. Camazotz is a place where the people have "conquered all illness [and] deformity," a description fitting the Hanso Foundation's mission "to further the evolution of the human race and provide technological solutions to the most pressing problems of our time." Accompanying the appearance of perfection in both is the strong suggestion that something about these places is just wrong.

The governance of both "utopias" is likewise extremely similar. In *Lost*, "the Others" are led by a single person who acts based on decisions made by the mysterious Jacob, whose very existence until Season Five was in question. The CENTRAL Central Intelligence of *Wrinkle*'s Camazotz presides over the people according to the wishes of "IT," an evil being that makes few appearances. Both IT and Jacob are treated by their followers as absolute rulers whose decisions should be obeyed without question.—**Sarah Bryant**

Y: The Last Man—We already knew that Hurley's preferred reading material on planes is comic books. On Oceanic 815, after all, he was reading a Spanish version of *Green Lantern/Flash: Faster Friends*, Part One (as we saw in "Exodus"), later seen in the hands of Walt ("The Pilot"). So it shouldn't surprise us when Hurley again chooses a graphic novel, a Spanish language installment of Brian V. Vaughan and Pia Guerra's *Y: The Last Man*, to take along on Ajira 316 ("316," 5.6). (In sharp contrast, Hurley's more high brow fellow traveler Benjamin Linus is reading James Joyce's modernist masterpiece *Ulysses*.)

Published from 2003 to 2008 in sixty issues and ten collected volumes, *Y*, as the subtitle suggests, is about Yorrick Brown, the last surviving Y-chromosome possessing human on the planet after all males are killed by a mysterious plague. (All male mammals, with the exception of Brown's Capuchin monkey Ampersand, have also died.) Perhaps Hurley found the series' subject matter compelling after his time on the Island, where infant mortality remains a conundrum.

At the time of Ajira 316's departure, Hurley has evidently read as far as *Y*'s third volume, "One Small Step," in which two male and one female astronauts, who had been on the International Space Station at the time the plague hit, return to earth. The men soon die, but the woman turns out to be pregnant.

Hurley no doubt purchased his copy of *Y* in a Los Angeles bookstore, but Jorge Garcia might have been given a copy by its author, *Lost* writer Vaughan, coauthor of such Season Four and Five episodes as "Catch-22," "Confirmed Dead," "Meet Kevin Johnson," "The Shape of Things to Come," "The Little Prince," "Namaste," and "Dead Is Dead." *Y: The Last Man*'s appearance is thus a somewhat unnerving *Lost* moment, one of the few in which the series becomes self-conscious. "Why does it make us uneasy to know," the great Jorge Luis Borges once asked, "that the map is within the map and the thousand and one nights are within the book of *A Thousand and One Nights*? Why does it disquiet us to know that Don Quixote is a reader of the *Quixote*, and Hamlet is a spectator of *Hamlet*? I believe I have found the answer: those inversions suggest that if the characters in a story can be readers or spectators, then we, their readers or spectators, can be fictitious" ("Partial Enchantments of the Quixote"). *Lost* incorporates many real fictional books into its fiction, but *Y*'s appearance in the text is a kind of stunt casting in which a fictional character, Hurley, reads a real fictional book written by a real author who himself contributes to the creation of the *Lost*verse in which his book is read. Does not the moment make the knowing viewer a bit uneasy?

ANCESTOR TEXTS

Alice in Wonderland—Perhaps the most prominent literary ancestors of *Lost* are Lewis Carroll's *Alice's Adventures in Wonderland* (shortened to *Alice in Wonderland* for many filmed versions of the story, including Disney's animated movie; Disney is a parent company producing *Lost*) and the sequel, *Through the Looking-Glass and What Alice Found There*. *Lost* regularly incorporates *Alice* imagery, themes, and even characters from Carroll's works, particularly the iconic White Rabbit.

Early in the series, writers borrowed the *Wonderland* character for the episode "White Rabbit" (1.5), a reference inspiring multiple interpretations, both literary and musical. "White Rabbit" is Jack's first backstory, in which viewers see the frazzled doctor reach a breaking point. In his peripheral vision, an exhausted and guilt-ridden Jack sees a man who resembles his recently deceased father, but when he turns to get a closer look, the man disappears. Locke later convinces Jack it doesn't really matter whether the vision is real or not, but what is important is what Jack does when he sees the vision. During this episode, Jack confronts his troubled memories of his father and follows the apparition/hallucination through the jungle until he finally discovers caves with a limitless supply of fresh water where Jack's awe-filled entry into this wonderland ends. Like Carroll's White Rabbit, the apparition of Jack's father appears and disappears suddenly to get the flashbacks moving again. Much like Alice, Jack and his fellow castaways must accept their predicament and quickly adapt to their new nonsensical and unpredictable world in order to survive.

At times, Jack himself even seems like a White Rabbit. Alice's White Rabbit is often nervous and flighty, rushing from task to task with a never-ending fear of being late. Immediately after the plane crash, Jack rushes from person to person, crisis to crisis, in his fear that he won't be in time to save the wounded. In later episodes, Jack acts like the White Rabbit, the character who stands up to the king and demands that Alice be allowed to testify at her trial. In a flashback (during "All the Best Cowboys Have Daddy Issues," 1.11), he stands up to his father during a medical inquiry into Christian Shephard's actions during a botched operation. His testimony leads to his father's dismissal as chief of surgery. The court in *Alice in Wonderland* parallels the board of inquiry in "All the Best Cowboys Have Daddy Issues." Jack also stands up for Juliet during her murder trial ("Stranger in a Strange Land," 3.9). He confronts Ben, forcing him to intercede on Juliet's behalf to lessen her punishment. Perhaps most importantly, Jack's testimony at Kate's trial ("Eggtown," 4.4) helps bring about her plea bargain. Although these actions take place long after "White Rabbit," they are still Jack's White Rabbit moments.

White Rabbit imagery also appears in several episodes as a sign of hope, impending fortune, and the reclamation of identity. In "Tricia Tanaka Is Dead" (3.10), Vincent arrives on the beach carrying a decomposing arm with a white rabbit's foot hanging off the decaying finger. Vincent leads Charlie and Hurley to the DHARMA Initiative van that not only brings the beachmates closer together but also rekindles the hope that has been lost on the Island and later saves Jin, Bernard, and Sayid from the Others in "Through the Looking Glass" (3.23). Again, the White Rabbit signifies entering a new realm when in "Some Like it Hoth" (5.13), Miles Straume discovers that he has the supernatural gift of communicating with the dead. In a flashback, young Miles reaches under a concrete rabbit statue and pulls out a spare key to an apartment. Once inside, he realizes that he has been hearing the voice of a recently deceased man.

The White Rabbit also makes an appearance in another childhood flashback in the crucial Ben-centric episode "The Man Behind the Curtain" (3.20). While trying to escape the confines of the DHARMA Initiative, young Ben Linus releases a white rabbit to test DHARMA's sonic fence. Ben's mother, Emily, suddenly appears and advises Ben to wait for his time to join the Others. With blonde hair and a blue and white babydoll style dress, Emily bears a striking resemblance to the Carroll's descriptions of Alice, as well as the Disney version of the young girl.

As Ben ages, he takes on many of the characteristics of Carroll's Humpty Dumpty and Mad Hatter, such as the desire to perpetuate confusion and a love of mind games. In "A Tale of Two Cities" (3.1), the breakfast scene between Ben and Kate is almost a duplicate of John Tenniel's illustration of the Mad Hatter's tea party. Other *Lost* scenes and shots also replicate Tenniel's illustrations ("White Rabbit," 1.5, "Fire + Water," 2.12, and "Flashes Before Your Eyes," 3.8).

The Season Three finale is entitled "Through the Looking Glass," which is a shortened title of Carroll's 1871 sequel to *Alice, Through the Looking-Glass and What Alice Found There*, in which Alice willingly steps through the looking-glass into an alternate chessboard world where time is not linear, and the poem "Jabberwocky" makes sense. In the finale, Charlie, who has much in common with Alice (i.e., unable to resist temptation and has difficulty distinguishing reality from dreams such as in "Fire + Water," and both Alice and Charlie are ultimately striving for identity, purpose, and maturity), stops the jamming signal inside the Island's Looking Glass station, clear communication is opened between the Island and the outside world. Though destroyed at the conclusion of the episode, the Looking Glass is a place where self-reflection occurs and difficult decisions are made.

The convoluted sequence of events leading to the Oceanic Six's rescue propels them into a new world—a version of home very different "Through the Looking Glass" than they remember from their pre-crash lives. In this new world, when Kate and Jack set up house together, Jack reads Aaron a bedtime story: *Alice in Wonderland*. He tells Kate that his father used to read the book to him. Perhaps in this way *Lost*'s writers remind us that the next generation also will see life from a very different perspective—or travel into strange new worlds again.

As in Carroll's *Wonderland* and *Looking-Glass*, *Lost*'s jungle is full of hidden marvels and dangers. Just as in the Alice worlds, multiple timelines and parallel worlds seem to exist on the *Lost* island as well. Also in Carroll's works and *Lost*, games (especially chess), riddles, communication, and language are key motifs, particularly the use of French. In *Through the Looking-Glass*, the White Queen guides Alice through a life-size chessboard, advising Alice to speak in French when English cannot suffice and to also maintain a keen sense of who she is. In "Whatever the Case May Be," Shannon regains her confidence as she utilizes her fluency in French to assist the survivors in deciphering Rousseau's distress call.

"White Rabbit" and "Through the Looking Glass" have popular counterparts in music, as well as literature. Jefferson Airplane's Grace Slick wrote "White Rabbit in Wonderland" in 1967, with trippy lyrics echoing not only Carroll's Wonderland but Jack's as well. Several artists named albums after "Through the Looking Glass"; Toto (another *Wizard of Oz* link) used this title for their eleventh album. Whether in literature or music, Carroll's stories inspire the creative use of altered states of mind or worlds peripherally linked to our own, in which anything can happen. *Lost* is only one of the latest creative endeavors inspired by this ancestor text.—**Lisa Williams**

"The Damned Thing"—One of three relevant stories in Ambrose Bierce's "An Occurrence at Owl Creek Bridge"—we discuss the title story from this collection, as well as the equally relevant tale "A Psychological Shipwreck," elsewhere in this guide—"The Damned Thing" is a terrifying account of an invisible monster. In a fashion made popular by Edgar Allan Poe, the story is told via a mysterious diary and a too-incredible-to-be-true story-within-a-story read at an inquest. With the horribly mangled corpse of Hugh Morgan front and center before the coroner and assembled jury, William Harker, a reporter and friend of the deceased, tells the tale under oath.

Morgan, whose rural way of life Harker has come to study as research for a novel, had for some time been aware of an anomalous "damned thing" prowling his property. Although it is apparently, invisible, its presence can be detected, as Harker himself explains:

I was about to speak further, when I observed the wild oats near the place of the disturbance moving in the most inexplicable way. I can hardly describe it. It seemed as if stirred by a streak of wind, which not only bent it, but pressed it down—crushed it so that it did not rise; and this movement was slowly prolonging itself directly toward us.

Though not initially terrified himself, Harker looks on in alarm as his host fires both barrels of his shotgun at the spot, a blast that evidently hits home, for it produces an agonized cry.

Brushed aside by something he can feel but not see, Harker then looks on astonished at a terrible struggle:

All this must have occurred within a few seconds, yet in that time Morgan assumed all the postures of a determined wrestler vanquished by superior weight and strength. I saw nothing but him and not always distinctly. During the entire incident his shouts and curses were heard, as if through an enveloping uproar of such sounds of rage and fury as I had never heard from the throat of man or brute!

By the time he reaches his host, Morgan is dead.

The jurors don't believe a word of Harker's account and find that Morgan died from an attack by a mountain lion, but in the diary he left behind (which the coroner is reading in the story's opening scene) we are given an explanation "from beyond the grave" of the killer's real identity.

The monster is so large that it can blot out the stars—

"Sept. 2.—Looking at the stars last night as they rose above the crest of the ridge east of the house, I observed them successively disappear—from left to

right. Each was eclipsed but an instant, and only a few at a time, but along the entire length of the ridge all that were within a degree or two of the crest were blotted out. It was as if something had passed along between me and them; but I could not see it, and the stars were not thick enough to define its outline."

> *—Like those sounds we cannot hear because they are beyond the capacity of the ear to discern, the monster is of a "color" not visible to human sight.*

Not exactly Smokezilla, to be sure—Bierce's being, for example, is not in the habit of passing judgment on those it encounters—but in size, lethal power, and inscrutability, alike enough to be an imaginative ancestor/relation of the Island's own Damned Thing.

Gilgamesh—*Gilgamesh* appears as the answer to #42 down in a crossword puzzle Locke works in "Collision" (2.8). Gilgamesh, a Sumerian epic poem describing the friendship between a king of the same name and the wild half-man Ekindu, is recognized as one of the earliest literary works. Divided into twelve tablets (or books), the narrative guides human understanding about the nature and worship of deities, provides the purpose of death and suffering, and offers insight on how to be a good person and live a fruitful life. *Gilgamesh* includes the myth of the great flood (which appears in several other literary and religious texts, including the Epic of Atrahasis and the Bible).

While *Gilgamesh* is most certainly ideal reading material for anyone given its historical significance and overall literary merit and influence on countless other important literary texts, the *Lost* fan has even more incentive to read this ancient myth. Since appearing late in Season Two, many have asked why *Gilgamesh* was such an important crossword clue. Some theorize that Mr. Eko is a character based off the wild and unruly Ekindu, citing the character's bizarre prophetic dreams and his journey with the ruler Gilgamesh, a character that may or may not remind readers of Locke. There's also a door that Gilgamesh fashions for the Gods, not unlike the Blast Door Locke discovers during "Lockdown" (2.17). But the main reason that every *Lost* fan should read *Gilgamesh* is that most literary scholars have noticed startling parallels between *Gilgamesh* and *The Odyssey*—another must-read literary text.

The Little Prince—"The Little Prince," named for a children's book by Antoine de Saint-Exupery, is the title of the fourth episode of Season Five of *Lost*. In the opening pages the narrator laments, "So I lived all alone, without anyone I could really talk to, until I had to make a crash landing in the Sahara Desert six years ago." A beginning recognizable enough to the *Lost* viewer, but what is more familiar in the book is the theme of "taming"—that people need relationships even though it makes them vulnerable—which is particularly prominent in the eponymous episode.

In the book, the little prince learns about "taming" through an encounter with a fox he meets after arriving on Earth. The fox wants to be tamed, telling the little prince, "It means to create ties." He says, "If you tame me, we'll need each other. You'll be the only boy in the world for me. I'll be the only fox in the world for you." This reminds the little prince of the rose he left behind on his planet for whom he feels responsible. By the end of the book, the narrator has been tamed by the little prince just as he was tamed by the rose on his home planet. In the end, though, he must let the little prince leave.

Nowhere in *Lost* is this theme of being tamed more apparent than between Kate and baby Aaron. In "The Little Prince," Kate fights to keep Aaron's true identity a secret despite the fact that someone, later identified as Ben Linus, wants to expose the truth. Kate has always been fiercely independent, but while she claims she only wants to protect Aaron, the truth is she needs Aaron just as much as Aaron needs her. During the flashback at the beginning of the episode, Kate tells Jack that she wants to keep Aaron. She tells him, "I can't lose him, too." As in *The Little Prince*, the line between wanting to protect something and being afraid to lose it is blurred.

Kate and Aaron aren't the only characters facing this kind of dilemma. Locke has also been tamed, though not by a person. In the book, the narrator realizes that he has been tamed by the little prince after he leads him to water, saving his life. The relationship between Locke and the Island exemplifies this dynamic: the Island has healed him, and so he feels responsible for keeping it safe. Like the fox says in *The Little*

Prince, "You become responsible forever for what you've tamed." In the same way the narrator feels responsible for the little prince, Locke feels responsible for the Island.

In the course of Season Five, Locke leaves in order to try to bring everyone back, and Kate gives Aaron to his biological grandmother so she can return to the Island and find Claire. Ultimately, Kate and Locke, like the narrator in *The Little Prince*, are forced to let go of what tamed them.—**Caty Chapman**

Lord of the Flies—Because *Lord of the Flies* (1954) has been one of the most often-read books in American secondary schools for more than thirty years, it would be surprising if it had not influenced the creators of an American television series about the survivors of a plane crash on a desert island. Indeed, the novel is evoked at least twice on the series, once by Sawyer in "…in Translation" (1.17): "Folks down on the beach might have been doctors and accountants a month ago, but it's *Lord of the Flies* time now"; and later by Charlie in "What Kate Did" (2.9), when he observes that the Tailies went "all *Lord of the Flies*."

Written by British novelist and Nobel Laureate (1983) William Golding (1911–1993), *Lord of the Flies*, of course, had its own ancestor text. Golding's novel can be read as a revision/repudiation of R. M. Ballantyne's popular Victorian novel, *The Coral Island* (1857), in which shipwrecked proper little subjects of the Queen build themselves the very model of a modern British society on a desert island. Golding, whose next novel, *The Inheritors* (1955), would tell the story of the eradication of Neanderthals by early *homo sapiens*, would take a much darker view of how the marooned might behave.

As every reader of *Lord of the Flies* (or its CliffsNotes) knows, Golding's English schoolboys don't fare quite as well as *The Coral Island*-ers. Survivors of a plane crash and of some distant war they appear to be fleeing (Golding quite intentionally never makes the context clear), the boys must choose between two possible leaders: the quiet and serious Ralph, who would establish, with the advice and counsel of pudgy, thoughtful, bookish, bespectacled, asthmatic Piggy, a fledgling democracy on the island, and the aggressive, cruel, and hedonistic Jack. Lured by the attraction of becoming boys-run-wild—painting their faces, hunting wild boar, enjoying the pleasures of the tribe—Jack and his followers triumph. The only thing they need from Jack and Piggy is the occasional use of the latter's glasses in order to focus the sun's rays to start a fire.

Early on, fear spreads that there is a "Beast" on the loose, and even though the fabled monster is only an air force pilot who crashed and died on the island, Jack finds it convenient to keep the myth alive in order to maintain control over his subjects. (The image of the dead pilot in Peter Brook's 1963 film version of *Lord of the Flies* is evoked in the image of Naomi hanging from a tree in "Catch-22" [3.17].) A final encounter between Jack and his hunters and Ralph and Piggy over their common future should they never be rescued results in Piggy's murder with a deliberately toppled boulder. As the forces of Jack stalk Ralph, all are saved by the *deus ex machina* of the British Navy. At the end, a naval officer inquires if the boys have put on a "jolly good show. Like the Coral Island."

A few micro-similarities between *LoF* and *Lost* exist (though hardly as many as *Gilligan's Island/Lost*). Both islands have an asthmatic inhabitant: *LoF*'s Piggy ("Sucks to your ass-mar," repeated by friend and foe alike, is one of the book's most familiar lines) and *Lost*'s dearly departed Shannon. Glasses play a role in each narrative: Piggy's broken, then stolen, lenses not only mark his character but help to drive the plot; and, on *Lost*, Jack (with an assist from Sayid), provides glasses for the headache-afflicted but constantly reading Sawyer (who, if he had been on *LoF*'s island, would have been one of the first to belittle Piggy). Both in *LoF* and on *Lost*, the desert islanders hunt boar for food. Both narratives have a resident "monster" (the real nature of which on *Lost* remains, at the time of writing, still mysterious).

In its approach to the formation of a new society apart from civilization, however, *Lost* follows a middle road between *The Coral Island* and *Lord of the Flies.* By the end of Season Three, the *Lost*aways have not reverted to barbarism, but they have not yet exactly built a stable social order either. For much of Season One, after all, they lived apart as two enclaves, those who remained on the beach and those who had moved to the caves. Though we have yet to see a severance anything like that of Ralph/Jack, we have seen oppositions developing between several pairs. Jack/Sawyer, Michael/Jin (over Sun), Kate/Sawyer (they fought over a briefcase and a place on the raft long before they felt caged heat),

Sayid/Sawyer, Locke vs. Boone/Jack/Charlie/Eko/Sayid, Ana Lucia/
Sawyer...And they have done their share of killing: Boone (indirectly
by Locke), Ethan Rom (by Charlie), Goodwin and Shannon (by Ana
Lucia), Libby and Ana Lucia (by Michael), Coleen (by Sun), Paolo and
Nikki (by everyone), Anthony Cooper (by Sawyer), Ryan Price (by
Hurley), Jason (by Sayid), Tom (by Sawyer), Naomi (by Locke). With
the emergence of the Others in Season Three and their manipulation
and cruel physical mistreatment of the *Lost*aways, the likelihood of a
Lord of the Flies–like rending of the Island's social fabric came to seem
all the more likely, and when we got to know the DHARMA folk in
Season Five, some of them seemed not the harmless hippies we assumed but perfect candidates for the tribe of *LoF*'s Jack.

Lost Horizon—See the entry in Must-See Television and Movies.

Moby-Dick—The opening tease of "The Incident" (5.16–17), the two-
parter that closed *Lost* Season Five and introduced us to the mysterious
Jacob, showed us the Island patriarch working away at a spinning wheel
and then meticulously weaving, warp and woof, a large tapestry, seemingly involving Egyptian themes, prior to checking his traps on the
beach and filleting and cooking himself a fish.

The scene, which went on to give us Jacob's amiable discussion
with his nemesis, the Man in Black/Loophole Man, while watching the
Black Rock approach, provoked endless web speculation, none of which
referenced its fascinating ancestor text, *Moby-Dick* (1851). Herman
Melville's philosophical masterpiece about the mad quest of the peg-
legged Captain Ahab for revenge against a mysterious white whale is
built around a loom/weaving metaphor.

Narrated by a young sailor named Ishmael who signs on board *The
Pequod* for its last voyage, the novel's first chapter, "Loomings," firmly
establishes, like "The Incident"'s tease, the theme of weaving. Later in
the novel, when Pip, the cabin boy, is pulled to the bottom of the ocean
after his foot becomes entangled in a harpoon line, he goes mad after
seeing, in the depths, "God's foot upon the treadle of the loom."

Most importantly, in "A Bower in the Arsicades," Ishmael has his
mind blown on a South Pacific island by the sight of a giant skeleton in
the midst of the jungle:

A great Sperm Whale, which, after an unusually long raging gale, had been found dead and stranded, with his head against a cocoa-nut tree, whose plumage-like, tufted droopings seemed his verdant jet. When the vast body had at last been stripped of its fathom-deep enfoldings, and the bones become dust dry in the sun, then the skeleton was carefully transported up the Pupella glen, where a grand temple of lordly palms now sheltered it.

Deep inland, like a certain slave ship out of place far from the ocean, the whale is a thing of mystery:

The ribs were hung with trophies; the vertebrae were carved with Arsacidean annals, in strange hieroglyphics; in the skull, the priests kept up an unextinguished aromatic flame, so that the mystic head again sent forth its vapory spout; while, suspended from a bough, the terrific lower jaw vibrated over all the devotees, like the hair-hung sword that so affrighted Damocles.

In the ever-curious Ishmael, the jungled whale inspires a new understanding of the weave of existence:

It was a wondrous sight. The wood was green as mosses of the icy Glen; the trees stood high and haughty, feeling their living sap; the industrious earth beneath was as a weaver's loom, with a gorgeous carpet on it, whereof the ground-vine tendrils formed the warp and woof, and the living flowers the figures. All the trees, with all their laden branches; all the shrubs, and ferns, and grasses; the message-carrying air; all these unceasingly were active. Through the lacings of the leaves, the great sun seemed a flying shuttle weaving the unwearied verdure. Oh, busy weaver! unseen weaver!—pause!—one word!—whither flows the fabric? what palace may it deck? wherefore all these ceaseless toilings? Speak, weaver!—stay thy hand!—but one single word with thee! Nay— the shuttle flies—the figures float from forth the loom; the freshet-rushing carpet for ever slides away.

The scene thus prompts our narrator's deepest metaphysics: the realization that God himself is a weaver and the universe itself a tapestry:

The weaver-god, he weaves; and by that weaving is he deafened, that he hears no mortal voice; and by that humming, we, too, who look on the loom are deafened; and only when we escape it shall we hear the thousand voices that speak through it. For even so it is in all material factories. The spoken words that are inaudible among the flying spindles; those same words are plainly heard without the walls, bursting from the opened casements. Thereby have villanies been detected. Ah, mortal! then, be heedful; for so, in all this din of the great world's loom, thy subtlest thinkings may be overheard afar.

Unlike Pip, the knowledge does not drive Ishmael mad but results instead in an acceptance, indeed a celebration, of the ultimate inscrutability of the "material factory" of existence.

Now, amid the green, life-restless loom of that Arsacidean wood, the great, white, worshipped skeleton lay lounging—a gigantic idler! Yet, as the ever-woven verdant warp and woof intermixed and hummed around him, the mighty idler seemed the cunning weaver; himself all woven over with the vines; every month assuming greener, fresher verdure; but himself a skeleton. Life folded Death; Death trellised Life; the grim god wived with youthful Life, and begat him curly-headed glories.

Just the sort of understanding, an embrace of the linked destinies of life and death, that Jacob himself seems governed by. For when his Nemesis/Loophole Man asks with tranquil antipathy in their colloquy beneath the statue, "Do you have any idea how badly I want to kill you?" the ever-calm Jacob replies simply, "Yes," and to his rival's insistence that "one of these days I'll find a loophole," Jacob answers with supreme equanimity, "When you do, I'll be right here."

When *Lost*'s warp and woof comes to a close, when its narrative tapestry is finished in May 2010, maybe then we will be able to make sense of "the thousand voices that speak through it."

The Mysterious Island—Like *Lord of the Flies, Robinson Crusoe,* and *Lost Horizon,* Jules Verne's 1874 novel about a group of five Northern POWs escaping by balloon from the American Civil War who crash land on a mysterious island in the South Pacific (2,500 kilometers east of New Zealand) is a no-brainer *Lost* ancestor text, as even dim-bulb Shannon, who refers to the castaways' new home as "Mystery frickin' island" in "Whatever the Case May Be" (1.12), seems to realize. Though hardly a rival of *Lost*'s island in mysteriousness, Verne's nevertheless offers its fair share of odd goings-on. One of the balloon's passengers impossibly survives a fall; guns and ammunition and a cure for malaria appear out of nowhere; a menacing pirate ship blows up, its crew slaughtered. The mysteries, however, are all explained when the novel turns out to be a chronologically impossible sequel to *20,000 Leagues Under the Sea* and the island the last sanctuary of Verne's scientific genius Captain Nemo. The builder and master of the *Nautilus* dies of old age, and the balooniacs escape a volcanic eruption that destroys Lincoln Island and make it back to civilization.

Verne's enigmatic atoll has no monster, no unexplained numbers, no ghosts, no creepy whispers, no time dislocation. But the two narratives do share arrivals by a balloon (recall the late Henry Gale from Minnesota?), pirates, dogs, the baffling arrival of supplies. These coincidences could be mere chance, but a shared orangutan named Joop—domesticated by the Union soldiers in *Mysterious Island*; the subject of controversial experimentation by the Hanso Foundation in *Lost*—confirm that *Lost*'s makers were familiar with Verne's book. And Darlton hint (in the DVD commentary to "The Man Behind the Curtain") that the Island's volcano, mentioned by young Ben's teacher in the episode, will make a reappearance before the series is over.

The Odyssey—The second of the great epic poems by the Greek bard known as Homer—a sequel, if you will, to *The Iliad*, the story of the Trojan War, *The Odyssey*, written sometime between 800 and 600 BC, tells the story of Greek hero Odysseus' long (ten year), arduous return home from Troy after a total of twenty years away from his beloved Ithaca, his son Telemachus, and his long-suffering wife Penelope.

Prior to the final episode of Season Two of *Lost* ("Live Together, Die Alone"), *The Odyssey* had shown no sign, other than being one of the foundational works of all western literature, of being a *Lost* Ancestor Text. The *Lost*aways have met many adversaries, fought polar bears, monsters, and human killers, but no deity like Poseidon or witch like Calypso, no Scylla and Charybdis or Cyclops (we hadn't met Mikhail/Patchy yet) or Siren, have threatened their lives or offered supernatural temptations.

But then, in the Season Two finale, we are properly introduced to

Penelope, Penny, the love, the constant, of Desmond's life, the woman he had deserted in order to embark on a round-the-world sailing race sponsored by her father Charles Widmore (using a boat given to him by Libby), in order to impress him, in order (as we learn in "Flashes Before Your Eyes" [3.8]) that he might fulfill his destiny as laid out for him by former resident Eloise Hawking: to crash on the Island, input, for years, the numbers in the Hatch, and be the one to turn the failsafe key and save the world.

Penelope Widmore, it is true, has not been required to fend off, as her Homeric namesake must, a score of suitors seeking her hand in the absence of her great love, but she has not been idle. As we learn in the "What the x&#*&?" final moment of Season Two, she has used her fortune to find her Odysseus by identifying the geo-synchronous location of electromagnetic anomalies, as tracked by her Portuguese researchers Mathias and Henrik. How it is that she knew Desmond would be found where such an irregularity is detected—that we still don't know. Had Penny been talking to Mrs. Hawking? Doubtful, because when they meet in the hospital after Ben shoots Desmond, they do not know one another. Why did Naomi—about whom Penelope knew nothing (as she told Charlie)—carry a photo of Desmond and Penny?

Des and Penny are reunited in Season Four's final episode (an end to their Odyssey set up in the brilliant and poignant "The Constant" [4.5]), but Ben had promised Charles Widmore (in "The Shape of Things to Come," [4.9]) to seek revenge for Keamy's murder of his daughter Danielle by finding and killing the daughter of his nemesis, and he comes close to making good on his vow in "Dead Is Dead" (5.12) until Des and Penny's son gives him pause and a wounded Desmond beats the crap out of him

We do not yet know what will become of Des and Penny, but with Penelope firmly established as one of *Lost*'s major players, with Desmond's odyssey elevated from minor tale to epic status, *The Odyssey* must now be considered as a prime *Lost* Ancestor Text.

Of Mice and Men—John Steinbeck's *Of Mice and Men* must have made a big impression on Sawyer. He reads it in prison, which helps when he later uses literary metaphors to spar with Ben Linus. In "The Brig" (3.19), Sawyer later wonders if Locke, like Ben a few weeks earlier, may be leading him to an isolated spot to trick or attempt to kill him; the con man tells Locke that he remembers the bunny. Sawyer's connection with the book seems to haunt him; he might pride himself on being as manipulative as George, but he could secretly fear being Lennie.

In the novel, friends George and Lennie begin work on a new ranch; they had to move on because large, strong, childlike Lennie unintentionally assaulted a woman, who pressed charges. As a manifestation of his childlike demeanor, Lennie likes to pet animals, but because he is mentally challenged, he does not realize that his touch is too forceful. He often kills the animals as he pets them. Nevertheless, he hopes one day to tend rabbits on his own farm. After all, rabbits are larger and might withstand his loving care.

In a fateful encounter with the flirtatious wife of his new boss' son, Lennie accidentally snaps her neck. Once more George and Lennie escape, but this time the friends cannot simply slip away. With a mob close behind them, George takes Lennie to a quiet spot where he tells him once more about their rabbit farm. Just before George kills him to "save" him from the mob, Lennie asks again if he can pet the bunnies. They become his last sweet thought.

During "Every Man for Himself" (3.4), Ben Linus tortures Sawyer with the idea that an implanted pacemaker can easily kill him if his heart rate becomes elevated. Ben even shakes to death a test bunny, also with a pacemaker, to prove his point. Although he later reveals that the bunny is fine, ever-skeptical Sawyer knows that this might be the second Bunny #8. (A similarly marked rabbit is mentioned in "On Writing," part of Stephen King's memoir; King is a *Lost* fan, and his books, such as *Carrie*, are mentioned in or are ancestor texts for the series.) Like the rabbit, Sawyer is a replaceable test subject.

Ben repeats lines from *Of Mice and Men*, which Sawyer recognizes. He asks if Ben/George has brought him on a long hike just to kill him. Sawyer, like Lennie, may not know his own cruel power over people; his words and actions kill relationships just as surely as his gun kills his enemies. Ben assures Sawyer that murder is not his intention, but he swiftly kills Sawyer's hope for escape when he explains that the Others live on a second island.

"A Psychological Shipwreck"—As we point out elsewhere, the appearance of a collection of stories by the nineteenth-century American writer Ambrose Bierce in the Swan invites investigation of several of the tales contained within as *Lost* Ancestor Texts (see also "An Occurrence at Owl Creek Bridge" and "The Damned Thing"). One such candidate is "A Psychological Shipwreck." As Jeff Jensen has suggested in his comprehensive, controversial *Lost* theorizing in *Entertainment Weekly*, this enigmatic tale about an ocean voyage, a love affair, and a transportation calamity that may or may not have happened is clearly worthy of our attention.

"Shipwreck" is narrated by an American merchant sojourning (in 1874) in Liverpool after the collapse of his business, who books a return home on a sailing vessel called, significantly, *The Morrow*. *The Morrow* carries only two other passengers, a young South Carolina woman and her black maid, traveling suspiciously alone after her traveling companions, a married couple, had both died in Devonshire. In a bizarre coincidence, the husband had the same name, William Jarrett, as the narrator.

The narrator finds himself attracted to his fellow passenger, Janette Harford, but reassures himself that it is not love he feels. One night, on the eve of the Fourth of July, he is overwhelmed by a bizarre notion:

It seemed as if she were looking at me, not with, but through, those eyes—from an immeasurable distance behind them—and that a number of other persons, men, women and children, upon whose faces I caught strangely familiar evanescent expressions, clustered about her, struggling with gentle eagerness to look at me through the same orbs. Ship, ocean, sky—all had vanished. I was conscious of nothing but the figures in this extraordinary and fantastic scene.

At the moment this strange inversion takes place, a book, Denneker's *Meditations*, lies in the lady's lap, and the narrator takes note of a perplexing passage suggesting the possibility of consciousness switching bodies.

A calamity, not fully explained, ensues, and the ship goes down. Later, the narrator finds himself on a steamer, *The City of Prague*, stranded because of a mechanical breakdown, on which he has apparently been traveling all along, accompanied by his friend Gordon Doyle, whose fiancé, Janette Hartford, is likewise on her way to America—on board the sailing vessel *The Morrow*.

Doyle is, of course, reading Denneker's *Meditations* as well (his fiancé had a second copy). Leafing through it, the narrator's attention is directed to the same passage—marked by Doyle—about swapping consciousness with another. At this point the story abruptly ends with these words:

A week later we were towed into the port of New York. But The Morrow *was never heard from.*

Needless to say, "A Psychological Shipwreck" considered as a *Lost* Ancestor Text lends fuel to the fire not only of that tiny band of "Two Plane Theory"[4] advocates (Bierce's tale, after all, has two ships), but all those fans who want to read the events of the series as in some way unreal/delusional/in-the-mind. The temptation to see the entirety of *Lost* as a "psychological shipwreck" begins with its opening shot (in "The Pilot") of Jack's eye. Is everything that then ensues, some have wondered, in Dr. Shephard's mind? It is safe to say that, when *Lost* finally reaches port (aka when the series ends), if it turns out it has all been somehow an illusion, we, and a huge majority of viewers who have completed the entire journey, will be mighty disappointed. Then again, at the end of Season Five of *Lost*, hardly any reason remains for such a reading.

Robinson Crusoe—Daniel Defoe's 1719 book about a man shipwrecked for twenty-eight years on an island is an obvious ancestor text for *Lost*. The original story has been popular for nearly three hundred years and so is the ancestor of several films and television shows. In October 2008, *Crusoe*, a TV series version of the tale obviously inspired as much by *Lost*'s success as Defoe's novel, began airing on NBC. It lasted for thirteen episodes, the last one airing in January 2009.

Defoe's hero may have written the survival handbook for the *Lost* castaways' behavior during Season One. These characters seem determined to survive after a wreck, whether by ship or plane, and they approach life on the island in remarkably similar ways. Crusoe is the only survivor from his ship and must rely only on himself for several years, until he saves the man he dubs Friday from cannibals and thus gains a companion for the remainder of his stay on the island. Although the *Lost* castaways share the workload among more people, they, too, gain new companions, such as the Tailies (after Season Two's "The Other

28 Days" and its aftermath) and Desmond, who officially joins beach society in Season Three. Instead of fearing cannibals, the castaways fear the Others, who favor abducting children and pregnant women, although they are also known to take other adults prisoner.

Crusoe's initial plan, one the modern castaways share, includes salvaging goods from the wreck, finding food and water, building a shelter, and setting up camp for the long haul. Both Crusoe and Michael build rafts, although Michael wants to use his to leave the Island instead of hauling supplies from the wreck, as Crusoe does. Crusoe easily finds a pure water source and soon begins to hunt birds and fish. Jack eventually finds fresh water in the caves; Locke hunts boar; and Jin fishes.

Robinson Crusoe shares other minor plot points with characters from *Lost:*

- Crusoe thankfully has scavenged goods from the ship before the wreckage is washed to sea. The castaways abandon the fuselage, after it has been stripped of usable parts and supplies, because a rapidly rising tide begins to wash away the wreckage.

- Crusoe's masted wooden ship may have looked similar to the *Black Rock* beached miles inland on *Lost*'s mysterious Island.

- Like Crusoe, whose family name originally is Kreutznaer, Sawyer abandons his family name (Ford).

- "Father issues" come into play in both stories. Crusoe fails to take his father's advice and live a comfortable, safe, middle-class life in England. Instead, he goes against his father's wishes and takes up a life of adventuring. The senior Crusoe warns his son that he will live a miserable life if he insists on going to sea, but Robinson disregards this warning. Later, stranded on the Island, Robinson remembers his father's words and wonders if God is punishing him, a question that Sun also asks herself. Several *Lost* characters disagree with their fathers or father figures and, on the Island, ponder their troubled relationships. More specifically like Crusoe, Desmond vows to prove his love Penelope's father wrong about her suitor's worth and goes to sea to win an around-the-world race; Charlie follows his interest in music, despite his father's objection, and often suffers because of his career and life choices; Claire disregards the prediction of the psychic (a possible father figure), who says she must be the one to raise her baby, or something bad will happen.

- Crusoe keeps a journal of his island life, as does Claire.

- While on the island, Crusoe talks to God and becomes more spiritual. Locke finds that the Island provides him with a miracle; he establishes his own dialogue with the Island, his deity. Eko and Charlie also periodically "find religion" on the Island.

- Crusoe is rescued from the island by the mutinying crew of a passing ship, similar to the inhabitants of *Lost*'s mysterious Island being found by the freighter folk. When Charles Widmore's mercenary leader, Martin Keamy, becomes too vicious for the freighter's captain and crew to abide, they turn against him. Helicopter pilot Frank Lapidis helps rescue the Oceanic Six plus Desmond, a direct violation of Widmore's orders.

Defoe's *Robinson Crusoe* became a popular novel in its time and succeeding centuries because it offered an escapist story that allowed readers to wonder what they might do in a similar situation. It put readers in an exotic location very different from their homeland and gave them the vicarious freedom to do exactly as they pleased. *Lost* provides similar escapist fare in an exotic location, but its themes more often illustrate how people must work together to survive.

Those who have never lived through such an ordeal tend to romanticize it as an "adventure" and don't understand just how traumatic the experience can be. The readers of *Robinson Crusoe* might have longed for their own escape to a remote island to do as they pleased, but they probably didn't understand the magnitude of Crusoe's life-or-death experiences, just as Hurley's parents, happily throwing their newly returned son an island-themed birthday party ("There's No Place Like Home," 4.14), have no idea of all that occurred before the rescue.

Solaris—Almost from the beginning, *Lost* fan speculation has been fanned by the frequent appearance on the Island of figures from the *Lost*aways' past. Early in Season One ("White Rabbit," 1.5), Christian Shephard appears to his son Jack. Dave, Hurley's "imaginary" friend from the Santa Rosa Mental Institute, arrives, challenges his sanity, and nearly lures him to his death ("Dave," 2.18). Mister Eko's brother Yemi appears to him in dreams and does lure him to his death at the hands of the Monster ("The Cost of Living," 3.5). A cat from Sayid's *Death and the Maiden*ish encounter with a woman he tortured in Iraq appears at Mikhail Bakunin/Patchy's in "Enter 77" (3.11). Locke's dastardly father shows up as "The Man from Tallahassee" (3.13). Is the Island, or perhaps the magic box Ben speaks of ("The Man from Tallahassee"), somehow able to materialize beings from the characters' memories?

In Stanislaw Lem's science fiction novel *Solaris* (1961), and in two film adaptations, Andrei Tarkovsky's 1972 Russian version and Steven Soderberg's 2002 American one (starring George Clooney and *Lost*'s Daniel Faraday, Jeremy Davies—as a physicist of all things!), a distant planet, covered almost entirely by a vast ocean, which seems to be a living sentient organism, is capable of reproducing, out of the minds and memories of all those humans who venture near it, almost exact, biologically functional replicas of individuals dear to them, and, although its motives in doing so are never fully understood, it seems to offer them as gifts and as experiments in understanding, despite disastrous results. Among its replications is the ex-wife of the novel's narrator, Kris Kelvin, a woman he helped drive to suicide years before.

At the novel's close, after enduring the agonizing second loss of his wife's double, Kelvin confides to Snow, the Solaris station's expert on cybernetics, that he has come, after a futile effort at comprehending Solaris' mysteries, to think of the planet-ocean as an aspect of an evolving ego, which in an early stage of development approached "the divine state" but "turned back into itself too soon" and became, instead of a god, an "anchorite, a hermit of the cosmos," completely under the sway of repetition, as witnessed in the endless formations—"mimoids"—gestated by its waters.

If we were to replace the name of Kelvin in the above account with that of John Locke (or perhaps Benjamin Linus), exchanging, too, "the Island" for each mention of "Solaris" or "the ocean," would we not be well on our way to transforming Lem's mind-boggling SF into something more *Lost*-like?

The Stand—The writers and creators of *Lost* have specifically stated on several occasions that Stephen King's 1977 novel *The Stand* never leaves the writer's room. On podcasts and in interviews, Abrams, Lindelof and Cuse repeatedly hint at the importance of the book, its characters, and storyline, "We took *The Stand*," Cuse would insist, for example, "and put it on an island." The parallels are indeed remarkable.

King's novel opens with an outbreak of a weapons-grade influenza virus in a secret government weapons facility in the California desert. When the quarantine protocol fails, one man is able to escape along with his wife and child, effectively exposing the rest of the United States population to a super flu popularly known as "Captain Tripps" that kills off 99 percent of the population. The novel chronicles the virus' effects and the plight of the immune as they struggle to find potable water and uncontaminated food in a post-flu world. They are involved in a deeper battle as well—one of good versus evil, God versus Satan, as survivors are divided into two distinct camps based on dreams and their inherent goodness (or evilness) as they travel to either Mother Abigail's camp in Boulder, Colorado (the "Free Zone"), or Randall Flagg's in Las Vegas, Nevada.

The threat of disease exists in both *The Stand* and *Lost*: In King's work, disease is the catalyst for all the novel's action. In *Lost*, we first hear of its presence on the Island when mentioned by Rousseau in "Solitary." The presence of disease reappears when Kate "Quarantine" stamped on the inner hull of the Hatch ("Man of Science, Man of Faith," 2.1), Desmond's inoculates himself daily, and the mural on the Swan station hatch wall pictorially depicts a deadly sickness. Whatever the disease is, Rousseau explicitly defines it as dangerous—dangerous enough to cause her to kill a crew of researchers that included her husband.

The most obvious parallels between *The Stand* and *Lost* exist in the characters. Several share similar traits and attitudes.

- **Frannie Goldsmith and Claire Littleton.** The first and most apparent is King's Francis "Frannie" Goldsmith and Claire Littleton. Both women are young and pregnant and struggle with the realities of their pregnancy in less than optimal conditions. Both keep a diary, exhibit similar fears about motherhood and raising their children, and have psychic experiences through dreams. Frannie repeatedly dreams of Mother Abigail, the emissary of goodness who beckons the survivors first to her old homestead in Nebraska and later to Boulder, Colorado. Claire dreams of the *Black Rock* and fuzzy details of her capture. Both are carrying children that have extreme significance: Frannie's child will be the first born in a post-flu world and will let the survivors know if the human race can hope for long-term survival, and Claire's child is born on an island that is in quarantine for an unknown disease. Eventually, both Frannie and Claire give birth to male children that do survive: Frannie's Peter fights off Captain Tripps, and Claire's Aaron survives a kidnapping initiated by Rousseau.

- **Larry Underwood, Harold Lauder, and Charlie Pace.** Charlie can be seen as a combination of two characters in *The Stand*: Larry Underwood and Harold Emery Lauder. Larry is a one-hit-wonder guitarist and singer with a history of cocaine use and has never been an all-around nice guy. He has let several people down in his life, including his religiously pious mother. At the novel's beginning, as Captain Tripps claims its first victims, Larry is on the run from California after blowing his advance from the record company and owing debt collectors forty thousand dollars. He journeys to New York to hide out with his mother. Larry's quasi-hit, "Baby, Can You Dig Your Man," appears throughout the novel, sung by Larry and other characters as an ephemeral thread between the characters and the old world, not unlike Driveshaft's "You. All. Everybody." Selfish and self-absorbed before the flu, he only gradually achieves redemption, mostly acquired through witnessing the horrific deaths of his mother and a traveling companion. Charlie, of course, mirrors Larry in his rock-star status and his drug use, but he calls to mind King's Harold Lauder as well, an inveterate loser devoted to Frannie Goldsmith.

When the two are the only survivors in Quantagnut, Maine, Harold positions himself in the role of protector for Frannie in a way similar to Charlie's desire to protect Claire. Mild-mannered and apparently harmless. Harold exhibits a streak of violence that is unexpected and uncontrollable—much like Charlie when he takes revenge on Ethan Rom for kidnapping Claire. In addition, both Harold and Charlie read their beloved's diaries.

- **Stuart Redman and Jack Shephard.** Stuart, or "Stu," Redman is a rough-and-tumble east Texan who escapes from the disease control center in Stovington, Vermont. Despite their obvious difference in education and a country drawl that might remind some of Sawyer, Stu most resembles Jack. Like him, Stu becomes a reluctant leader, forced into his role because no else is there to do it. He uses deadly force only when necessary, a policy Jack also follows. And both serve as "shepherds" for their wayward "flocks," placed in control of the group without requesting the position. When Stu's traveling party is joined by a man with an appendicitis, Stu finds a medical textbook and attempts to save the man by performing an impromptu appendectomy—a surgery that mirrors Jack's futile effort to save Boone. Stu exhibits the same degree of stubborn control that Jack aspires to have and does not want to give up—even after his patient has died from blood loss.

  Named Marshal of the Free Zone following Mother Abigail's death, Stu becomes a psychic superconductor, receiving prophetic visions from the beyond. Jack takes on the role of the Island's only doctor and its unconventional leader, delegating responsibilities, such as burial of the dead, finding a water source, and ushering the survivors to the caves, and eventually warming to his role as protector and leader. But Stu and Jack are both coaxed into this role by others, Glen Bateman and John Locke, respectively, who suggest that good, strong leadership is central to the continuity of the new society that they hope to form.

- **Glen Bateman, Trashcan Man, and John Locke.** Locke's character can be understood as an interesting (and conflicting) combination of King's Glen Bateman and the "Trashcan Man." Glen Bateman is a retired sociologist, painter, and all-around philosophical good guy. Accompanied by an Irish Setter (named Kojak) that he found post-flu, Bateman is both practical and realistic: he sees the promise in the social and psychological realities brought about by the flu, the capacity to build a new world in place of the old, predicts the coming order of things, attempts to explain away the supernatural elements all the survivors are experiencing, and remains benevolent throughout the course of the novel. Like Glen, Locke contemplates the needs of their new society long before the other survivors. Like him, he is a counselor and spiritual facilitator for others (see Chapter Four). Unlike Locke, however, Glen is not a firm believer in the spiritual elements of the survivor's experiences. Locke's profound and un-blinking faith in the Island does resemble the strange religiosity of *The Stand*'s Trashcan Man, who, while manic and unquestionably insane, believes in the spiritual dimension 100 percent.

- **Rita Blakemoore and Shannon Rutherford.** King's Rita Blakemoore is rich and insufferable, and it is only through Larry Underwood's help that she is able to make it outside of New York City alive. Rita is accustomed to the finer things in life, has a frivolous attitude, and has no idea how to take care of herself—all characteristics shared by Shannon Rutherford. Rita tries to hike in stylish heeled boots, pops a Valium when reality is too much for her, and is constantly nostalgic about the life she once had; Shannon sunbathes in a bikini and gives herself a pedicure while others seek to recover from the crash. And both Shannon and Rita prove themselves to be extraneous to their stories: Rita kills herself (a drug overdose); Shannon is shot by Ana Lucia.

- **Kate as Lloyd Henreid and Nadine Cross.** In the pre-crash world, Kate Austen is a fugitive. She stands accused of murder-ing her biological father, Wayne, organizing a bank robbery, and bringing about the death of Tom, her high school sweetheart. The character most similar to Kate is Lloyd Henreid, a criminal by nature who survives on the body of the man in the adjourning cell and a rat for weeks following the flu outbreak, before Flagg offers him redemption. Lloyd is Flagg's "soldier," his right-hand man, and experiences a redemption based on accepting the spe-cial status Flagg offers him.

From the moment the Marshal is knocked unconscious as the plane goes down, Kate proactively works to secure her own survival. Unlike Lloyd, however, Kate does not appear to intend to serve (or desire to serve) evil, but she does struggle with the concept of goodness. In "What Kate Did," she desperately longs to be good, condemning Jack for his goodness and her mother's bad choices as the reason that, forever tarnished and marked with badness, she can never be *truly* good.

Nadine Cross in *The Stand* struggles with the teeter-totter of good versus evil. She tries to make good by joining up with Larry Underwood, for she sees the capacity for transformation in him and knows he is a "good" man. But, Nadine is drawn inexplicably to the west and Randall Flagg. She is to be his bride, his intended, and in that respect believes herself to be evil. Nadine is attracted to both Larry and Randall in a way that mirrors Kate's attraction for both Jack and Sawyer. As much as Kate wants goodness for herself, and possibly believes that Jack's good nature might finally redeem her, she is drawn to Sawyer. Ultimately, Nadine chooses Flagg and regrets her choice, eventually killing herself in a final attempt to repent.

- **Mother Abigail, Mr. Eko, and Rose.** Mother Abigail is the penultimate "good" character in *The Stand*. She is 108 years old, communicates with the other survivors through psychic dreams, and has pipeline access to the word of God. She is benevolent and warm and good—all qualities that inspire others to travel across the country to join her. The African American Mother Abigail has traits similar to both Rose and Mr. Eko on *Lost*. Rose, after all, is spiritual and has unwavering faith in her husband's survival, despite his being in the tail section. She prefers to dry her laundry on a clothesline (as does Mother Abigail), and appears to exhibit certain psychic tendencies similar to Mother Abigail's.

  In the first half of Season Two, Mr. Eko appears to be religious or spiritual to some extent. He pays penance for those that perished in the crash and the Others he killed on their first night on the Island by observing forty days of silence. He carries a stick that he carves as he makes his journey across the Island. And he tells Locke an obscure Old Testament story about the long forgotten King Josiah. Eko's references to scripture are similar to Mother Abigail's—the elderly mother often references scripture in the course of the book, occasionally as hidden clues.

- **Joe/Leo and Walt Lloyd Porter.** Nadine Cross and "Joe" find Larry following the death of Rita Blakemoore, and Larry spends a great deal of time helping to care for the two. Nadine found Joe in a grocery store, abandoned, mute, and feral. The child cannot communicate and often reacts with a predatory anger toward those that try to touch or confine him, and it is only with careful provocation that he emerges from his silent shell. When the boy finally becomes comfortable with Nadine and Larry, he informs them that his name is Leo, and from that moment on, Leo acts as a psychic conductor, knowing things about people that no ordinary child would know. Leo is first to notice Harold's deceit and perceives Nadine's darkness as soon as she commits herself to her "destiny" as the Dark Man's bride. Leo's psychic ability is similar to Walt's on *Lost*: both boys are able to perceive the thoughts and feelings of others, and both can "read" the goodness or badness inherent in others. The boys also share an interesting vengeful streak: Leo attempts to stab Larry several times as he sleeps; Walt burns down his father's first raft so they cannot leave the Island. Seeking mentors, they both form relationships with men other than their father: Leo seeks out and bonds with Larry, and Walt grows close to Locke.

- **The Black Rock.** A "black rock" exists in both the novel and *Lost*. Randall Flagg's symbol, worn by his followers, is a black stone marked with a red flaw, on more than one occasion is referred to as "the Black Rock." The Black Rock in *The Stand* is able to change shape and meaning—Flagg turns it into a key on more than one occasion—the key to the demonic kingdom that all his followers are promised.

  The *Black Rock* in *Lost*, first mentioned in the paranoid mumblings of Rousseau, is a marked location on her map and a place on the Island that she avoids. By the end of Season One, we learn that the *Black Rock* is a run-aground, masted slave ship of unknown age and origin that, among other things, houses some very old dynamite. Rousseau's hesitation to go on board the ship indicates that the place is more frightening and sinister than she is willing to say. The ambiguity of the ship's name (and unanswered questions about its meaning or how it got on the Island) closely parallels the ephemeral concept of the black rock that Randall Flagg's followers wear.

- **Animals.** Animals appear as symbolic in both *The Stand* and *Lost*: Randall Flagg often appears as a crow or sends out packs of gray wolves to do his bidding and spying. Rats swarm the cornfields in front of Mother Abigail's homestead, and she attributes the rodents to "The Devil's Imp"—Randall Flagg.

  On the Island, the Others have sharks and polar bears that appear to display significance—especially that shark emblazoned with a DHARMA logo. A black horse may be the animal embodiment of Kate's dead father, and Charlie is inspired to break his heroin addiction thanks to a magnificent Moth.

  Kojak in *The Stand* and Vincent on *Lost* are both extraordinary dogs. Kojak survives a few encounters with the Dark Man's wolves and tracks across the country looking for his owner, Glen Bateman. Vincent goes missing on several occasions in Seasons One and Two, most notably his disappearance and reappearance following the crash. Kojak is even the point of view character for a passage in the course of *The Stand*, a dog's-eye-view of his journey and all the perils encountered along the way. Damon Lindelof admits that he had initially hoped to close out the first season with an episode from Vincent's perspective but discarded the idea after news of the concept leaked out onto the Internet.

- **Us vs. Them**. *The Stand* is often billed as a battle between Good and Evil, Flagg and Mother Abigail, Us versus Them. The survivors of Captain Tripps choose sides and regroup in Las Vegas and Denver. *Lost* is filled with similar measures. The survivors of Oceanic 815 are initially pitted against the Others as they plot from their two camps. Factions emerge within their groups as well. In Season One, arguments erupt over whether or not to make camp at the beach or move into the caves. In Season Four, the remaining castaways must choose to go with Locke to the Barracks or follow Jack back to the beach. Season Five turns the tables when the Others become "Us" against the Richard Alpert's Others. In each case, like *The Stand*, the division between the two groups is further represented by the different locations they inhabit.

- **Spies and Spying.** Spying is pivotal to the narrative of *The Stand*, as the Free Zone elects to send out three spies to explore the west and learn more about Randall Flagg. The Others in *Lost* have also used at least one spy, Goodwin, to ascertain the "good" and "bad" survivors from Oceanic Flight 815 before he is killed by Ana Lucia. Although the writers have never established Ethan Rom or Nathan as Others, the audience has collectively assumed them to be spies.

- *The Stand* **Miniseries.** The filmed version of *The Stand* was a network television miniseries event in 1994, starring Rob Lowe, Molly Ringwald, and Gary Sincse. Some notable additions to the filmic text appear to influenced *Lost*. The dog Kojak is a yellow Labrador Retriever in the miniseries, not an Irish Setter, and truly resembles Vincent. The black rock necklace Flagg's followers wear is completely black, without the "red flaw" described in the book.

  In the miniseries Harold delivers two lines that are not in the book but echo with *Lost* significance. He says to Frannie that their survival of the flu is as lucky as winning the "Megabucks Lottery." Hurley's winning lottery ticket on *Lost* was from none other than Megabucks. When Harold turns against the committee in the Free Zone and makes a bomb with dynamite, he explains that dynamite sweats nitroglycerin—a line that Arzt echoes prior to his death in "Exodus" (1.23).

Until the end of the series, it is impossible to know every parallel between *The Stand* and *Lost*. Several characters, most notably Sawyer,

Ana Lucia, and Michael, have no clear ancestors in *The Stand*. In time, these connections may appear, as well as even greater resonance between the two texts.—**Hillary Robson and Tyler Hall**

Stranger in a Strange Land—The ninth episode of *Lost*'s third season, the almost completely forgettable "Stranger in a Strange Land," owes its title to a 1961 novel of the same name by the controversial American science fiction writer Robert Heinlein (1907–1988). His four decades of prolific authorship earned Heinlein a variety of labels: "a conservative, a militarist, a Calvinist, a sexist, a libertarian, a solipsist, and even a fascist," and none of his books seem harder to classify than *Stranger*, an epic novel about a young man, raised by Martians on the Red Planet, named Valentine Michael Smith, who becomes, upon his return to Earth, the founder of a new religion centered on "grokking," a philosophy of oneness and love with all people and things. In the psychedelic 1960s, *Stranger* became a campus bestseller. In his short life, Smith has many adventures and may have changed the nature of human history through his influence, but he does not go to Thailand and engage in outlaw tattooing. *Stranger* is an ancestor text in name only.

Walden Two—Even if unaware that *Lost* cocreator, Damon Lindelof, has been interested in B. F. Skinner since an undergraduate at New York University, the attentive *Lost* viewer might well have concluded that the pioneer behavioral psychologist was a presence on the Island.

In the "Orientation" film, after all, Marvin Candle actually evokes his name:

The DHARMA Initiative was created in 1970, and it is the brainchild of Gerald and Karen DeGroot—two doctoral candidates at the University of Michigan. Following in the footsteps of visionaries such as B. F. Skinner [there is a jump cut/splice here] imagined a large scale communal research compound where scientists and free thinkers from around the globe could pursue research in meteorology, psychology, parapsychology, zoology, electromagnetism, and utopian social [splice] Danish industrialist and munitions magnate Alvar Hanso whose financial backing made their dream of a multipurpose social science research facility a reality.

And although Lindelof and Cuse deny they had Skinner in mind in creating Sawyer's cage in the Season Three "miniseries," the temptation to see the enclosure as a "Skinner box" and its push-the-right-combination-of-buttons-and-win-a-fish-biscuit as a classic example of Skinnerian "operant conditioning" is hard to deny.

Skinner's most important book is probably *Beyond Freedom and Dignity* (1971), but his utopian "novel" *Walden Two* (1948) is the most likely candidate as a *Lost* ancestor text. Hardly a novel at all, *Walden Two* is more of a Socratic dialogue between Frazier, the founder of the eponymous utopian community of the book, and Burris and Castle, two visitors to Walden Two. Set just after World War II, the book was supposedly inspired by Skinner's contemplation of the social problems caused by returning war veterans.

Season Five's extended stay (with Sawyer, Juliet, Miles, Jin, Hurley, Jack, and Kate) in DHARMAville shows life with the Initiative to be anything but utopian. From bottom (the disgruntled, abusive father Roger Linus) to top (the inept Horace Goodspeed, the despicable future-suicide Radzinsky), DHARMA seems anything but a happy place.

MUST-SEE TV AND ESSENTIAL MOVIES

The Adventures of Brisco County, Jr.—One of Carlton Cuse's early (1993–1994) ventures in television as an executive producer was with *The Adventures of Brisco County, Jr.*, a FOX series scheduled in the Friday night slot preceding *The X-Files* and later relegated by TNT to Saturday morning reruns. However, *Brisco* was far from a typical Western or a children's show. Part comedy, part science fiction, part drama, and part buddy series, its snappy dialogue defied the "Thank you, ma'am" and "This town ain't big enough for the both of us" school of Western dialogue. Double entendres and comments on 1990s' culture (that's 1990s, not 1890s) permeated the episodes. For example, an Elvis impersonator becomes a recurring character, and a slab of beef placed on a bun is eternally saved from being known as a "cow patty" by Lord Bowler's timely comment.

Cuse, who created *Brisco* with Jeffrey Boam, also wrote the teleplay or story for seven episodes spanning different genres and playing with popular culture icons. "The Orb Scholar," the second episode in the series, begins the mythology of the mysterious orbs. Episode 20, "Bye Bly," concludes the orb saga with a time-traveler denouement, as thief-from-the-future John Bly is stopped and the orbs returned to their rightful place in time.

Playing with timelines during a multi-episode story arc is perhaps the clearest link between *Brisco* and *Lost*. During the latter's Season Three, Desmond sees flashes of the future. His present-time actions revolve around these glimpses of another timeline; he tries, usually in vain, to change or preserve the "future that was," depending on what seems to benefit him or his friends the most.

Desmond frequently saves Charlie from his "future" death: being electrocuted by lightning, drowning, breaking his neck, becoming impaled by an arrow. Although Desmond decides to let Charlie die one time, he saves him at the last second ("Catch-22," 3.17). (It seems that Charlie has to decide to die—as he does in "Through the Looking Glass," 3.23—before Desmond can't save him or "bring him back.") Brisco, too, has the power of life or death over pal Bowler, who dies helping Brisco during a shootout. Because Brisco has been honorable in stopping Bly and then returning the orbs to their rightful owners from the future, he is allowed to travel back in time a few minutes to try to save Bowler. Brisco succeeds, and Bowler lives.

Seasons Four and Five continue the time travel theme far more elaborately than anything in *Brisco*'s limited number of episodes, but Cuse still managed to work his long-time interest in time travel into the series' mythology. When creating *Lost*, he admitted that time travel as a theme in the series "was something that we'd known about from very early on, but it just couldn't be deployed until we got within striking distance of the end of the show."[5] Although *Brisco* lasted far fewer episodes than *Lost*, Cuse made sure that the most significant story arc revolved around the mysterious future orbs and their trip through time, periodically intersecting the timeline of the series' hero.

Lost also shares other story elements with *Brisco*. The concept of killing main characters—or teasing viewers with that idea—is nothing new to *Lost*. *Brisco*'s last episodes portrayed Brisco's and Bowler's deaths by firing squad. Viewers later find out that the duo faked their demise. Cuse and Lindelof staged similar "fake" deaths for Charlie and Shannon during Season One (although later in the series the death scenes became real).

Plays on words also grace both series. *Brisco* features a lawyer named Socrates; *Lost*'s characters include John Locke, Rousseau, Edmund Burke, and (Desmond) David Hume. *Brisco*'s "chapter" or segment titles include "The Blast Supper" and "Spur of the Moment" (from the pilot); an episode about Dixie Cousins is titled "Deep in the Heart of Dixie." *Lost*'s first-season episode titles often refer to song titles or lyrics, such as "Born to Run" (1.22), or play with the theme of the episode, such as "Whatever the Case May Be" (1.12), about the marshal's briefcase. Although this pattern becomes less noticeable in later episodes, it periodically resurfaces, as in the *Alice in Wonderland* allusion in the third-season finale, "Through the Looking Glass," and the Henry Gale (Ben Linus) *Wizard of Oz*–themed "The Man Behind the Curtain."

Brisco County, Jr., and Jack Shephard share similar "daddy issues." Jack, like Brisco, fails to gain his father's approval and support while his father is alive. Like Brisco's father, Jack's dad dies before father and son work out their differences. Jack, like Brisco, sees his father's ghost (or hallucinates the visions) and gains insights from seeing the apparition.

Cuse demonstrates an attraction for a "buddy" theme in *Brisco*, later echoed in *Nash Bridges* and *Lost*. (Cuse worked with Daniel Roebuck on both *Nash Bridges* and *Lost*.) Brisco's and Bowler's sometimes prickly but strong friendship evolves during the season as the two share adventures: Charlie and Hurley similarly bond on the Island. As in all series in which Cuse is involved, a wide variety of often quirky characters come together to pool their disparate knowledge and skills for the greater good in plots occasionally otherworldly. Although Cuse doesn't blatantly steal from his previous work, supernatural or mystical elements, father/son relationships, and the themes of friendship frequently turn up in a Cuse series.

Alias—J. J. Abrams' spy drama *Alias* (2001–2006) has whisked its audience to a thousand and one exotic locations, with main character and series heroine, Sydney Bristow (Jennifer Garner), in an array of flashy (and often revealing) costumes and disguises. But the premise of *Alias* isn't just about the couture: Abrams has said the original concept came from his WB network semi-hit *Felicity*, which inspired him to concoct a storyline that centered around a college student who just happened to be a spy. (*Alias*, according to Abrams, "was the result of wanting to do 'something with dramatic stakes a few notches higher than the romantic turmoil of a college coed'" [Dilmore 22].) Add a mythos concerning prophetic Renaissance inventor Rambaldi, who created devices that can destroy the world, and a dysfunctional father-daughter relationship, and a new cult hit was born.

The series was initially dependent on standard cliff-hanger endings that prevailed through much of the first season, while Sydney tried to keep her secret lives secret: she juggled working as a double agent both for the CIA and against the nefarious SD-6, which she'd previously thought was a black ops division of the CIA. Her best friends, roommate Francie (Merrin Dungey) and reporter Will (Bradley Cooper), were kept in the dark, thinking that she worked for an international bank, Credit Dauphine. Her boss at SD-6, Arvin Sloane (Ron Rifkin), functioned as Sydney's prime nemesis for the duration of the series (in the finale becoming immortal, though buried alive), and her relationship with her father, fellow Season One double agent Jack Bristow (Victor Garber) traveled through a dizzying array of emotional ups and downs.

Sydney endures the loss of her fiancé, Danny, in the pilot episode after revealing her spy status to him (he is killed by SD-6). She witnesses her best friends, Will and Francie, destroyed as a result of her secret lives—Francie is killed and cloned by the second and third season baddie, the Covenant, and Will is put into the Witness Protection Program. She learns that her mother (Lena Ollin) was a traitor—a spy for the Russians against the United States—and that her death when Sydney was a child was a lie told to protect her. In the five seasons of *Alias*, Sydney found out her dead mother was actually alive; lost her memory; worked as an assassin for the government; saved the world—repeatedly; fell in love with her CIA handler; took down SD-6, the Alliance of Twelve, and the Covenant; discovered a long-lost pair of aunts (one evil, one semi-evil); and had all of her eggs stolen. Add to the mix that she's a key figure in the apocalypse predicted by Rambaldi, whose creepy inventions and even creepier designs on the future world somehow always manage to figure into each season's story arc.

The connections between *Alias* and *Lost* are manifold. Despite the action-packed drama on each series, both are primarily character driven. In both *Alias* and *Lost*, intrigue and mystery imbue the characters.

The taciturn and occasionally brutal Jack Bristow may remind viewers of both shows of the hard-edged but tender Sayid. The quirky techno-hip-geek Marshall (Kevin Weisman) might be seen as a (slightly smaller) mirror image of the funny (yet cursed) Hurley, or maybe even Charlie Pace. The characters of both J. J. Abrams series share depths unusual for these kind of shows. Without their inner turmoil, neither show would have much of a life expectancy.

Sydney's emotional trials and tribulations are often set against the backdrop of life-or-death situations not unlike the challenges the castaways of *Lost* face. Sydney had to MacGyver herself out of many situations while in "spy mode," requiring the audience to suspend disbelief in a way occasionally required by *Lost* as well. The mythology of *Alias* enlists fans to become experts on all things CIA, spy or black ops, and the existence of a prophecy involving the series' heroine has engaged more than one fan on wild goose chases, solving the Rambaldi prophecy—futile quests well known to the zealous *Lost* fan. Other tie-ins between the two series include the destination city of Sydney, Australia, and the number 47—a prominent fixture in *Alias* that makes a brief appearance on *Lost* in the pilot episode (a tally number of survivors). Terry O'Quinn (John Locke) spent two seasons on *Alias* as FBI Assistant Director Kendall, and *Alias* regular Greg Grunberg made an appearance as the short-lived, pulled-out-of-the-cockpit-by-the-Monster pilot in the series pilot. (He's very briefly visible in "Exodus" as well.)

Never a big success in the ratings, *Alias* benefited greatly in its fourth season from having the more successful *Lost* as its lead-in. *Alias'* better Season Four numbers were in part the result of viewers who tuned in for the new Abrams series and stuck around for the older one. If they didn't budge from their seats, even at the end of each show, they got to see twice that rapidly moving, red cartoon automaton and hear the children's voices scold "Bad Robot"—the name of J. J. Abrams' production company, responsible for both shows. Even without that signature, the careful viewer might well have guessed *Lost*'s and *Alias'* shared genesis.

Talking about his two Bad Robots with *Cinefantastique*, Abrams had a lot to say about his more successful younger child:

If eight or nine million people are watching Alias *and sixteen or seventeen million people are watching* Lost, *then it says that* Lost *is doing better than*

Alias. *But if a show is doing well enough to stay on the air, the experience from my point of view is fairly the same on both shows. As long as you're on the air and doing well enough to sustain, you don't really experience an enormous difference in the creation or the reception of the show.*

In fact, from Abrams' perspective as executive producer, "The job is exactly the same. The numbers are different, but you're still trying to do a good show. I've always been really proud of *Alias* and of the viewership of the show. There's something special about it being a cult show."—**Hillary Robson**

Back to the Future—Robert Zemeckis' 1985 science fiction comedy was a box-office smash. It tells the story of high schooler Marty McFly, who is accidently carried thirty years into the past in a DeLorean time machine built by local mad scientist Doc Brown and finds himself faced with intimidating challenges: confronting a familiar bully, introducing rock and roll to Chuck Berry, making certain his mother and father fall in love (because otherwise he will cease to exist), returning to the future.

Given the centrality of time travel to Season Five, it was probably only a matter of time until *Back to the Future* came up. In "Whatever Happened, Happened" (5.11), as Hurley and Miles debate the implications for all their destinies of Sayid's attempted murder of young Ben, *Back* is very much on the former's mind. Remembering that Marty McFly's image begins to disappear from a photograph he brought with him from the future after his presence in the 1950s make his parents' mating less likely, Hurley begins to worry that he too will be wiped away:

Miles: What the hell are you doing, Tubby?
Hurley: Checking to see if I'm disappearing.
Miles: What?
Hurley: "Back to the Future," man. We came back in time to the Island and changed stuff. So if little Ben dies, he'll never grow up to be big Ben, who's the one who made us come back here in the first place. Which means we can't be here. And therefore, dude? We don't exist.
Miles: You're an idiot.
Hurley: Am I?

Miles: Yeah. It doesn't work like that. You can't change anything. Your ma-
niac Iraqi buddy shot Linus. That is what always happened. It's just...we
never experienced how it all turns out.
Hurley: This is really confusing.

Indeed it is. At the end of the season we are still not sure whether
Hurley's worries are justified or whether Jack, Sawyer, Sayid, Hurley,
Miles, Kate, and Juliet have made it "back to the future" alive.

Buffy the Vampire Slayer, Angel, Firefly—Episodic television in the
first decade of the twenty-first century owes a substantial debt to the critically acclaimed series created by Joss Whedon. *Buffy the Vampire Slayer*
(1997–2003), *Angel* (1999–2004), *Firefly* (2003–2004), and now *Dollhouse*
(2009–), though never big Nielsen successes, nevertheless made possible
multigenre, character-driven shows with fantastic themes.

Lost cannot be said to be directly under the influence of the
Whedonverse; so far, *Lost* has given us no chosen ones, no demons, no
vampires, no spaceships. Still, *Lost*'s credits are studded with the names
of key writers and directors who came to the series with the experience
of working for Whedon still fresh in their minds. Major Whedon collaborator David Grossman, director of twenty-one episodes of *Buffy*
and *Angel*, did *Lost*'s "The Greater Good." *Buffy* director (and television veteran) Tucker Gates directed "Confidence Man" (1.8), "...In
Translation" (1.17), "Born to Run" (1.22), and "I Do" (3.6). Marita
Grabiak, who worked on three Whedon series, directed "Raised by
Another" (1.10). Daniel Attias, who helmed two Season Five episodes
of *Buffy*, directed the pivotal episode "Numbers" (1.18), cowritten by
other key Whedon collaborators, David Fury and Brent Fletcher, who
had also written a Season Five *Angel*. Fury also authored "Walkabout"
(1.4), "Solitary" (1.9), and "Special" (1.14). Drew Goddard, author of
three episodes of *Buffy*'s final season, has written/cowritten "Outlaws"
(1.16), "The Glass Ballerina" (3.2), "Flashes Before Your Eyes" (3.8),
"The Man from Tallahassee" (3.13), and "One of Us" (3.16) for *Lost*.

No single episode better exemplifies the Whedon touch than
"Numbers," written and directed by Whedon alums. Its comic attention to detail (the chicken on Hurley's fast-food work shirt in the first
flashback, for example), its dark, absurdist humor (the dispassionate

death of his grandfather during Hurley's appearance on TV as the lottery winner), its mixing of pathos and humor in the same scene, its self-referentiality (Hurley complains to Rousseau about the Island's perplexing mysteries, especially the Monster, with a kind of impatience that suggests he might just be a regular watcher of the series in which he appears: "I want some freakin' answers!")—all of these are Whedon signatures.

Cast Away—*Cast Away* (2000) must have played a role in the chain-of-inspiration for *Lost*. An Oceanic Airlines plane (FedEx plane) crashes after a terrifying in-flight incident on (near by) an island in the South Pacific; the story then tracks the struggles of the survivors (the only survivor) of the disaster to survive on the Island. Was Lloyd Braun's bare-bones idea for the series in fact a case of what is now sometimes called "kleptonesia," a conveniently forgetful "borrowing," from the Zemeckis/Hanks film? Perhaps, but the basic idea, in whatever form, is not exactly high concept nor terribly innovative.

Tom Hanks—who purportedly brought the idea for the film to Robert Zemeckis—plays Chuck Noland (No-land), a FedEx efficiency expert, whose life is ruled by the clock. Jetting all over the world to spread the company gospel of on-time delivery (the film opens in Moscow in what *Slate* critic David Edelstein deemed "an overture that plays like an especially grandiose Federal Express commercial"), Noland is sent off to Asia on Christmas day to deal with an emergency but never arrives. The air cargo plane on which he's the only passenger goes down over the ocean in what Edelstein rightly describes as "the most harrowing plane crash ever filmed (or computer-generated)," and he makes it, thanks to a life raft, to a nearby island where he will spend four years. Except for a volleyball, a fellow survivor he names Wilson (he gives it a face painted with his own blood), Noland goes it alone, and the film follows his solitary struggles: to crack coconuts, make fire, stay sane, build a raft. He makes it to sea and is rescued. The film's ineffective final act shows Noland trying to reenter a world where the love of his life (Helen Hunt) has married another man and he is now an alien.

By multiplying the number of survivors by forty-eight (with fourteen the center of focus)—a move that was a necessity for an ongoing series, *Lost*, of course, radically alters *Cast Away*'s subject matter. In just over one hundred days of *Lost* time, exponentially more has happened to the *Lost*aways than transpired in Noland's four years. With no fellow survivors nor Others on his island, Noland's interactions can only be with the contents of washed-ashore FedEx parcels (including the one containing his Fridayish volleyball), nature (like *Lost*, *Cast Away* is full of beautiful seascapes), and, most importantly, himself. *Cast Away* is more *Robinson Crusoe* than *Lost* or *Lord of the Flies*.

Crossing Jordan—A long-running American television series on NBC, a drama, set in Boston, about a psychologically troubled, crime-solving medical examiner named Jordan Cavanaugh (Jill Hennessy), *Crossing Jordan* was one of the least well-known successful series of the last twenty years. In over 120 episodes of a six-season run (2001–2007), it attracted little buzz and almost no academic interest and was treated rather shabbily by NBC, which routinely moved it all over its schedule. But its creator, Tim Kring, gained notoriety with his successful (for one season at least) new series *Heroes*, as has *Jordan* alum Damon Lindelof (who wrote nine episodes, 2001–2004) as one of *Lost*'s cocreators. Other *Lost* directors—Michael Zinberg, Steven Williams, Karen Gaviola, Roxann Dawson—and writers—Lynne E. Litt, Liz Sarnoff—likewise worked on *Crossing Jordan*.

Disaster Movies—As a producer, writer, and director, one of J. J. Abrams' mission statements has long been "Take a B-genre and do it A." One clear and distinct "B" *Lost* ancestor is the disaster movie. Both Abrams and Lindelof espouse their great love of movies like *Airport* (1970), *The Poseidon Adventure* (1972), *Earthquake* (1974), *Towering Inferno* (1974), all from the disaster movie's golden age, the 1970s. Whether the star "vehicle" is a severely damaged jumbo jet, a capsized cruise ship, a city devastated by a 7-on-the-Richter-Scale-tremor, or a huge skyscraper on fire, the formula is the same. An incongruously diverse assemblage of people, usually walking stereotypes, more often than not played by a conglomeration of not quite A-list stars, mouthing clichéd dialogue and bearing complex, usually troubled personal histories, are thrown together in some kind of catastrophic situation and must, despite their tendency to clash, overcome their selfish concerns and strive heroically for the common good. *Lost* elevates this blueprint to "A" by making its characters, largely played by unknowns, anything-but-stereotypes, "goosing" the challenges the survivors face, resolutely resisting the cliché in word and deed, and experimenting with narrative structure in radical new ways.

Fantasy Island—This slab of cheese might seem to occupy the opposite end of television's imaginative spectrum from *Lost*, because the show, which aired from 1978 to 1984, was doggedly reliant on conventional plots and canned emotions, and offered a haven to familiar actors on the down sides of their careers and ingénues willing to take on the flimsiest of roles. The stories of folks both rich and "ordinary," hoping to live out long-harbored dreams of physical prowess, sexual conquest, financial triumph, and victory over themselves tied up neatly at the end of each episode, with a friendly farewell to the local wizard, Mr. Roarke (Ricardo Montalban), and his diminutive assistant, Tattoo (Herve Villechaize). This was comfort food, as prepared by Swanson's—everything clearly packaged and presented, in strong contrast to the most complicated serial in the history of network television.

But, as Roarke might say in one of his moments of sententious gravitas, there is more here than meets the eye—not least in terms of context and emotional logic. Each show begins when a plane, in rather different circumstances, lands on a tropical island, an island whose mysterious ability to stage the wishes and nightmares of its visitors remains unsolved. (The opening credits of *Fantasy Island* were in fact filmed in Hawaii.) Both islands serve as blunt instruments of self-knowledge and redemption—quite unfairly in the case of the older show, because its guests paid for pleasure and invariably left with hard-earned moral instruction. Indeed, the charmed circle of the Island serves in each program as a place where powerful figures can run psychological experiments on those who have signed up willingly (in the case of the DHARMA recruits), or are trapped against their will (in the case of the Losties). Roarke operates as a precursor to Ben, Jacob, and Charles Widmore—a powerful, controlling figure who manipulates human prey for his own ends; while he may have projected a far more genial persona than that gang of Machiavels does, Roarke was essentially a punishing superego masquerading as a liberating id, enacting the tension between law and freedom, or obligation and anarchy, that *Lost* has also explored.

Beyond those similarities of geography and theme, the two series flourished as hybrid constructs, invested in the gamut of televisual genres and styles. While *Lost* has carved out a roiling intersection of science fiction, adventure yarn, family drama, and quest narrative, *Fantasy Island*, in its much less extravagant way, also created itself out of a heterogeneous heritage. The key genre of the so-called golden age of television in the 1950s was the anthology—shows like *Playhouse 90* and *Studio One*, essentially black box theaters which could be filled in and emptied out every week, with any kind of formula or concept that the producers cared to put on. That flexible hour, by the late 1970s, had vanished from the schedule. *Fantasy Island* revived the anthology, even more explicitly than did its Saturday-night companion, *The Love Boat*, which was inevitably confined to the Lido deck and cramped cabins. Instead, *Fantasy Island* could move omnivorously from fairy tale to detective story to sex farce to courtroom drama—and, most significantly, to stories of the past. Two of the first seven episodes involved Westerns—a genre that had dominated the landscape in the 1960s through such vehicles as *Gunsmoke* and *Bonanza*, but which had disappeared by 1978. This archaeological practice speaks to half of *Lost*'s genetic composition—married to the vast serial sprawl is the anthology-as-revival, endlessly shifting from Sayid's troubled Iraq to Jack's Oedipal hospital conflict to Sun and Jin's Romeo and Juliet to Kate's modern-day Bonnie Parker. Just as *Lost*'s producers recycle Hawaii weekly to resemble Oxford, Sydney, and New York, so does the show prosper by reinventing shopworn types—the Loner, the Loser, the Bad Girl, the Alpha Male, the Funny Fat Guy, the Wronged Man; this flea-market aesthetic may look like postmodern brilliance on *Lost*, and it may look like Hollywood hackery on *Fantasy Island*, but in each case, you have a show marking its difference from everything else on the air by plundering television's conventional past.

And if that juxtaposition of past and present offers the recipe for *Lost*'s trademark flashback structure—bouncing back and forth in each episode between the history of one character and the ongoing drama of the group—*Fantasy Island* likewise deploys a bifocal process. As always with *Fantasy Island*, its version of stereo looks much tamer than that of *Lost*: each episode simply ping-pongs between two storylines over the course of the hour. But that design is shared by very few

shows in television history; procedurals stick to one story from beginning to end, and serials traditionally navigate among at least three
different stories. While that doubleness in *Lost* has always depended
on shifts in time, *Fantasy Island* also dipped into temporal dislocation;
the very first installment (a two-hour TV film, which triggered the
series a year later) included a woman who wanted to flash-forward to
the future—by feigning her death and witnessing her funeral—and
a man who wanted to travel to the past—by returning to a wartime
scene of lost love. By the end of the first season, the give-and-take
between two separate parts often manifested itself within storylines,
as bit players in one character's fantasy themselves turned out to
be paying customers on a thrill ride. That reduplication extended
to the guest stars, many of whom turned up in multiple roles over
the show's six-and-a-half-year run, thereby making their appearance
histories themselves a subliminal, ongoing narrative. In its much less
ambitious way, *Fantasy Island* stands with *Lost* in that small group of
TV shows that have blended fixed formula and boundless variety, the
mystical and the mundane, savvy nostalgia for television's history and
canny awareness of television's present.

It needs to be pointed out, as well, that both shows nicely capture
the sensibility of their respective eras, as embodied by that era's pre-
siding spirit. In the case of *Lost*, that spirit is J. J. Abrams, whose capa-
cious old/new, familiar/groundbreaking synthesis (equally explicit in
his earlier anthology/serial mash-up *Alias*) defines the first decade
of the twenty-first century; in the case of *Fantasy Island*, that spirit
is Aaron Spelling, the tortured artist who gave us *Charlie's Angels*,
Dynasty, and *Beverly Hills, 90210*, all disposable, and all at the front
and center of the zeitgeist.—**Sean O'Sullivan**

Forbidden Planet—We won't know for sure whether the 1956 science
fiction classic *Forbidden Planet* is or is not a *Lost* ancestor text and may
not until the mystery of the Island's Monster (aka Smokezilla) is solved
once and for all. *Forbidden Planet*, directed by Fred M. Wilcox from a
screenplay by Cyril Hume (no relation, we presume, to Desmond), from
a story by Irving Block and Allen Adler, tells of the arrival of United
Planets Cruiser C-57D, captained by Commander John J. Adams (Leslie
Nielsen before he got his comic genius on) on Altair 4, a distant planet

formerly the destination of the *Bellerephon* expedition, which hasn't been heard from in twenty years. The previous explorers, we learn, have all mysteriously died, leaving only the ship's philologist, Dr. Morbius (Walter Pigeon), and his daughter Altaira (Anne Francis).

Morbius introduces the visitors to the amazing world of the Krell, a highly advanced but now extinct civilization on Altair 4, whose miraculous machines still function beneath the planet after thousands of years. Morbius reveals that he has been using their magical technology to boost his own brain power. Soon after arrival (and soon after the all-male crew begins lusting after Altaira) a mysterious, invisible monster attacks C-57D and kills several members of the crew, triggering Morbius' fear that the force that wiped out the *Bellerephon*'s crew, and apparently exterminated the Krell as well, may have returned. On its next attack, C-57D's forces manage to make the beast visible using an electrical grid and discover that it is a powerful being of pure energy.

In a final showdown at Morbius's home, the monster is revealed to be a "creature from the Id"—Morbius' id to be precise—a Freudian nightmare writ large and all powerful, and it is only when the doctor, in keeping with Shakespeare's *The Tempest*, a key inspiration for the filmmakers, acknowledges his Calibanish monster as his and dies in the process, that all are safe.

Because we know that *Forbidden Planet* influenced such major figures as *Star Trek* creator Gene Roddenberry ("Requiem for Methuselah" was also a *Tempest* wannabe) and Joss Whedon (in the movie *Serenity*, C-57D appears several times on the planet Miranda—the name of sorcerer Prospero's daughter in *The Tempest*, the point-of-origin for the Reavers); because echoes of *Forbidden Planet* appear too in *Babylon 5* and *Rocky Horror Picture Show* and *Halloween*, it seems only natural to wonder if Abrams, Lindelof, and Cuse might have borrowed their conception of the Monster from it as well. Might Smokezilla be the manifestation of some inhabitant of the Island? At the end of Season Five, the web was abuzz with speculation that perhaps the Monster might be somehow connected to Jacob's loophole-seeking nemesis.

We should note, too, that *Lost*'s Rousseau, like Morbius the survivor of a scientific expedition mysteriously wiped out, stands as another *Forbidden* echo.

Fringe—As we write, *Fringe* (FOX, 2008–) has only aired one season, but a show often hailed as "the next *Lost*" and cocreated by J. J. Abrams, this time in collaboration with *Transformers* and relaunched *Star Trek* scribes Roberto Orci and Alex Kurtzman, has already announced itself as must-see for *Lost* fans. Produced by Abrams' Bad Robot, *Fringe* is a kind of *X-Files* for the twenty-first century. A team made up of eccentric/brilliant scientist Walter Bishop (John Noble), his son Peter (Joshua Jackson), and FBI agent Olivia Dunham (Anna Torv), assembled by Homeland Security's Philip Broyles (Lance Reddick), investigates/does battle with the Pattern, an emerging series of incidents, perfectly suited to episodic television, involving "out there"/occult/cutting edge/fringe science, from reanimation to telepathy.

As if inviting a linking of the two series' audiences, *Fringe*'s pilot, which broke *Lost*'s record as most expensive ever, began with a horrifying in-flight incident on a passenger jet. Other *Lost/Fringe* intersects come to mind: *Fringe*'s showrunner, Jeff Pinkner, worked on *Lost* as a writer and producer, and Bryan Burk produced both series; Reddick is on both shows (he played the Charles Widmore assistant Matthew Abaddon on *Lost*); Michael Giacchino has written the original music for both; in the first episode of *Fringe*, a character holds a airline ticket for seat 108—the sum of, 4, 8, 15, 16, 23, 42, *Lost*'s mysterious numbers. Several characters or places share names with *Lost* characters: Charlie (Pace and Francis), Walter (Lloyd/Porter and Bishop), John (Locke and Scott), Claire as a character and St. Claire's Hospital where Walter Bishop lived for seventeen years. In addition, *Fringe* science takes to the next level disciplines in science and pseudo-science studied by the DHARMA Initiative and Hanso Foundation on *Lost*. *Fringe* takes "science" and types of experiments to the next level.

Like *Lost*, *Fringe* is generating an Internet fan blitz. Check out the *Fringe* wiki at fringepedia.net. Not surprisingly, fans of both series salivate online at the possibility, to-date not even contemplated, of a crossover of the two verses, but Season One, which ended with Olivia in an alternate reality America in which the Twin Towers are still standing but the White House has been destroyed, seemed ready to take risks equal in magnitude to *Lost*'s time-tripping Season Five.

Gilligan's Island—Imagine, if you will, a television series in which the following events transpire:

- Marooned on a Pacific island, castaways try to retool a radio into a transmitter.

- One of the Island's new residents is fabulously wealthy. Another is certain he has won millions in a sweepstakes.

- An airplane is discovered in the jungle.

- The new residents are besieged by recurring strange dreams.

- The Islanders construct a golf course.

- The newcomers discover that the Island is already inhabited by another castaway from a foreign land.

- The Island turns out to be inhabited by mysterious others.

- One of the survivors is afflicted with amnesia.

- Another survivor is expected to perform surgery under primitive conditions.

- Plans are made to build a vessel in order to escape.

- A member of a rock group is on the Island.

- One of the castaways is believed to be a criminal, perhaps a murderer.

- The Islanders discover that their paths have crossed before their fateful journey.

- A mystery attaché case is found.

As a reader of a book on *Lost*, no doubt you are rolling your eyes at such belaboring of the obvious. The series in which these events take place is, of course, the one that inspired you to read these pages. Even an honorable mention winner in a *Lost* trivia contest can probably identify each of them, chapter and verse. But they were not original with *Lost*. Each of these narrative events can be found as well in a series often considered to be one of the most idiotic in the history of television: *Gilligan's Island*, a half-hour sitcom about a seven-member sight-seeing party on the charter boat S. S. *Minnow* shipwrecked on a South Pacific island.

Running on CBS from 1964 to 1967, *Gilligan's* cast included the Skipper (Alan Hale), a burly, usually jovial, former Navy officer; Thurston Howell III (Jim Backus), a supercilious billionaire who made his fortune on Wall Street; Lovey Howell (Natalie Schafer), his snobbish wife; Ginger Grant (Tina Louise), a beautiful, flirtatious, self-important, and vapid actress; Mary Ann Summers (Dawn Wells), a beautiful, honest, down-to-earth girl-next-door from Kansas; the Professor (Roy Hinkley), a high school teacher with a PhD, who possessed an extraordinary breadth of scientific knowledge and was fluent in multiple languages as well; and, of course, Gilligan (Bob Denver), the *Minnow's* second mate, the Skipper's "Little Buddy" and all purpose screw-up (his comedy of errors deep-sixes every possibility of rescue), who finds himself quite happy in his new home.

Some of the *Gilligan* Seven likewise share traits in common with the *Lost* Fourteen. When the *Gilligan's Island* Fan Club website describes one of the characters as "display[ing] little tact, blam[ing] the Skipper for the shipwreck, and…always trying to break the castaways' laws and bribe others…sneaky, untrustworthy, conniving, greedy and corrupt," the *Lost* fan might well think, if we substitute Sayid for the Skipper as the recipient of blame, that it is (all together now!) Sawyer being described. The Professor certainly reappears in *Lost* as well, although his functions are divided among several different characters: Jack and Leslie Arzt (however briefly) exhibit some of his scientific knowledge, Sayid and Locke inherit his Mr. Fix-it-ness and Locke his survival skills, and at least a trace of his felicity for language emerges in Shannon. The Howells' wealth is passed on to the far more "Dudely," far less pretentious, Hurley. Thanks to the ever-evolving, deliberate revelations of their backstories, *Lost*'s central characters escape their types and become complex moral human beings we find difficult to judge. The "stupendous stupidity" (Bianculli 123) of *Gilligan's Island* asked nothing from us. When Steven Johnson argues in his recent *Everything Bad is Good for You: How Today's Popular Culture is Actually Making Us Smarter* that today's bad TV is a lot smarter than yesterday's version, he might well have made *Gilligan* the poster child for the brainless, implausible TV of several decades past.

Most laughable of all (not meant as a compliment) were the series' preposterous plots. For being a "desert island," *Gilligan's* location was primary destination for a wide variety of strange visitors. An eccentric pilot drops in. A bankrobber makes the island his hideout. A World War II Japanese sailor turns up—twice. An exiled dictator arrives. Two Russian cosmonauts land. A rock group makes the Island a hideout from their fans. A mad scientist finds the island a perfect locale for his mad science. A film producer crash lands and wackiness ensues. Other visitors include a surfer, an eccentric painter, a butterfly collector, a game-show contestant, and a big-game hunter. In a 1981 *Gilligan's Island* special that ran fourteen years after the series was cancelled (aka, "put out of its misery"), even the Harlem Globetrotters showed up. The voracious need of television to fill air time somehow transformed Gilligan's island from a land of the lost into a magnet for the farcical and the inane. If the writers of *Lost* decide to import a lepidopterist just to liven things up, fans and critics will proclaim immediately, loudly, and with one voice that their beloved show has "jumped the shark."

Strangely, *Gilligan*, like *Lost*, was full of elements of the fantastic and science fiction. *Gilligan* would offer us episodes in which characters become mind readers, are turned into zombies, switch bodies, and become robots. A robot plummets from the sky and lands on the island. The castaways acquire a rocket pack; find a space capsule; and discover a meteor that causes premature aging. A NASA satellite bound for Mars mistakenly lands on the Island and sends back to Houston pictures of the castaways thought to be proof of extraterrestrial life. Every other episode of *Gilligan's* third season makes use of bizarre dream sequences, in one of which *Gilligan's* becomes an on-trial Jekyll and Hyde, Mrs. Howell is Mary Poppins, and Mary Ann plays Eliza Doolittle. *Gilligan* resorted to such motifs not because of a true generic affinity for them but because they made possible the generation of new stories. Finding new material was a special challenge for *Gilligan*'s makers, who had to churn out, in keeping with the network demands of the day, over thirty episodes—36, 32, 30—in the show's three seasons.

But for all their shared plot and character elements, *Gilligan's Island* can hardly claim to be a true *Lost* ancestor. *Gilligan* was always lost-at-sea, devoid of any direction, never for a moment aspiring to be anything more than silly rubbish. *Lost* aspires to be suspenseful, mind-blowing, engaging, inventive, memorable. The islands of *Lost* and *Gilligan* are not even in the same archipelago of the imagination.

Jurassic Park—Seeking to reassure Paolo in "Exposé," Nikki insists they not fear the Island's Monster because they are not "in Jurassic Park." Michael Crichton's novel now seems almost prehistoric as an ancestor to *Lost*. The "don't mess with Mother Nature" or even sterner "playing God with species creates problems you can't begin to imagine" theme has been used many times, and the special effects that once seemed innovative in Steven Spielberg's cinematic version seem, well, jurassic in comparison to *Lost*'s Smokezilla, much less the level of dinosaur effects showcased in films like Peter Jackson's *King Kong*. Nevertheless, *Jurassic Park* and *Lost* share an island setting in which scientific "breakthroughs" run amok and threaten the Island's inhabitants.

Lost Horizon—Not only does the series share "Lost" in the title, but James Hilton's novel and two resulting films (one a musical) have a plane crash in common. Frank Capra brought the novel to the screen in 1937, a much more dramatic and true-to-the-book version than a 1970s musical remake. However, all versions use a plane crash in a mysterious mountain location as the plot device for the survivors to change their lives.

In *Lost Horizon*, a hijacked plane crashes in China; the pilot is killed, and the survivors must figure out where they are and how they are going to survive. Capra's film then tracks the story of the five Westerners who are rescued by the inhabitants of the utopian Shangri-La. Hidden from the rest of the world by high mountains, the inhabitants live in a mystical harmony. The visitors undergo profound changes as they spend time in the Valley of the Blue Moon, similar to *Lost*'s "redemption" theme.

As in *Lost*, the survivors are not alone. Though equally mysterious as the Island's Others, the inhabitants of Shangri-La are friendlier. *Lost Horizon*'s characters often parallel those who are *Lost*. The survivors include a self-interested criminal who gradually becomes more "socialized" to the group (i.e., Henry Barnard, Sawyer), a sensitive man who brings humor to the story (i.e., Alexander Lovett, Hurley), and a man interested in the spiritual possibilities of his surroundings (i.e., Chang, Locke).

Lost Horizon's crash survivors learn that Shangri-La can provide them with long life; the valley intends to keep them there, and bad things happen to those who try to leave. Richard Alpert certainly has a long life, as do Jacob and his nemesis. *Lost*'s "living dead" characters also survive, it seems, because they are connected with the Island. Leaving, or staying away for good, also proves difficult for the castaways. Even Ben, who tells Locke that once he leaves, he won't be able to return, manages to come home to the Island. With Eloise Hawking's data, Ben, the Oceanic Six, and Frank Lapidis crash once again on the Island. The Island, like Shangri-La, clings to its inhabitants.

Time works differently in Shangri-La, and the time travel subplot during *Lost*'s Seasons Four and Five explains that time differences on- and offshore are one reason why leaving the Island is so difficult. When the "Donkey Wheel" falls off track, several characters bounce among different Island time zones and see glimpses of the recent and more distant past. Time becomes an important element both to *Lost Horizon* and *Lost*, as does the timelessness of a mysterious, mystical place.

Nash Bridges—Given that *Lost* masterminds Damon Lindelof and Carlton Cuse met while writing for *Nash Bridges* (a show the latter created) and *Lost* directors Tucker Gates, Robert Mandel, and Greg Yaitenes and writer Lynne E. Litt also contributed to it, the set-in-San Francisco police drama, a CBS show which ran for 122 episodes between 1996–2001, must stand as an important, though unlikely, *Lost* ur-text.

With *Miami Vice* star Don Johnson as its eponymous, frequently divorced, yellow-Barracuda-convertible-driving, stylish, yet totally professional cop hero, the head of a police Special Investigation Unit in San Fran, *Nash Bridges* was full of interesting supporting characters, including former stoner comic Cheech Marin as his partner Joe Dominguez

(Marin would, of course, later migrate to *Lost*, where he would play Hurley's dad). The cast also included Jeff Perry (now Meredith Grey's father on *Grey's Anatomy*) as techno-wiz and Deadhead Harvey Leek; James Gammon as Nash's somewhat demented father Nick; *Baywatch* alum Yasmine Bleeth as Caitlin Cross, and Daniel Roebuck—*Lost*'s dead-by-dynamite Doctor Arzt—as corrupt cop Rick Bettina.

The roster of guest stars on *Nash Bridges*—a partial list would include Gonzo journalist Hunter S. Thompson, transvestite extraordinaire RuPaul, wrestler Stone Cold Steve Austin, *Sex and the City*'s Cynthia Nixon, 1970s sex goddess Valerie Perrine, tabloid journalist Geraldo Rivera, controversial baseball great Barry Bonds, Springsteen saxophonist Clarence Clemons, singer Willie Nelson, B-movie queen Shannon Tweed, and *Laverne and Shirley*'s (and *League of Their Own* director) Penny Marshall—was truly impressive.

The Prisoner—In the mid-1960s, right in the middle of global upheaval including the Cold War, space race, and various land wars, such as the U.S. involvement in Vietnam, a UK television series captured viewers' interest with its unsettling take on reality. Forty years later, during another era of global turmoil, *Lost* is doing the same.

In *The Prisoner*, a former government employee (most likely a spy) known only as Number Six is incarcerated and monitored by unknown people in "the Village," a seaside resort from which no one can escape. Is Number Six part of an experiment? Is he a political prisoner? Exactly what's going on? Those were fan questions throughout the series' run—questions similar to those from *Lost* fans not only as Oceanic 815's survivors learn about their bewildering island during the first season, but as more people are heard whispering, glimpsed watching, or caught monitoring the castaways' behavior. The Others' ability to monitor the castaways seems like a variation of *The Prisoner*'s plot, especially when Ben Linus reveals that some lucky few can leave, but only he determines how and when. Even after the ways off or onto the Island become better understood by the end of Season Five, a "prisoner" quality remains in the series because someone—such as Jacob or his nemesis—may be the still-unrevealed force behind the mystery. Even off island, in the supposedly "normal" world, the Oceanic Six discover that "others," such as Ben, Charles Widmore, or even Jeremy

Bentham, can follow their every move and track them down. No one, whether on an isolated island or anywhere in the metropolitan world, is immune from observation. In this sense, we are all prisoners of modern society and its ubiquitous surveillance.

The Prisoner's Village resembles the Others' compound, with colorful houses mocking normalcy and providing a home from which its inhabitants cannot escape. On the outside, the Village and the Others' community seem like friendly places with all the amenities needed for a happy life, but they belie a more sinister reality from which the inhabitants feel compelled to escape. Number Six and, in *Lost*'s Season Three, Jack face repeated interrogation and mind games; Number Six and Karl endure attempted brainwashing. Like Number Six, Jack is a strong man unlikely to break under duress but is severely tested; his vow to escape becomes a primary reason for living. Even in Season Five, Jack often flounders through Ben's games to get Jack to convince the Oceanic Six to return to the Island. Strange as it may seem, especially when we know just how much Jack wanted to escape the Island, he also feels imprisoned in his Los Angeles life and is compelled to return to the Island.

An important icon for *The Prisoner* was Rover, the large white balloon sent either to pacify or suffocate potential escapees. It could appear anywhere at any time, and because video surveillance covered the Village, Rover could easily be dispatched to avert problems. *Lost*'s Smoke Monster apparently serves a similar purpose as a "security device," although its method of operation is even creepier than Rover's. In *Lost*'s Seasons Four and Five, Smoky plays judge and executioner more often, condemning Keamy's men to death but permitting Ben, who confesses he allowed Alex to die, to live. Surveillance and punishment are two themes common to both series that, not surprisingly, becoming popular with audiences during times of international stress and mistrust.

Questions of free will also become important elements of both series. Juliet refuses to follow Ben and questions the Others' belief in free will when everyone around her is manipulated into acting against their better judgment. Dan Faraday suggests that the variables, not just the constants, determine what happens, and even past events may be changed. With hope that he might change the past and thus the future, Jack sets out to challenge time's status quo. The Prisoner also prefers self-determination and refuses to become a number instead of a man; he may not understand exactly what goes on behind the scenes in the Village, but he rebels against being manipulated into giving his captors information. Both *The Prisoner* and *Lost* explore what makes us human and how "civilization" attempts to break us into easily controllable drones.

Even the series' fandoms parallel each other. Fans of *The Prisoner* demanded answers as they tried to figure out the series' meaning and determine exactly who Number Six was and what he had done. They went so far as to hound Patrick McGoohan, not only the star but a director, writer, and series creator, who had toyed with the ideas leading to *The Prisoner* for years before the series made its way onto television. As a result, McGoohan reportedly went into hiding to avoid fans' fervor. In pre-Internet fandom, *The Prisoner*'s devotees went to extremes to talk with the series' actors and writers, as well as each other. Although only seventeen episodes were broadcast, *The Prisoner* achieved cult status and spawned numerous novels, games, and comic books, and a new series has been promised for a few years. *Lost* fans are well known for their similar involvement with the series, although the Internet provides us with outlets for exploring conspiracy theories and sharing information that not even Number Six could have dreamed up forty years ago. Although *Lost* and *The Prisoner* explore similar sociopolitical themes in different ways, they both are examples of innovative, thought-provoking stories that respond to times of upheaval and global uncertainty.

Solaris—See the entry in Ancestor Texts.

Star Wars, The Empire Strikes Back, Return of the Jedi—George Lucas' original *Star Wars* trilogy (now films 4, 5, 6 of a never-to-be-completed cinematic epic) was so influential back in the day that it could be claimed as an ancestor text for virtually any work of science fiction in the last quarter century, including *Lost*, but with "Some Like It Hoth" (5.13) the Lucasverse actually touched down on the Island—in 1977. The episode's title, a mash-up of the masterful Billy Wilder film (*Some Like it Hot* [1959]) and the name of the ice-planet on which Luke Skywalker finds himself at the beginning of *Empire* (1980), hinted at what was to come. Before its end—before Daniel Faraday returns from Ann Arbor ("Long time, no see," the physicist remarks to Miles)— Hurley has revealed to the ghost whisperer what he is writing in that

DHARMA notebook: the script of *Empire*. Now living in the very year in which, far away, off-island, *Star Wars* was changing the landscape of modern film, Hurley has decided to be the one, not Leigh Brackett and Lawrence Kasdan, to author, fanboy style, the sequel.

In a story titled "Pierre Menard, Author of *Don Quixote*," Jorge Luis Borges tells the tale of a Cervantes scholar, who, after steeping himself in the life and times of the Man of La Mancha's creator, sits down to write his own version of the great novel, and he succeeds, producing, word for word, the same book as Cervantes, though his is judged to be "infinitely richer." It is doubtful, given his problems with rudimentary orthography ("How do you spell 'bounty hunter'?" he asks Miles) that Hurley's alternate *Empire* would have surpassed the original.

Hugo nevertheless hoped, with 20/20 hindsight, to create a sequel precluding unfortunate later plot developments—especially the lamer-than-lame Ewoks of *Jedi* (1983), and with DHARMA's new cook's down-to-earth, wise grasp of the trilogy's exploration of fatherhood, the Reyes version was likely to enhance that theme. If Luke had only recognized Darth Vadar as his true father, Hugo understood, he might not have lost his hand, a second Death Star might not have been destroyed, and we would have not had to endure the Ewoks. And if Miles would only forgive *his* real dad, Pierre Chang, perhaps another hand might be spared.

Survivor—Mark Burnett's inventive castaway reality series *Survivor* premiered in the United States on CBS in 2000. The original premise: sixteen castaways are forced to "outwit, outlast, and outplay" fellow contestants while creating a "new society" on a deserted island as they are competing for a million dollar reward. The series secured a several-season reign at the top of the Nielsen's and has consistently remained in the top ten during new-run episodes.

Separated into two tribes of eight, the contestants spend thirty-nine to forty-one days roughing it in the middle of nowhere, without any modern conveniences or potable water. The castaways forage for their own food (many of the early seasons included a tin of rice for sustenance, but viewer demand for harsher conditions eventually led to full deprivation); locate a water source, build a shelter, start a fire, and compete in biweekly challenges for both reward and immunity. Every three days, the losing team has to face the dreaded Tribal Council, where one is ceremoniously voted off the Island.

When Lloyd Braun, former head of programming for ABC television, suggested a drama with *Survivor*-like undertones—the show that would eventually become *Lost*—the reception was less than warm. *Survivor*'s appeal to audiences is based on the dramatic component of the challenges and tribal council sessions; group dynamics were simply a sideshow. Marrying *Survivor*'s high concept to drama and suspense required a significant outside force—in the case of *Lost* a big-island mystery that could keep the emotions running high and the audience hooked.

Lost is often linked to *Survivor* in the print media; the first season was often described as "*Survivor* meets *Lord of the Flies* meets *The X-Files*." Mid-Season One, FOX's *Mad TV* offered a parody of the series, where the *Lost* castaways journey through the dense jungle to discover Jeff Probst, who prompts them to participate in a reward challenge.—**Hillary Robson**

To Kill a Mockingbird—In "The Cost of Living" (3.5), Juliet pretends to be putting in a video of *To Kill a Mockingbird* when she instead secretly communicates to Jack her request that he kill Ben during surgery.

To Kill a Mockingbird was Robert Mulligan's award-winning 1962 adaptation of Harper Lee's award-winning 1961 novel about lawyer Atticus Finch's courageous defense of a black man erroneously accused of raping a white woman in Depression-era Alabama. Gregory Peck won an Oscar for his portrayal of Finch. Equally as memorable was child actor Mary Badham's performance as Atticus' young daughter Scout, who narrates both novel and film as an adult.

The Twilight Zone—During the pilot episode of *Lost*, the camera pans to a dark sky teeming with stars, a now-iconic *Lost* image. The shot lingers as the stars twinkle over the castaways. The scene emphasizes the survivors' loneliness and their feeling of being so small in the scope of the universe. According to series' cocreator Damon Lindelof, this scene also welcomes castaways to *The Twilight Zone*.

When *Lost*'s writers and creators were growing up, they loved TV series like Rod Serling's masterpiece. During *Lost*'s first three seasons, fans revisited the *Zone* when they watched *Lost* episodes dealing with everything from parallel universes to time travel to technological problems to sentient machines. Of course, people suffering from their own paranoia and misinterpretation of information create their share of *Twilight Zone* moments, too. Like *Lost*'s island, the *Zone* is a familiar land with weird twists that play with and prey on the imagination.

Like *The Twilight Zone*, *Lost* sets precedents that change the nature of television. Before the end of Season Three, the creative forces behind the series negotiated an ending date for *Lost*: 2010. Although Seasons One through Three involved numerous experiments to determine how best to tell such a complex story while retaining the highest number of viewers, the final "formula" will be sixteen consecutive episodes for each season, Four through Six, broadcast each year between February and May. *Lost*'s show runners, primarily Lindelof and Cuse, received what they wanted: a finite number of episodes in which to tell a compelling story. ABC received what it wanted, too: an award-winning series that, even with slippage in the ratings, continues to break storytelling ground for three more seasons. Like *The Twilight Zone*, *Lost* will never be duplicated, either in content or in the way the story is told.

Although Serling is often solely credited with *The Twilight Zone*'s development and success, much as J. J. Abrams is often singularly praised for *Lost*, Serling worked with two other writers to craft what many viewers and critics believe is one of the finest science fiction shows ever. Charles Beaumont and Richard Matheson shared writing credits with Serling for the series' episodes. These writers are well known in their own right; in fact, Stephen King, among other writers, has noted Matheson's influence on his writing. In a six degrees of separation way, Matheson influenced King, who, in turn, influenced Abrams, Lindelof, Cuse, and other *Lost* writers through *The Stand*. The science fiction community is indeed incestuous.

The Twilight Zone provided a different kind of television viewing in the 1950s and 1960s; audiences were accustomed to linear story lines enacted live like a televised play. Science fiction with possibly multiple interpretations offered a new experience, and many viewers were not quite ready. Nevertheless, *The Twilight Zone* built Serling's reputation and begat science fiction knockoffs for generations. *Lost*, too, is a different type of storytelling, one that challenges "standard" television programming, invites imitation, but sometimes is difficult for casual viewers to accept.

As *Lost* has progressed, its plot threads share similarities with many themes that made *The Twilight Zone* a success; like *Zone*, *Lost* at times seems more like science fiction, but it never completely entered that realm until Season Five. During the first season, the drama emphasizes how the castaways survive after the plane crash. Mysteriously, most of the forty-eight survivors have only minor injuries, when no one should have lived. *The Twilight Zone*'s flights of fancy include "The Odyssey of Flight 33," in which a plane breaks the time barrier and lands in a prehistoric past, and "The Arrival" of a plane whose passengers mysteriously vanished, leaving an empty plane to land.

Even an "outer space" episode suggests a possible interpretation for *Lost*'s castaways' survival. Richard Matheson's "Death Ship" describes the fateful landing of a spaceship near the wreckage of another space vehicle. The crashed spaceship and its dead crew are identical to the newly arrived vessel and its "live" crew, who begin to hallucinate visions of dead friends and relatives. The crew become convinced they are dead, only to "wake up" back in their spaceship, preparing to land on the planet.

Throughout *Lost*'s first four seasons, fans and critics speculated about the fate of Oceanic 815 and its passengers, and the theories sound remarkably similar to those brought to life on *The Twilight Zone*. Season Three's "D.O.C." concludes with the startling revelation that Oceanic 815's fuselage had been found in a trench off Bali, all passengers dead, although the castaways on the Island seem very much alive. Although it now appears that the crash was faked (by Charles Widmore), the possibility of parallel universes, time discrepancies, and other *Zone*-themed explanations don't seem out of the question.

The introduction of the Others into *Lost*'s plot begins an escalation of fear, distrust, and social disintegration, not only for the castaways but the more established Others. Determining who is friend or foe, Us or Them, becomes the motivation for espionage, lies, murder, and betrayal, a theme that reaches its flashpoint during the Season Three finale. The series illustrates just how "lost" people can become when they find it impossible to trust even their supposed friends and how far they might go in trying to protect themselves. *Lost* reflects a current Western culture of fear, similar to the Cold War fears during the time of *The Twilight Zone*.

One of the *Zone*'s most famous episodes, "The Monsters Are Due on Maple Street," highlights this fear—a rumored alien invasion seems real when one street after another loses electrical power, and all equipment, including cars, fails to work. One man, however, can start his car, an act that leads to his neighbors' suspicions that he is one of the "aliens." Lights in a few homes flash off and on during the blackout. Certain that the invasion is happening and their street infiltrated by "aliens," neighbors take up arms to fend off these invaders, leading to the accidental shooting and death of an innocent man. The neighborhood plunges into chaos, just as the real aliens, watching from a distance, have predicted. They don't need to invade Middle America; neighbors will soon turn against each other and destroy themselves. By the end of Season Three, *Lost* destroys its own Maple Street.

Other themes, including time travel, space travel, nuclear war, death and the afterlife, and sentient machines, may be tangentially linked to *Lost*. The *Zone*'s first season includes "Mirror Image," a Serling-penned tale in which bus traveler Millicent Barnes discovers that she has a double. Although Millicent is convinced that only one of her selves can survive in this world, the man to whom she tells this story is convinced that she's crazy. His idea abruptly changes, however, when he discovers his own double. The second-season "Back There" sends a modern man, Peter Corrigan, back in history to the day before President Lincoln's assassination. His attempts to change history fail, but one man who heard Corrigan in the 1860s paid attention—back in his own time, Corrigan meets the ancestor of the man who profited from knowing information from the future. In another episode, "The Parallel," astronaut Major Gaines returns to earth, convinced that he is a colonel in a parallel universe. His superiors, colonels themselves, scoff, until they receive a message from "Colonel Gaines." During Season Three, *Lost* plays with similar themes, especially in scenes involving Desmond, who becomes convinced that he knows—and might be able to change—the future. Time travel and parallel universe theories have become more popular among fans to explain *Lost*'s convoluted plot twists.

Lost borrows from the *Zone* in other ways, too. Both series title an episode "The Whole Truth," although the plots radically differ. *Lost* references "An Occurrence at Owl Creek Bridge," which becomes a peripheral ancestor text for the series, in "The Long Con" (2.13); *The Twilight Zone* broke tradition by bringing a French film of the short story to U.S. television.

Lost shares common themes and values with *The Twilight Zone*. The best episodes make viewers think; they scramble audiences' perceptions of the way the universe works; they have a message, although they seldom are heavy handed in delivering it. They bring in elements of the fantastic, but, as characters and viewers discover, the worst monsters come from our imaginations. Human acts resulting from fear, paranoia, and "group think" often provide the greatest terror.

Twin Peaks—The ABC television series *Twin Peaks* (1990–1991) would count as a *Lost* ancestral text even if it hadn't figured prominently in the thinking of both the network executives and show creators who put *Lost* on the air in the fall of 2004. Virtually every important maker of end-of-the-millennium and early twenty-first-century TV, from Joss Whedon to David Chase to J. J. Abrams, has spoken of their debt to David Lynch and Mark Frost's bizarre tale of Special Agent Dale Cooper's investigation of the murder of prom queen Laura Palmer in the small Northwest town of Twin Peaks. ABC knew full well to expect something out of the ordinary from Lynch (director of *Eraserhead, Elephant Man,* and *Blue Velvet*) and Frost (*Hill Street Blues*), though they may not have anticipated a woman who communed with her log, a dancing dwarf, unforgettable dream sequences, crime-solving through Tibetan rock throwing, and a supernatural parasitic serial killer named BOB. Described in one early press story as the "show that will change TV," *Twin Peaks* quickly became a cultural event but flamed out early in its second season, abandoned by a once-huge audience that quickly grew weary of its difficult-to-follow metaphysics and over-the-top quirkiness.

But the thoroughly postmodern (it riffed on/sampled scores of movies, TV shows, and works of literature, from *Double Indemnity* to Arthurian legends) and genre-mixing (was it a soap opera? a sitcom? a police procedural? an FBI drama? a coffee commercial?), *Twin Peaks* did make it possible for television creators to think outside the box. It is hard to imagine ABC allowing J. J. Abrams and Damon Lindelof to morph the basic "plane crashes on an island" idea into the series *Lost* has become without the splendid failure of *Twin Peaks* in its collective past.

Though not quite as PoMo as *Twin Peaks*, *Lost* certainly is genre-bending. As we watch, we are never quite certain which genre-spectacles to don in order to facilitate our close reading of either its present-tense or backstory narratives. An old Sufi tale describes how several men touching different parts of an elephant offer dissimilar reports on the reality before them. Depending on where we encounter the *Lost* elephant, we too might well make very different genre reports.

As Jack operates (in present and past tense), we may think we are watching a medical drama. When Boone sleeps with his stepsister Shannon or Sun and Jin's marriage goes awry, we may think melodrama. As terrifying noises fill the night and a mysterious Monster roams the Island, we are afraid *Lost* may turn out to be horror. In the aftermath of Oceanic 815's crash (and in the frighteningly realistic flashbacks to the catastrophic event that broke the plane apart), we might well think we are watching a disaster movie. Flashback after flashback incrementally revealing the backgrounds of all the major characters might mislead us into thinking *Lost* is really an anthology drama. Its many mysteries—Locke's inexplicable ability to walk, the baffling appearance on the Island of Jack's father, Walt's psychic ability, the magical power of the numbers that have altered Hurley's life—might make us think *Lost* is some kind of supernatural tale, an exercise in what is sometimes called the fantastic. With Season Five's narrative bending time travel, the series stepped emphatically out of the science fiction closet. *Lost*, of course, never insists on how we should understand it, and in this openness to mystery lies its greatest debt to *Twin Peaks* and its most significant heir, *The X-Files*.

We have detailed elsewhere the many "conspiracy theories" *Lost* has inspired in its avid fans. That, too, we should note in closing, is *Twin Peaks'* legacy. One of the first television series to truly energize its fan base (see Henry Jenkins' essay in *Full of Secrets*), *Twin Peaks* inspired obsessive theorizing; its long-delayed answer to its "Who Killed Laura Palmer" central question only fed the flames. In addition to nominating all the usual subjects, fanatics would also suggest that Laura's murderer was (a) an often-used-as-a-transitional-image traffic light and (b) the ceiling fan in Laura Palmer's house. Crazy people enjoy TV, too. But then again, we did learn in *Twin Peaks: Fire Walk with Me*, the series' feature film prequel, that BOB, Laura's actual killer (using her father as his agent), traveled throughout weirdsville via the electrical system, including that ceiling fan at the top of the stairs...

The Wizard of Oz—Even before the title of *Lost's* three-part Season Four finale—"There's No Place Like Home," clearly a reference to Dorothy's signature line in Victor Fleming's classic 1939 film, *The Wizard of Oz* had already come to the Island. Anyone who's seen the movie version remembers Dorothy's Uncle Henry. He isn't the smartest man, leaving the handling of Miz Gulch to his wife, but he's polite and sincere. Nevertheless, he undoubtedly is the head of the family. Henry Gale of Kansas might be considered a good figurehead for his small family. Although as the man of the household he oversees the farm and its workers, audiences understand that he really isn't the one in charge.

Lost may have appropriated the character name of Henry Gale as an original wink to yet another ancestor text. "Fake" Henry Gale says he arrived on the Island in a bright smiley-faced balloon, but he merely takes the name of the balloonist he buries ("One of Them," 2.14). Gale's driver's license lists an address of 815 Walnut Ridge Road in Wayzata, Minnesota. Although Wayzata is featured in the TV series *90210*, Minnesota was the home state of Judy Garland, the movie's Dorothy.

Ben Linus may borrow the name Henry Gale, but he is more akin to another *Oz* character, the Wizard himself. Ben's Season Three backstory, appropriately named "The Man Behind the Curtain" (3.20), recalls a pivotal scene in *The Wizard of Oz* when Toto tugs back the curtain hiding the man manipulating controls to project the Wizard's powerful image. "Pay no attention to the man behind the curtain," the Wizard proclaims, but the secret is out: The Great and Mighty Wizard of Oz is merely an average man who puffs himself up in order to frighten followers and maintain control of Oz (itself a wink to Australia, departure point for Flight 815).

Perhaps the "man behind the curtain" is the real Ben Linus. For years he keeps his followers in line with threats and a few magic tricks, but he is just as much stuck in Oz as they are. Since the sky turned purple and then the submarine blew up, no one seems able to leave the Island (until the Season Three finale reveals that at least Jack and Kate do make it back to LA). Michael and Walt, who earlier received permission (and coordinates) to head for home, may never be able to return to the Island, á là the "wizard" flying away from Oz but being unable to visit, even if he so wished. Although Walt again seems to "teleport" his essence as a vision to a castaway, this time Locke ("Through the Looking Glass," 3.22–23) sees the vision; much like the Wizard's disembodied head, Walt only appears as a holographic image to dispense his wisdom. One man with some of the answers, Ben technically may know how to leave the Island but so far hasn't been motivated to take that one-way trip; he warns Jack that he doesn't know what he's doing by communicating with a boat waiting off shore; "rescue" from the Island seems to be Jack's undoing. Although he tries to return to his "Oz," Jack's travels across the Pacific seem futile.

A late Season Two fan comparison between *Lost* and the movie noted parallels between *Oz* and *Lost* characters: Ben (the Wizard), Dorothy (Kate), Scarecrow (Jack), Tinman (Sawyer), and Cowardly Lion (Hurley). Kate, the spunky Dorothy, runs away from home in the Midwest (Kate's Iowa instead of Dorothy's Kansas). Scarecrow Jack seeks knowledge and develops a close friendship with "Dorothy." Sawyer needs a heart, or at least to show it more often, and Hurley's lovely locks are reminiscent of the Lion's curly mane. Like the Lion, Hurley shows surprising courage as the story progresses. Although this analogy works within the framework of late Season Two episodes, further plot development in Season Three renders it less tenable.

Although Ben controls the lives of those he keeps captive (early in Season Three), he doesn't provide the group a "quest" that may help them gain what they most desire. He does, however, promise Jack a way home if Ben's tumor is successfully removed ("The Glass Ballerina," 3.2) but then is unable to fulfill his part of the bargain ("The Man from Tallahassee," 3.13). Locke receives a "quest" that, if he succeeds, permits him to join the Others and "come home" to the Island rather than leave. Like the Wizard demanding proof of the Wicked Witch of the West's death (her broomstick), Ben requires Locke to bring the dead body of his father ("The Brig," 3.20). Locke successfully shoulders this burden, which rids him of the father he hates and initiates him into Others' society.

The original L. Frank Baum *Oz* adventure was published in turn-of-the-twentieth-century America, just when the rise of technology began to encroach upon rural society. On the Island, the Hatches and Others' community have higher levels of technology than the castaways' "rural" community on the beach. The struggle to gain technology, and then manage and maintain it, is as much a part of the Island's history as of Baum's America. Like the diminishing rural communities, by the end of Season Three, the beach community is not as "natural" as it originally was; contact with the Others and ever-increasing presence of technology essentially changes the way the castaways live.

The X-Files—One of *Lost*'s key characters, Hurley, does share a last name with Agent Monica Reyes (Annabeth Gish) from *The X-Files'* final season (2001–2002), and Robert Patrick (Agent John Doggett on the series [2000–2002]) and Terry O'Quinn (who appeared in a second season episode ["Aubrey," 2.2] and in the first *X-Files* movie [1998]) do show up on *Lost*—as Hibbs, the man who sets up Sawyer to kill his namesake in Australia in "Outlaws" (1.16), and Locke, respectively. FOX's *The X-Files* (1993–2002) shared fewer story elements with *Lost* than *Gilligan's Island* or even *Lord of the Flies*, and yet it stands as a key ancestor text in many respects.

Created by Chris Carter, *The X-Files* followed the investigations of two FBI special agents: the "I want to believe," open-to-all-things-occult, convinced "the truth is out there" Fox Mulder (David Duchovny) and the medical doctor and skeptic Dana Scully (Gillian Anderson), assigned to investigate the agency's most "out there" cases. (The series had its own ancestor texts, of course: the Watergate hearings, television programs like *The Night Stalker* [ABC, 1972–1975] and *Twin Peaks*, books like John Mack's *Abduction: Human Encounters with Aliens* [1994].) The show became first a cult hit and then a mainstream success that played a pivotal role in the establishment of FOX as a bona fide network.

Its fan base was rabid, producing some of the most brilliant, comprehensive, and ingenious websites to date and penning tons of fanfiction that not only consummated (at last!) the PST (Prolonged Sexual Tension) of Mulder/Scully but slashed all sort of other characters as well, including Mulder and Director Walter Skinner. But FOX was not kind to its fans, often shutting down sites for copyright infringement when they were contributing mightily to the series' growing popularity. In a later century, the creators of *Lost* would stroke the very fans FOX would counterproductively alienate.

Though *Lost* has no FBI agents and offers no police procedural, it does replicate *Files*-ish traits: its pairing of believer and doubter (on *Lost*,

Locke and Jack, respectively); its casting of relative unknowns in its key roles (Matthew Fox as Jack and Evangeline Lilly as Kate, replicate the Duchovny/Anderson pairing—both the male leads were somewhat better known; both the women were complete unknowns). Perhaps the greatest similarity between the two series lies in their similar openness to mystery.

The X-Files was a show so resistant to closure—to satisfactory resolution of the myriad questions each individual story, and its overarching "mythology" episodes, introduced—that it even self-referentially joked about it. "Whatever 'out there' truth Mulder and Scully discovered in the hour—whatever evidence they accumulated, by means of his intuitions or her careful science, of the existence of the paranormal or the supernatural or of vast conspiracies—dissipated or evaporated before the closing credits" (Lavery 243). In *Lost*'s *Black Rock*, Dark Territory, Others, polar bears, the Monster, the Hatch, we find echoes of *The X-Files*' reliance on its own recurring mysteries: the alien bounty hunter, the black oil, the Cigarette-Smoking Man, the Syndicate, the Well-Manicured Man, the bees, the alien rebels, supersoldiers...By the end of its run, however, many, if not most, *X-Files* regulars had grown tired of its mysteries-without-end. Marketing, on TV and in print, constantly promised that our questions would be answered, but they never were and even more were raised.

Writing about *The X-Files*' unhappy end in *The Chicago Tribune*, Joshua Klein would, not surprisingly, think of *Lost*: "TV watchers may currently sense a similar situation in the mysterious *Lost*, the finale of which angered viewers by failing to answer any of the many questions raised during its first season." Klein asked the man himself, *X-Files* creator Chris Carter, what he thought of *Lost*.

I'm a big fan of J.J. Abrams. I think he's really creative, and I'm a big fan of what he does. But I know there are pits to fall into, and you've got to avoid them every step of the way. It takes a lot of thought and gut instinct. I can tell you that with mythology shows, if you stumble, you fall.

Lost's makers are well aware of the dilemma, and demonstrate in podcasts and interviews and, most of all, in their negotiated end point for their vast narrative, their clear desire to avoid taking a fall.

CHAPTER TWO

THE *LOST* PLAYLIST

For their son's birthday party, Carmen and David Reyes throw a faux island fling. Guests sip fruity drinks and wear colorful leis. Even the Hawaiian music promises a tropical paradise ("There's No Place Like Home," 4.12).

Flash.

Back on the real island, flaming arrows blaze the beach. The castaways' camp burns. All is chaos. "Head for the trees!" Sawyer commands. Frogurt pauses a moment too long. Without looking behind, the survivors flee into the jungle. Slashing strings and drums pound just as fast as the survivors' feet ("The Lie," 5.2).

Flash.

Bernard herds Kate, Sawyer, and Juliet toward his and his annoyed wife's cottage near the beach. It's quiet and peaceful in their garden, representing the idyll Rose and Bernard have made of their "retirement." Although Juliet turns down Bernard's gracious offer of tea, she wistfully wishes to return...once the current crisis is averted. A lush cello solo reveals the retirees' tender love story trapped on their island of no return ("The Incident," 5.15).

For five years, composer Michael Giacchino's score has elevated these and other widely diverse visualizations of *Lost* life, making each relationship musically memorable or amplifying the pulse-pumping percussion to highlight dangerous scenes. *Lost*'s original score, however, is only part of the soundtrack to our—and the characters'—myriad stories. His award-winning compositions subtly underscore the danger, pathos, and joy of island living; by carefully selecting instruments and tones—and knowing just when music should enter and leave a scene—he creates a unique soundtrack for this rare television series.

Music unites viewers and characters through mutually remembered songs and artists, reminding us that music is a common note in our lives. It sets the scene in many ways: through characters who sing or play instruments on the Island and in their flash-forwards, time travels, and back stories; in the background popular music from roughly the past sixty years; by references to bands (real or imagined); and with that haunting original score. Music helps characters find themselves; it's the ultimate "comfort food" for the soul. In this chapter, we look at the many ways that a selection's lyrics, theme, time period, or pace creates a mood and enhances audiences' understanding of a scene.

THE MUSICAL CASTAWAYS

As the lone identified professional musician/songwriter/singer on the Island, Charlie Pace sings snippets of songs in several episodes in Seasons One through Three. They range from the high-pitched chorus of "You All Everybody" (sung twice in the pilot episode, including a scene cut from broadcast but appearing on the Season One DVD extended episodes, or when parodied during "Fire + Water" as "You All Every Butty"—an advertisement for diapers) to the Kinks' "He's Evil" ("The 23rd Psalm," 2.10). More memorably (and better in tune), he plays bass and sings with DriveShaft ("Homecoming," 1.15; "Fire + Water," 2.12; "Greatest Hits," 3.21). During back stories' quieter moments or between island crises, he plays guitar or composes songs. For three seasons, Charlie's life really was all about the music. We don't know if music plays a part in his rather active afterlife, but "ghost" Charlie's heaven probably includes at least a few jam sessions. As the Righteous Brothers reminded us, "If there's rock 'n' roll in heaven, you know they have a helluva band."[6]

A surprising number of other characters manage a few bars here and there. Before Claire agrees to give up her soon-to-be-born child for adoption, she asks the prospective parents to promise to sing "Catch a Falling Star" to the baby ("Raised by Another," 1.10). She quickly and self-consciously sings a few lines to make sure they know the song. For Claire, motherhood involves little things like bedtime lullabies; if she won't be there to sing to her baby, she wants him/her at least to have that comfort from someone else. Such a sweet song as "Catch a Falling Star" provides an ironic twist to Claire's wishes once she crash-lands on the Island. Perry Como's lighthearted recording lends an eerie note to "Maternity Leave" (2.15) as Ethan Rom plans to give Claire's baby to "a good family"—the Others—but Como's rendition eventually shows Claire's dream comes true.

When Kate sings "Catch a Falling Star" to Aaron, and then Como's version plays in the background as she and her adopted son walk to Cassidy's front door ("What Happened, Happened," 5.11), long-time fans remember that this song is associated with Aaron and his many "mothers." This time, the music provides yet another character connection, but it also brings the "Catch a Falling Star" sub-sub-sub-substory to its conclusion. Season Five provides answers and returns to niggly points in the story as rewards or Easter eggs to faithful viewers. The music helps satisfy audiences who want to tie up every loose end, and the song choice in scenes like this does so subtly but memorably.

Even when only a few days old, Aaron brings out surprising musical talent among the castaways. When Charlie runs out of songs for the crying newborn, he asks Hurley to help out. The big man bursts into a rousing rendition of James Brown's "I Feel Good"—which only makes Aaron cry more loudly ("The Greater Good," 1.21). The music becomes not only part of the characters' "dialogue," but the way they sing and their song choice let audiences know more about them. Hurley is *Lost*'s "feel-good" character, and the song that comes immediately to his mind reflects his propensity to find the lighter side of island life.

Almost any occasion can spark a song. Desmond drunkenly sings "The Celtic Song" for his favorite football (soccer) team after downing a bottle of Mariah Vineyards' finest ("Catch-22," 3.17). He mostly mumbles the chorus, as sung by Glasgow's Celtic fans: "For it's a grand old team to play for / For it's a grand old team to see / And if you know

the history / It's enough to make your heart go / Nine in a row."[7]
Desmond only makes it roughly through the first three lines before
Brother Campbell "fires" him as a monk.

Buoyed by the possibility of escape from the Island, Sawyer sings
Bob Marley's "Redemption Song" ("Exodus," 1.24) as he sets sail on
the raft near the end of Season One. The song may have been an em-
bedded spoiler for what is to come, as the first line is "Old Pirates, yes,
they rob"—perhaps alluding to Walt's kidnapping from the "Pirate-d"
Others. Sawyer again sings (albeit badly) during "Stranger in a Strange
Land" Irving Berlin's "Show Me The Way To Go Home"—it seems
sailing gets Sawyer in the mood for serenading. That's not the only
thing: he also knows the value of music to set the mood. When he
suggests Kate share a little "afternoon delight" ("Catch-22," 3.17), he
not only cites the title of a 1976 Starlight Vocal Band hit but promises
a mix tape to get her in the mood after she declines his invitation. Kate
is suitably impressed, although surprised, when Sawyer later hands her
a cassette of Phil Collins' greatest hits ("borrowed" from Bernard).

Even the most serious characters relax by playing the piano, and almost
every season introduces yet another surprising pianist. On the eve of Jack
and Sarah's wedding, the couple massacre "Heart and Soul" on the piano;
Jack is the more accomplished musician, but he lets Sarah peck a few notes
("The Hunting Party," 2.11). Jack's cold feet before marriage should have
signaled a greater concern about the doomed relationship. The couple's
marriage will echo the disharmony in their prewedding duet.

When Jack plays piano solo in his "home" at the Others' encampment ("Left Behind," 3.15), the scene again echoes Jack's feelings: he
is hopeful at the possibility of going home, but he is also alone and
lonely. When Kate sees Jack playing the piano in such a "normal" setting, she suddenly realizes just how much she doesn't know about him.
Music reveals a very different side to Jack and, as with other characters,
subtly indicates his deepest feelings.

In a scene mirroring Jack's solo during his stay at New Otherton,
Ben also de-stresses in a similar way ("The Shape of Things to Come,"
4.9) by playing Rachmaninov's "Prelude in C Minor." The camera in
his scene mimics Kate's quiet entry into the same house, but instead
of Kate watching Jack, the camera allows the audience voyeuristically
to watch Ben in what seems to be a rare unguarded moment. He, like

Jack, becomes absorbed in the solace of making music, a revealing insight into the common interest of two increasingly desperate leaders.

Dan Faraday wasn't always such a stickler for science. Until his mother, Eloise Hawking, convinces him he only has time for physics, young Dan spends much more time playing piano. His favorite selection seems to be the popularly retitled "(I'm Always) Chasing Rainbows," officially known as Chopin's "Fantaisie Impromptu" ("The Variable," 5.14). Either name ironically underscores what gentle Dan's life might have been had he been free of his parents' control. As he plays, the strict metronome ticks away the time he's allowed to enjoy music, as well as his shortened life.

The popular lyrics "I'm always chasing rainbows...My dreams are just like all my schemes / Ending in the sky" illustrate Ellie's inability to change her son's future; her schemes don't save her son's life. The next lyrics, "Some fellas search and find the sunshine / I always look and find the rain / Some fellas make a winning sometime / I never even make a gain,"[8] could be Dan's part of their song. By always trying to gain his mother's and father/mentor Charles Widmore's acceptance, Dan sacrifices his personal life in favor of physics. His work, however, ends up bringing memory loss, pain, and death. He should have been a brilliant, successful scientist (or perhaps better yet, a talented musician), but his ability to cheat time ends up being as elusive as a chased rainbow.

When Dan's mind shatters after failed time-travel experiments at Oxford, he once again escapes to the comfort of his music. When his mother arrives to encourage him to turn again to science, as well as head to the Island, Dan is playing a broken version of the tune. The rainbows he likely would've chased, music and love with an adoring girlfriend, become replaced with his parents' ambitions that he learn how to control time travel.

Even on the Island, Dan uses a music metaphor to explain the left-behinds' increasingly hazardous leaps in Island time. "We're not on the song we want to be on," he explains as a way to compare their jumps through time to a skipping phonograph record ("LaFleur," 5.8).

Although the characters have fewer reasons and less time to sing or play during Seasons Four and Five, audiences still can see how, on a fundamental level, music uncovers emotions usually kept beneath the surface and links disparate characters.

CHOOSING THE RIGHT SONG FOR THE SCENE

Paying attention to the lyrics, as well as the artist, time period, musical genre, and emotional timbre of a song, is crucial to getting the most out of *Lost*'s story line and real-world soundtrack. Not only does song selection often expose hidden parts of a character's personality, but it also can foreshadow what will happen. For five years, *Lost*'s carefully selected song choices add depth to scenes like the following:

- Until the batteries finally die, Hurley spends relaxation time on the beach listening to music through his headset ("House of the Rising Sun," 1.16).

- "Delicate" by Damien Rice, plays over scenes of the castaways' beach camp and abruptly stops right before Sun removes her coverings to stand in her bikini, marking her freedom ("...In Translation," 1.23). Here, lyrics also may foreshadow what we soon come to learn about Sun's extramarital affair, as the content of the song deals with a secret love affair.

- Willie Nelson's "Are You Sure" ("...In Translation," 1.23) must echo the feelings of the uncertain castaways beginning to realize rescue isn't coming any time soon: "The lonely faces that you see / Are you sure that this is where you want to be? / These are your friends / But are they real friends?"[9] At this point the alliances among castaways are still tentative, and true friendships have yet to be forged from sharing continued dangers.

- During a flashback in which we learn more about Shannon, Dave Matthew's "Stay (Wasting Time)" plays in the background, another foreshadowing perhaps—as Shannon is killed at the end of the episode ("Abandoned," 2.6).

- Staind's "Outside" plays in a bar as Ana Lucia hunts down the man who caused her to lose her child, Jason McCormick. The bitter lyrics mirror Ana Lucia's frame of mind: "And I taste / What I could never have / It's from You"[10] ("Collision," 2.16).

- Desmond's return to Penny in "Flashes Before Your Eyes" (3.8) features Sarah McLachlan's "Building a Mystery,"[11] a song that refers to a "beautiful, strange man" (Desmond).

- Nikki dances to "Rump Shaker" in "Expose" (3.14) right before her death scene in the mystery drama of the same name.

- Even after the Hatch implodes, Hurley still finds recorded music. Three Dog Night's "Shambala" brings back memories of his childhood; it blasts from the 8-track while Hurley and Charlie joyride in the DHARMA Initiative's van ("Tricia Tanaka Is Dead," 3.10). Hurley's music lightens the mood and gives viewers—as well as castaways—a respite from drama. The trend of "bouncy" music continues in that blast from the past when Miles and Hurley ride in the van, this time as bona fide members of the DHARMA Initiative. Captain and Tennille's 1975 hit, "Love Will Keep Us Together," is appropriate for their discussion of how they respectively communicate with the dead, a talent that links them despite their many other differences ("Some Like It Hoth," 5.13).

- Charlie occupies a sidewalk singing Oasis's "Wonderwall" in "Flashes Before Your Eyes" (3.8) (and in "Greatest Hits" [3.21]). The lyrics, "Maybe you're gonna be the one that saves me," reflect Charlie's need to save his friends and family, always a strong motivator in his life. They also specifically foreshadow his impending death, which Desmond tells him is necessary in order for Claire and Aaron to be rescued from the Island.

- Bonobo's "If You Stayed Over" ("The Economist," 4.3) appropriately summarizes Sayid's desire for a normal life with a woman he loves—a future denied to him on or off the Island. As he makes love with Elsa, the lyrics taunt him with possibilities: "If I breathe in the future / Breathe out the past, yeah / Savour this moment / As long as it lasts."[12]

- Our first introduction to country music lover Dr. Pierre Chang shows him listening to Willie Nelson's "Shotgun Willie" while he completes his morning routine ("Because You Left," 5.1); this scene is similar to Desmond's early morning routine in his first moments on screen in the Hatch. Chang later tells Hurley and Miles that his baby son was named for his wife's favorite musician, jazz legend Miles Davis ("Some Like It Hoth," 5.13).

"LaFleur" (5.8) brings back the 1970s with a vengeance, and later episodes encompassing island life from 1974–1977 cover the musical gamut of the era. The DHARMA Initiative's boogie nights fill the compound with song: Tony Orlando and Dawn's "Knock Three Times" ("LaFleur," 5.8), Captain and Tennille's "Love Will Keep Us Together" ("Some Like It Hoth," 5.13), Albert Hammond's "It Never Rains in Southern California" (Some Like It Hoth," 5.13), and, for special gatherings like new initiates' orientation, Blue Image's "Ride Captain Ride" ("Namaste," 5.9). Members of the older generation may pay less attention to pop rock, preferring jazz classics. When not whipping up a batch of truth serum or interrogating visitors, Oldham prefers an afternoon with Ella (Fitzgerald). "I Can't Give You Anything But Love, Baby" is the torturer's unlikely welcome theme when LaFleur and Sayid call ("He's Our You," 5.10). These and other scene-setting songs capture the Island's past and create just the right mood to explain life in the DHARMA Initiative.

The way that music is edited within a scene also powerfully supports the visuals and dialogue of even an "ordinary" scene, such as Kate's visit to Sawyer's New Otherton home in "Eggtown" (4.4). Making himself at home, Hurley starts watching *Xanadu* on TV, but Sawyer, who prefers to read, asks him to turn down the volume. Their interplay is interrupted when Kate knocks at their door. Just as Olivia Newton-John entices her love to "open your eyes and see what we have is real,"[13] Sawyer opens the door and takes off his glasses; he truly sees Kate as the woman he wants and, soon after, invites her to stay with him in the Others' abandoned town. Sawyer pictures a sheltered life there; he and Kate can share a little house and enjoy a few comforts while remaining secluded from the rest of the world (a fantasy come true with Juliet during Season Five). For Sawyer, this scenario would be ideal, his version of Xanadu as a mystical, perfect place where predestined love can overcome obstacles of time and space (and the clichéd long arm of the law). Kate, on the other hand, doesn't believe that life can be so simple, especially for (emotionally stunted and morally challenged) con artists like she and Sawyer. "Xanadu," as a theme song and a romantic ideal, converge in this scene and provide insights into Sawyer's more romantic, less pragmatic side.

CHANNELING THE DEAD

Ever notice how many songs featured on *Lost* are by now-dead artists? The list is long, including Glenn Miller, Patsy Cline, Bob Marley, Otis Redding, Perry Como, Skeeter Davis, Cass Elliot, Kurt Cobain, and Buddy Holly. Although some lived to see old age, most of these artists died unexpectedly while relatively young. Some, such as Miller, Cline, and Holly, died in plane crashes. Of course, songs by living bands and artists also provide a soundtrack for the castaways' *Lost* lives, but somber music often sets the mood, not so much because of the lyrics or melody but for the images it evokes of artists once popular but now gone.

After Sayid finally fixes the radio for Hurley ("The Long Con," 2.13), they test it on a quiet starlit night on the beach. Sayid finally tunes the radio so that it pulls in a song—Glenn Miller's "Moonlight Serenade." Appropriately, Sayid and Hurley are serenaded in the moonlight, but sci-fi–friendly Hurley feels compelled to comment that maybe the signal is coming from another time. Given Desmond's later penchant for playing with timelines and Season Five's travels in time and space, Hurley may have been right. *Lost* has a way of bringing back the dead, or at least making their presence heavily felt by the castaways.

Buddy Holly's "Everyday" recreates the 1950s as young Emily prepares for her date with an unseen "older man" against her mother's wishes ("Cabin Fever," 4.11). Irony, a frequent element in pairing music with scene, permeates Emily's happiness (and a lighthearted love tune) with the next scenes of the teenager being hit by a car and prematurely giving birth to baby John. The lyrics "Every day it's a-getting' closer / Goin' faster than a roller coaster / Love like yours will surely come my way"[14] also ironically foreshadow the mother's (and, much later, the son's) difficulty in finding true love. As loyal *Lost* fans know from previous flashback episodes, Emily's "love" is con man Anthony Cooper, who uses Emily not just for sex but to meet adult John in order to "steal" his kidney. Mentally unstable adult Emily sets up her son in exchange for cash.

John doesn't fare much better on his own. Although as a newborn he overcomes illness as a result of being born several months prematurely (and as an adult regains mobility after being paralyzed in a fall), he can't seem to overcome commitment issues in order to love. When he gives his heart completely—to his birth parents, for example—he ends up bitter and disappointed. When girlfriend Helen truly loves him, John manages to squander what may be his one chance at happiness ("Walkabout," 1.3; "Lockdown," 2.17; "The Man from Tallahassee," 3.13). Within this context, Buddy Holly's cheerful vocals promising love just around the corner seem as naïve as the teenager trying to look sexy for her big date but having no idea how sinister he may be.

Patsy Cline's artistry provides the perfect soundtrack to Kate's pre-island life, although other characters, such as Christian Shephard, also appropriate Cline's country sound for sad life stories. The lyrics of the much-used "Walkin' After Midnight" seem appropriate for Kate and Christian in "Left Behind" (3.5), "Two for the Road" (2.20), and "What Kate Did" (2.9); both characters search for the missing ones they love. Even Cassidy, who talks with Kate while the song plays in the background, has lost Sawyer, the man she loves but who abandoned her.

Cline's haunting voice describes loneliness and longing: "I'm out walking after midnight out in the moonlight / Just hoping maybe you're somewhere walking after midnight searching for me." The lyrics and lazy tempo capture the feeling of being lost and alone. The title "Leavin' On Your Mind" aptly fits Kate, discovered trying to slip away from the ranch where she's been hiding out ("Tabula Rasa," 1.3). As her former employer Ray Mullen drives her toward town, they discuss the universality of Patsy Cline music—a last fond moment between the two before Kate realizes that Ray plans to turn her in for the reward money.

Even after Kate has been living on the Island for three months, Cline's music continues to haunt her. "She's Got You"[15] foreshadows Kate's split from Sawyer, who remains in New Otherton with Locke's followers when Kate returns to the beach and Jack. In the song, a woman looks at the mementos of her now-ended love affair; all that has changed in her life is that someone else now has her lover, but her feelings for him haven't changed over time. Kate listens to this song while she waits for Sawyer ("Eggtown," 4.4) in his house, but she suspects that their respite in the Others' "paradise" will be short lived. The lyrics indicate a future Kate separated from Sawyer but still somewhat in love with the man she can't have: "I got your memory / Or has it got me? / I really don't know / But I know it won't let me be." A later episode ("Something Nice Back Home," 4.10) reveals Kate's future with Jack, and, true to Cline's "prediction," Kate jeopardizes what could be a normal married life to fulfill a promise to Sawyer. Cline's music always provides an appropriate musical metaphor for Kate's emotional rollercoaster of a love life.

When Kate and Sawyer become separated in time and space, Patsy Cline aptly summarizes their estrangement. Much of the music in Season Five is an Easter egg to long-time fans who know how a song or an artist highlighted character relationships in previous seasons. When Patsy Cline music is playing in the background of a Kate scene, as it does several times in Season Five, fans recall that music from this artist has played in each significant emotional event or pivotal turning point in Kate's story throughout the series. The music becomes a signifier that another key moment is taking place. When Cline's "I've Got Your Picture, She's Got You" again filters through the background of Kate's reunion with Cassidy ("What Happened, Happened," 5.11), not only do fans understand that Kate has never really had Sawyer, even when she thinks that he loves her, but that Sawyer often "belongs" to another woman just when Kate wants him. This recurring theme, musically as well as in the Kate-Sawyer dynamic, sadly illustrates the break in the couple's relationship, one that can never be truly repaired or healed.

Within an entirely different "love" context, young Katie unsuccessfully tries to persuade her best friend Tom to join her in crime. She attempts to shoplift a New Kids on the Block lunchbox, but Tom only stands and watches. When the clerk catches her, however, Jacob intervenes. He asks, "You're not going to steal anymore, are you?" during a pivotal moment in her life ("The Incident," 5.17). In the background, once again, is Cline's voice, this time singing "Three Cigarettes in an Ashtray." Although the title is deceptively grown up, the first stanza's lyrics indicate a theme emerging in young Kate's life: "Two cigarettes in an ashtray / My love and I in a small café [the inseparable Katie and Tom in a small convenience store] / Then a stranger [Jacob] came along / And everything went wrong."[16] Like Pavlov's puppies, we immediately tune in to Cline's voice in a Kate scene to find additional layers of meaning buried shallowly beneath the dialogue.

Whereas Cline's melancholy love songs provide both text and subtext for Kate's romantic entanglements, Cass Elliot's music offers ironic counterpoint to Desmond and Michael's embittered lives. Elliot's hits are better known for upbeat lyrics and a bouncy beat; her classic pop hits "Make Your Own Kind of Music" and "Getting Better Every Day" emphasize just how far from perfect, or even normal, these characters' lives are.

Cass Elliot's cover of "Make Your Own Kind of Music" offers emotional irony in Desmond's scenes ("Man of Science, Man of Faith," 2.1; "Flashes Before Your Eyes," 3.8). Stuck in the Hatch for what he thinks quite possibly may be the rest of his life, Desmond plays the bouncy 1970s pop tune as part of his morning routine—wake up, exercise, eat breakfast ("Man of Science, Man of Faith," 2.1). He has little control over his life, a mockery of the song's theme of self-determination. Even when he sees "flashes" of the future, shortly after the Hatch implodes, he wavers between grasping at hope that he can change the future and despairing that fate thwarts his actions.

When Desmond hears "Make Your Own Kind of Music" from a jukebox in a London pub, he thinks he knows the future: a fight will soon erupt. The song ends, but the brawl doesn't occur. Desmond concludes that the premonition was wrong. During a second night in the bar, however, he rejoices when his vision comes true after the same song plays on the jukebox. He was only a night too early with his prediction, and for a fleeting moment, he believes he just might be able to change the future and permanently regain his life with true love Penny. Before he can celebrate this possibility, Desmond inadvertently gets in the way of an angry patron, takes a punch to the head, and wakes up back on the Island ("Flashes Before Your Eyes," 3.8). Even when he is reunited with Penny at the end of Season Four ("There's No Place Like Home," 4.14), he has trouble making his own kind of music without interference from people he met on the Island. During Season Five, a dream/memory leads Desmond to travel first to Oxford and then to Los Angeles in his search for Mrs. Hawking, a journey that threatens his and his family's lives ("Because You Left," 5.1; "Dead Is Dead," 5.12).

"It's Getting Better" ("Meet Kevin Johnson," 4.8) provides an ironic accompaniment to the life of Michael Dawson (soon to be known by the freighter folk as Kevin Johnson). As the episode opens, Michael prepares to commit suicide. While Elliot cheerfully sings about life getting better every day, Michael accelerates his car toward a metal dumpster. Although he and Walt are living in New York, just as he planned if he ever left the Island, Walt refuses to talk to him, and Michael can't live with both the loss of his son and his guilt over what he did to get them home.

The ghosts, quite literally, of Michael's past continue to plague him on his new job on the freighter headed to the Island. Michael plans to blow it up, only to hear Cass Elliot's refrain eerily playing once again and Libby, one of the women he killed, beseeching him not to detonate the bomb. The upbeat music also recalls Cass Elliot's sad and untimely death after giving the world a series of life-affirming hits. Even "happy" music unearths some serious truths on *Lost*.

Each artist becomes identified with a character or place. Table 1 provides some character insights based on the music that accompanies one or more scenes from Seasons One through Five.

THEY'RE PLAYING YOUR SONG

Song(s)	Artist	Character	Reason
"Walking After Midnight," "She Has You," "Two Cigarettes in an Ashtray"	Patsy Cline	Kate	Kate explains in her first flashback that Patsy Cline's music is played everywhere. No matter where or when Kate travels, Cline's songs of regret or missed opportunities fit the pivotal moments of Kate's life.

Song(s)	Artist	Character	Reason
"Redemption Song"	Bob Marley	Sawyer	Sawyer may seem ready for commitment to a relationship, but he always longs for freedom in an outlaw life. LaFleur redeems Sawyer when he becomes the DHARMA Initiative's security chief and accepts Juliet as his significant other.
"Downtown"	Petula Clark	Juliet	Although this song encapsulates the fantasy life of muffin-baking, finger-burning, book club hostess Juliet of the Others, we first don't see the bravado and loneliness implied by the song. It all makes sense, a few years later. Ben makes Juliet a commando; LaFleur makes her smile.
"Make Your Own Kind of Music"	Cass Elliot	Desmond	Des wants to follow Elliot's advice but finds it difficult when he frequently is forced to do others' bidding. He just can't seem to get rid of that Island influence.

Song(s)	Artist	Character	Reason
"It's Getting Better"	Cass Elliot	Michael	Only when Michael does the right thing—sacrifices himself for his friends—does his brief remaining life get better.
"Wonderwall"	Oasis	Charlie	Charlie knows he needs to save people, but he so often needs saving.
"Good Vibrations"	Beach Boys	Charlie	Confident musician Charlie does what no one else can do—play this song as a code—and ends up saving at least some of his friends.
"Catch a Falling Star"	Perry Como	Aaron	Claire and Kate may wish on a falling star to give Aaron the kind of life he deserves; Aaron needs to catch and hold onto those elusive memories of his "parents."
"(I'm Always) Chasing Rainbows"	Harry Carroll (but also covered by Perry Como)	Dan	Dan always chases rainbows, but he fails to get a happy ending in life or death.

Song(s)	Artist	Character	Reason
"Scentless Apprentice"	Nirvana	Jack	Jack at his messed-up best fits the song well. He can't escape the pain of off-island living, especially as he drives to the funeral home to view Locke's/Bentham's body. Unfortunately, this theme plays a bit too often in LA.
"I Can't Give You Anything But Love, Baby"	Ella Fitzgerald	Oldham	Oldham might not be able to give anything but love, at least with his laughably good truth serum, but he certainly takes memories with a vengeance. Oldham seems like an eccentric gentleman from his tastes in music and décor, but he becomes an oddly efficient torturer.

MAKING THE BAND

Popular music for more than four decades has been defined by culture-influencing bands: the Beatles, Rolling Stones, Beach Boys, Doors, Supremes, Righteous Brothers, Metallica, Lynyrd Skynyrd, Police, U2, and so many others. Think of the pop cultural implications of the British invasion on U.S. counterculture in the 1960s or the Bee Gees on disco in the 1970s as only two examples. Making the band became a dream for would-be stars who wanted the celebrity and perks afforded to rock stars. During the intervening decades, the popularity of certain groups has signaled cultural changes, and young fans' idolatry of band members can influence everything from fashion to slang to sociopolitical activism. The rise of a group's or an artist's popularity often accompanies shifts in popular consciousness and trends in popular culture.

Even *Lost*'s characters find their lives interconnected with pop bands. Charlotte Lewis's delirious recollections of her DHARMA Initiative childhood include Geronimo Jackson, one of the series' recurring bands. Perhaps this band's popularity with the DHARMA Initiative explains the album Charlie and Hurley find nearly thirty years later in the Hatch ("The Hunting Party," 2.11). (Possibly the uptight and later suicidal Radzinsky brought his record collection when he began his exile as one of the Hatch's resident button pushers.) Locke follows pop bands throughout his life; his high school locker sports a Geronimo Jackson poster, and he later listens to DriveShaft.

Two bands helped shape *Lost*'s early musical history, and references to them or their band members surprisingly continue through Season Five. The inclusion of 1970s hits as the DHARMA Initiative's happier (i.e., pre-Purge or pre-Jughead-detonation) era underscores the pervasive influence of bands on even the most isolated community; mostly forgotten hit makers of yesteryear live again in these episodes. Older fans may reminisce just what they were doing in 1977 when they, as well as the DHARMA Initiative, listened to the Captain and Tennille or Tony Orlando and Dawn.

Bands' fortunes wax and wane with the sales of their songs, however, and even the most influential groups seldom stay on top for long. The desire to be one of the few who attain such stardom motivates many young musicians to form bands and attempt to turn professional. It's no wonder that *Lost* has explored how musicians find and lose themselves in celebrity as much as in the music.

Although bands haven't been as important to plot developments in Seasons Four and Five, they still occasionally pop up to remind us of their importance to the overall story. DriveShaft once was synonymous with castaway Charlie Pace, and early in the series Charlie's identity is so tied to DriveShaft's fleeting fame that he automatically assumes people know him because of the band. DriveShaft has one hit, two albums, and a few European tours before its perhaps not-so-tragic demise; a belated "Greatest Hits" collection becomes popular after Charlie's reported death. Although DriveShaft provides Charlie with a wider audience and greater opportunity as a songwriter, it simultaneously restrains his unique—if not as commercially viable—artistic voice.

Geronimo Jackson memorabilia turn up in flashbacks and on the Island, with more references in Season Five than ever before. This band also represents a bygone era in music and American history, fading quietly into obscurity. *Lost*'s focus on has-beens fits the series' motif, but they also represent the majority of musicians who struggle to be on top, even briefly, but are more likely (and lucky) to scrape out a living doing what they love. *Lost* bands make audiences think about why fame seems so important and what people will do to keep or regain it. A closer look at Geronimo Jackson and DriveShaft provides greater insight into "making the band" and the popularity of these groups with *Lost* fans.

Geronimo Jackson

A lesser *Lost* mystery, but one causing fan speculation early in the series, is whether or not Geronimo Jackson ever was a real band. On the Season Two DVD, writers Edward Kitsis and Adam Horowitz mention that the band existed briefly in the San Francisco area in the late 1960s. Kitsis explains that Geronimo Jackson released one album, tried to make that perfect second album but couldn't, and disappeared after a Woodstock appearance in 1971. According to the writers, like so many young musicians in the 1960s, Kentuckian Keith Strutter eventually migrated to San Francisco, where he founded the band.[17] Later, official podcasts claimed similar information.[18] Some fans even supported that statement by writing online about their memories of seeing the folk rock group at Woodstock. However, these memories are often questioned by other fans—the only online documentation of the group is fan speculation (e.g., one fan site mimicked a real Geronimo Jackson site for a few weeks before taking it down in 2005), and no paper trail leads back to the group. Most *Lost* fans think that the band is yet another long-running inside joke for the series' creators.

Even *Lost*'s characters provide contradictory "evidence" about the band's popularity, although it undoubtedly was a real group in their fictitious world. Charlie, who claimed to be an expert on all music, never heard of Geronimo Jackson ("The Hunting Party," 2.11), but the members of Locke's commune, closer to Locke's age than Charlie's, have ("Further Instructions," 3.2). When newcomer Eddie sports a band T-shirt, commune leader Mike asks him if he liked the band. Although Eddie isn't a fan, his father was, and Eddie wears his vintage shirt. Some fans speculated that Mike's interest comes from being a member of the mysterious band. Yet another theory posits that Geronimo Jackson was the DeGroots' band.[19]

The band makes three appearances in the first half of the series: "The Hunting Party" (2.11; Hurley discovers the album), "The Whole Truth" (2.16; Locke flips through albums, including *Magna Carta*), and "Further Instructions" (3.2). Geronimo Jackson's yellow-and-orange logo even turns up in *Lost* Puzzle #1, The Hatch, which promised insights into the series' mysteries. In Season Four, a Geronimo Jackson poster flashes on screen as young John Locke opens his school locker ("Cabin Fever," 4.11). The DJ at Hurley's surprise party stacks a Geronimo Jackson album among the discs to spin ("There's No Place Like Home," 4.12). Season Five episodes include a number of Easter eggs featuring Geronimo Jackson. Charlotte wants the music turned up so she can hear the band ("This Place Is Death," 5.5). A DHARMA Initiative fan wears a band T-shirt ("LaFleur," 5.8), and a concert poster adorns the cafeteria's wall ("He's Our You," 5.10). The band's "Dharma Lady" becomes background music twice: as the song playing in Jin's van when he discovers his old friends from Oceanic 815 arriving in 1977 ("316," 5.6) and during the new recruits' orientation ("Namaste," 5.9). *Lost* makes the most of the band's peak popularity in setting the right tone for the DHARMA Initiative's most glorious decade.

In mid-2006, the band gained notoriety beyond episodes when lyrics and references popped up frequently in The *Lost* Experience. DJ Dan's podcasts proclaimed that the band's founder, Keith Strutter, also had been a member of the band Karma Imperative,[20] a name strangely similar to the DHARMA Initiative. Rachel Blake's blogs also quoted lyrics, and The *Lost* Experience incorporated information by and about the band throughout the game. Geronimo Jackson adds depth to DHARMA-infused island culture and prods fans to speculate ways that musical cues and clues can unravel the story's many mysteries.

DriveShaft

Music often provides an ironic counterpart to characters' lives, and Charlie Pace is a key example. He lives in the *Lost* story, years after his death, through his legacy of friendship instead of his fame as a rocker, although the most symbolic reminders of Charlie are his DS ring and guitar case. During Season Five, these symbols become important Easter eggs (or potential foreshadowing of Charlie's Season Six return). As well, Charlie's likely namesake, Charlie Hume, continues the presence of a young British "Charlie" in the saga.

Unlike so many other characters who are gone and apparently forgotten, Charlie gains immortality in the minds of his friends (and thus in the story) for who he became on the Island, not as a famous Oceanic 815 victim. Nevertheless, DriveShaft wove its often mindless lyrics into the series' first half just as surely as Jacob wove the Oceanic Six into the fabric of island space-time. DriveShaft isn't Charlie's most significant contribution to *Lost*, but the band helps describe the musician's growth into more than a one-note character.

DriveShaft is not a real band, although series' fans continue to treat it like one, even after Charlie's death. The band likely has been derived from Oasis; both Mancunian bands share a musical style as well as two frequently feuding brothers, one named Liam, fronting the band. Charlie plays Oasis' "Wonderwall" twice during Season Three: when Desmond recognizes him from the Island as he plays for money near a subway station ("Flashes Before Your Eyes," 3.8), and a similar scene without Desmond, when a sudden rain shower breaks up the crowd and Charlie's path intersects that of a young woman being mugged in a nearby alley ("Greatest Hits," 3.21).

As noted earlier in this chapter, "Wonderwall" lyrics seem to haunt Charlie's final days, and saving others is a recurrent theme in his backstories: Jack's rescue from a cave-in ("The Moth," 1.7); his mother telling him to save the family with his music and his Island vision/dream of saving Aaron ("Fire + Water," 2.12); the previously mentioned confrontation with Nadia's London mugger ("Greatest Hits," 3.21); and that fateful handwritten message before he drowns ("Through the Looking Glass," 3.23). Even after his death, a surprisingly solid "ghost" Charlie tries to look after his surrogate family, especially Hurley and Aaron. He frequently chats with Hurley, who, after initially freaking out over the encounters ("The Beginning of the End," 4.1), shares his friend's messages with Jack ("Something Nice Back Home," 4.10). Until all his friends are "saved" from their island troubles, Charlie seems determined to stick around.

DriveShaft isn't an Oasis clone, however. The first season *Lost* DVD includes a commentary about the making of DriveShaft ("Backstage with DriveShaft," Disk 7). Inspiration for the band's lyrics comes from many places: inane dialogue from a talk show (leading to "You All Everybody" as a song title), the series' creators' feelings about music from their generation, and Dominic (Charlie) Monaghan's interest in music and ability to identify with rockers.[21]

In *Lost* canon, the band's name is derived from a family heirloom, a DS ring passed from a relative, Dexter Stratton, to Megan Pace, to her older son Liam, who then hands over the ring to his brother when he believes Charlie is more likely to become a stalwart family man someday. Ironically, Charlie becomes the misfit who dies before fathering a child (Liam gains sobriety after the birth of daughter Megan). Before his one-way mission to the Looking Glass, Charlie passes on his treasured DS ring to surrogate son Aaron ("Greatest Hits," 3.21). In a scene fraught with symbolism, Claire fails to find the ring in Aaron's crib as she and her son prepare to leave the beach; the ring, enlarged by close-up, remains behind in the empty crib while Claire walks away with the baby. With all the frenzied activity surrounding the arrival of the freighter folk, Charlie's DS ring seems to be long lost. In a late Season Four interview, Emilie (Claire) de Ravin admitted that she, too, wondered what happened to that ring[22] and if this thread someday would be woven into the story. It was in Season Five. On a return trip to the long-deserted castaway camp, Sun finds the ring in the remains of Claire's hut.

Sun has a history of finding lost rings. She loses her wedding ring ("… And Found," 2.5) after Jin leaves on the raft, only to find it again—just when she learns she's pregnant. She once again believes Jin is lost to her when the freighter explodes, but she agrees to return to the Island when Ben presents her with Jin's wedding ring, a sign he survived ("This Place Is Death," 5.5). These rings represent promises that seem to be broken and relationships torn by separation that somehow become mended. Now that Sun has found the DS ring, perhaps it, along with Jin's wedding ring, will be returned to their owners in Season Six.

Charlie's DS ring symbolizes the band's importance in his life and the musical legacy he hoped to pass on to a new generation. The other key symbol of Charlie-as-musician, his guitar case, more accurately represents his continual love of music and gift of himself; this symbol becomes a more potent reminder of Charlie's life to those who knew him well, such as Hurley.

Throughout Charlie's island life, the guitar case, seen more often than the guitar itself, represents the real musician. In "The Moth" (1.7), he mourns the loss of his guitar in the crash and agrees to exchange his drugs for Locke's knowledge of the guitar's location. Once reunited with his prized possession, Charlie gives up drugs and begins to create music more often. He frequently composes songs on the beach, and even when Desmond proposes Charlie join him on a hike into the jungle, the musician asks if he can bring along his guitar ("Catch-22," 3.17). When Hurley returns to the Island via Ajira Airways 316, he brings a guitar case (presumably Charlie's), hanging onto it even when he crash-lands in a lagoon. Again, ironically, the drowned Charlie's guitar case helps keep Hurley afloat when he panics after waking up in the water ("316," 5.6). Even when Charlie is no longer a regular character in the story, these symbols remind viewers that Charlie's life was music and hint that there may yet be more to his song.

DriveShaft's and Charlie's Real-World Popularity

Perhaps based on Monaghan's popularity (as well as his and fellow former hobbit Elijah Wood's high-profile deejaying and highly publicized interest in undiscovered avant garde bands), DriveShaft received a lot of attention early on from *Lost* and *Lord of the Rings* fans. In 2004, after one line of "You All Everybody" in the pilot episode and the song's later guest appearance on another J. J. Abrams' series, *Alias*,[23] fangirls clamored for more. Rumors buzzed that DriveShaft might release an album.

Fans soon created fake DriveShaft websites and began to develop their own merchandise. "You All Everybody" and "Saved" can be downloaded from the DriveShaft MySpace site. This site remains open and, by the end of Season Five, maintained more than 3,000 friends and had almost 80,000 site views, up 20,000 from the previous year. A *Lost* "tribute" band called You.All.Everybody shares series-related songs on their

MySpace website (http://www.myspace.com/youalleverybodyband), including "Nerve aka Charley's [sic] Song."

One of the best fan sites, the realistic Second Tour of Finland—The Unofficial DriveShaft Site—provides notes from and an interview with Liam Pace; lyrics for several CDs; biographies of band members Charlie and Liam Pace, Adam "Sinjin" St. John, and Patrick Gleason; a swag shop; and fanvid tributes that feature clips of Monaghan himself as often as clips of Charlie. On September 22, 2007 (three years after the crash of imaginary Oceanic 815), a memorial event raised funds for the real Make Poverty History campaign. At that time, the site officially closed, although it continues to be available for fans who want to light a virtual candle and post a tribute to Charlie. Seven hundred candles burned soon after "Greatest Hits" and "Through the Looking Glass" were broadcast; fans have since added thousands of new tributes, lighting more than 3,900 candles by mid-2009.

Of course, fan interest initially led to mass-produced DriveShaft merchandise. As soon as the band's CD cover briefly appeared on screen in the Hurley backstory "Everybody Hates Hugo" (2.4), unofficial merchandise, including T-shirts, as well as officially licensed products, showed up online. The attention-grabbing, red-and-black DriveShaft logo on the CD mirrors the band's tempestuous offstage life. The briefly shown logo and Charlie's DS ring provided the patterns for other merchandise. Creation Entertainment sold official red-and-black DriveShaft coffee mugs and a "bloody rock god" Charlie T-shirt; the fan club once gave logo bumper stickers to new members. The "prize" accompanying McFarlane Toys' Charlie action figure is a life-sized DS ring. Like many aspects of *Lost*, fictitious DriveShaft developed a real-world presence, not only in the series' marketing campaigns but in fandom. Even at the end of Season Five, fan-created merchandise and official products continue to be sold online.

Perhaps with all the attention given to DriveShaft, and with many of Charlie's or Monaghan's fans angry over the character's demise, it's not strange that the post-death popularity of Charlie Pace mimics that of real dead-before-their-time rockers. Morbid fascination with famous people (especially hard-living rock stars) who die suddenly or horrifically often increases an artist's posthumous popularity. *Lost* briefly touches on this phenomenon when Naomi tells Charlie about a huge memorial service for him and the resurgence of DriveShaft in the wake of his reported death and the discovery of Oceanic 815's fuselage ("Greatest Hits," 3.21). Charlie and DriveShaft refuse to stay dead, at least in *Lost*'s fandom.

THE GENIUS OF MICHAEL GIACCHINO

Michael Giacchino's award-winning scores are becoming synonymous with J. J. Abrams' TV series and films. In 2008–2009, Giacchino added *Star Trek* and *Fringe* to his long list of Abrams-related projects, and he composed the scores for *Up* and *Land of the Lost*. In a May 2008 review of Giacchino's music for *Speed Racer* (a film starting Matthew [Jack] Fox), *iF Magazine* reported how well the composer has "scored" with such well-publicized films as *The Incredibles*, *Ratatouille*, *Mission Impossible 3* (written and directed by Abrams), and *Cloverfield* (produced by Abrams). Even in the *Speed Racer* review, *Lost* was prominently mentioned. Soundtrack Editor Daniel Schweiger reminded *Lost* fans that they should be grateful that "Giacchino is still bringing all of his big-screen inventiveness to the engaging, jungle-driven rhythms of the ABC show."[24]

Now that their association is firmly cemented, it seems strange to remember that when Abrams first approached Giacchino about writing a score for *Alias*, the composer was surprised and didn't know what to expect. After working with Abrams on that series, however, Giacchino didn't need to receive a formal invitation to work with *Lost*; he naturally became a part of this series from its inception. His original soundtrack (aided by other songwriters, including Abrams) incorporates unusual sounds to highlight the Island's creepiness; even plane wreckage serves as percussion at times. The recurring original themes enhance each scene's emotional impact.

Giacchino is no stranger to film, television, or video games; he has a great deal of experience with storytelling through music. For a composer, he has an interesting academic background in film as well as music. Giacchino studied at Juilliard but also earned a film degree from New York's School of Arts. He has won a BMI award, an Annie, and an Emmy—for *Lost*—as well as being nominated for a Grammy. Nevertheless, his creative process for *Lost* differs from his many other projects.

To retain an element of surprise and to stay in the moment (so that audiences also have a sense of anticipation as they watch a scene), the composer scores one scene at a time and doesn't skip to the end of a script to see how the episode ends. In this way he creates "uncomfortable" music, "something completely opposite what you would have [expected] in an action or jungle setting."[25] Like Lost's story, the soundtrack offers something different and unexpected. Giacchino insists that the series' original music should make audiences understand what it means to be spiritually lost; he "wanted something *not* typical for what you would get about a show about characters stranded on an island."[26] Reviewers and fans agree that Giacchino succeeded in his musical mission.

Giacchino, like many other creative talents behind Lost, is well known among the series' fans. Whereas the composers behind most other television shows, past or present, are seldom recognized in public, Giacchino has a higher profile. During a panel at the first official Lost fan convention, presented by Creation Entertainment in June 2005, Giacchino joined writers and producers Javier Grillo-Marxuach, Damon Lindelof, and Bryan Burk to talk with fans about the behind-the-scenes' aspects of the series. Since then, Giacchino has been interviewed on official Lost podcasts, and fans visit his website (www.michaelgiacchino.com) for the latest news about Lost and his many other projects.

Soundtracks for Seasons One–Four

Lost is highly unusual in today's television production: it incorporates an original orchestrated score into each week's episodes. One of Giacchino's initial fears about composing for the series was that he wouldn't be able to work with a live orchestra, a process generally deemed too expensive and time consuming for the fast pace and tight budgets of most series. Nevertheless, Giacchino got his wish and incorporates unusual combinations of instruments into his orchestra, which records the Lost soundtrack in Los Angeles' Eastwood Scoring Stage.

The resulting soundtracks were released in March 2006 (Season One) and October 2006 (Season Two), May 2008 (Season Three, with two disks), and May 2009 (Season Four). Although some cuts are the same (e.g., the Main Title or "*Lost* opening theme" on the first three CDs), each soundtrack's selections highlight character themes and major plot points of that season's episodes. As the series progresses, Giacchino varies the themes established for key characters, even Smoky. The composer compares *Lost*'s complex story to an opera, with music being a crucial element of both:

Themes in opera develop in the course of the storytelling. We've been able to develop these themes and make them more complex and less complex as needed. You almost need a chart about what goes where, who belongs to what. Characters have themes, and objects and rooms, the Smoke Monster, and they all have their own ideas and weird thematic ideas attached to them.[27]

The first CD's twenty-seven tracks have titles like "Oceanic 815" and "I've Got a Plane to Catch" to illustrate key scenes from the first season. Season Two's musical highlights in twenty-six tracks include the hauntingly beautiful "Rose and Bernard" as well as the harsh, suspenseful "Peace through Superior Firepower." Season Two's CD offers more musical variety, but both soundtracks capture the series' extremes in emotion and evoke memories of specific episodes. Season Three's two-disk soundtrack was released almost a year after episodes were first broadcast. Similarly, Season Four's soundtrack arrived almost a year after that season's finale, but the wait, according to reviewers, was well worth the delay. The twenty-six cuts include the evocative and, to many fans, best original composition, "There's No Place Like Home"; this haunting theme summarizes all emotions when the Oceanic Six first step off the cargo plane to return to their former lives.

The CDs have received good reviews from critics and fans, which might seem unusual for a television soundtrack featuring no famous covers or hummable tunes. The brilliance of *Lost*'s soundtrack, and a likely reason why it won Giacchino an Emmy after Season One, is that it captures the changing mood of the Island and its inhabitants. The music foreshadows the danger of the Monster or the Hatch, but it also poignantly conveys the castaways' mercurial emotions in response to their plight. *iF Magazine*'s soundtrack editor glowed that the first season soundtrack "dazzles with its hodge-podge of cool styles, alternating from bold melodies to exotic percussion and castaway poignancy. It's almost enough to make you wish they'd never get rescued so that Giacchino could continue to spin out such tantalizing, complex stuff."[28] A fan's product review of the Season Four soundtrack compares Giacchino with legendary film composer John Williams and enthuses that "Giacchino does a wonderful job of blending the different motifs of all the various characters, events, and emotions he has created throughout the years. Season Four was definitely his best work of the show since the groundbreaking first season."[29]

The Significance of an Effective Soundtrack

Giacchino creates themes for characters and then interweaves those themes with the on-screen action. One of the composer's favorite characters is Hurley, whose life blended of comedy and tragedy allows Giacchino to create some lighter moments in the score. Hurley has three themes, including one introduced during "Numbers," Hurley's first backstory episode. When Hurley first hears the lottery numbers, odd, quizzical sounds begin. These few weird notes recur during several scenes. Whenever Hurley believes the eerie numbers might be creating havoc, the theme again begins. The upbeat, syncopated "I've Got a Plane to Catch" underscores Hurley's lighter moments, such as dashing through the Sydney airport to catch Flight 815. Reviewer Nick Joy called it the "most bizarre cue" on the CD, "a jaunty 'Flying Down to Rio' Calypso-type affair,"[30] probably because such a lighthearted theme is unexpected within the darker context of the series. The second season collection showcases a theme for quieter moments, such as when Hurley distributes food from the Hatch. "Hurley's Handouts" features a guitar gently strumming an upbeat tune; a violin next plays a wistful counterpoint to the main melody. No matter which other instruments playing other characters' themes become part of the song, Hurley's continues in the background; his theme's presence in the song, just like Hurley's in the scene, holds everything together.

Rose and Bernard receive their own self-titled theme in their backstory "S.O.S." (2.19), the episode in which Bernard comes to understand that he and Rose can't leave the Island because she is unafflicted by a terminal disease as long as she stays. Their song is a bit sweet, a bit sad. As the melody deepens, more instruments are added: The opening piano sequence gives way to a cello solo before violins take up the same theme, this time with a cello counterpoint. Unlike many *Lost* themes, this song lacks an abrupt, scary, or surprising conclusion. Instead, the peaceful ending is a testament to Bernard and Rose's enduring relationship, a theme that continues through what likely is fans' last look at the couple at the end of Season Five. The poignant love theme again highlights the characters' abiding love but now emphasizes the peace and acceptance they find on the Island.

Giacchino's selection of instruments to create a variety of sounds, from the symphonic to the weird, is unusual. Not only are parts of the fuselage used to create unusual percussion,[31] but traditional instruments are used in unexpected ways. The score relies on trombones, a string section (including harp), percussion, and piano. To create what bass player Karl Vincent calls "auditory hallucinations,"[32] Giacchino might use odd note combinations to create a more sinister effect. "You don't often get beautiful harp lifts on *Lost*," Giacchino explains, "but you do get the lower five notes."[33] Striking one lower-register note ominously in a scene literally harps on the danger quotient. Strings used in more traditionally uplifting themes illustrate hope and exhilaration; Giacchino's score contrasts the "danger" scenes with the beautiful "Parting Words" as Jin, Michael, Walt, and Sawyer depart on the raft at the end of Season One. As the makeshift craft gains speed and the Island-bound castaways run along the shore to say farewell, the score soars, increasing in number of instruments and volume. Danger is never far away, however; the final notes—the single-note "bong" of a harsh harp—reminds viewers of the series' darker undercurrent.

More typical of *Lost*, scary scenes involving the likelihood of death or the introduction of a new danger require Giacchino to make the audience just as nervous as the castaways. Season One's "Toxic Avenger" harshly introduces percussion instruments that aren't easily distinguished, which matches the anxiety factor. The unusual use of percussion—lots of sticks, clangs from unidentifiable sources—creates a running pace and thrumming beat in Season Two's "Peace through Superior Firepower." The single harp note, heard in similar scenes, warns of new danger. Season Four's "Bobbing for Freighters" provides another action piece, this time highlighting the dramatic demise of the freighter and its crew.

Deciding when not to include music, thus making music more important when it is used, sometimes helps to build the appropriate mood. Silence, or the occasional sound effect, can increase a scene's emotional punch. Three life-or-death scenes involving Charlie clearly illustrate Giacchino's judicious use of musical themes. When Kate and Jack discover Charlie hanging from a tree ("Whatever the Case May Be," 1.12), they desperately cut him down and try to revive him. The score provides an ominous death knell—a single note tolling Charlie's apparent demise. While Jack performs CPR, the music stops; the only sounds are Jack's and Kate's frantic pleas. The absence of music appropriately illustrates the absence of life signs. When Charlie gasps for air and unexpectedly comes back to life, a more traditional score begins and adds to the emotional impact of the castaways' reunion.

A similar pattern builds tension in "Greatest Hits" (3.21) and "Through the Looking Glass" (3.22–23). Strings underscore the emotion in Charlie's decision to undertake a suicide dive to open a jammed communication link. The music switches to thrumming "danger sounds" as he swims toward the moon pool inside the Looking Glass station. The music ends with his entry into the (surprise!) not flooded station, and Charlie's gasps become the primary sound. The audience also can breathe again as the scene's tension briefly ebbs.

During the season finale, "Other" Mikhail shows Charlie a grenade—pin pulled—just outside a porthole. When the grenade explodes, the chamber—possibly the whole station—will be flooded. To stop Desmond from entering the communication room to talk with Penny, and thus be in harm's way, Charlie seals it off the only possible way: from the inside. Once he accepts the inevitability of his death, his piano theme from previous episodes rises for several bars; a single violin enters, and the poignant music "remind[s] the audience that the person they're losing is someone they were…quite fond of."[34] Desmond and Charlie have no dialogue, but a warning message written on Charlie's hand becomes his final words. The music, emphasized by lack of dialogue, elevates the emotional scene. As the *Connecticut Post*'s Amanda Cuder noted in the first of a series of music-related *Lost* blogs, "Charlie's death was particularly sad, as he was one of the show's most effective and sympathetic characters. Initially depicted as self-involved and morally weak, he eventually proved sensitive, brave, and even heroic. The music associated with him reflects his many layers."[35]

With such game-changing plot shifts and emotionally wrenching scenes in Season Three's final two episodes ("Greatest Hits" and "Through the Looking Glass"), perhaps it's not surprising that music from these episodes makes up the second disk of the two-disk soundtrack. Whereas musical highlights from "Greatest Hits" plays for almost eighteen minutes, the soundtrack from "Through the Looking Glass" is fifty-eight minutes long! The length alone is testament to the significance of Giacchino's score to the storytelling complexity and overall emotional impact of *Lost*.

Despite being shorter, the one-disk soundtrack to Season Four provides plenty of listening pleasure, including reworked (the best to date) themes associated with Desmond and Penny ("The Constant") and Sayid ("Lost Away—Or Is It?"). The recurrence of musical themes and the careful matching of music with action make *Lost*'s soundtrack crucial to a scene's dramatic or comedic elements. The visual context, however, is lost on a CD, and although musical cues undoubtedly alert fans to the scenes which a track originally enhanced, many listeners may have to rely on the CD's playlist to figure out which music accompanies which scene. If anything is criticized about the CDs, usually it is the choice of titles, which sometimes are groaningly bad puns.

The first season CD includes "Booneral" (played during Boone's funeral) and "Shannonigans." Season Two's "I Crashed Your Plane, Brotha" echoes Desmond's accent and his horrified confession during a pivotal scene. "Bon Voyage, Traitor" mirrors fans' thoughts toward Michael as he abandons his friends and heads for home with son Walt. Of the sixty-seven tracks on two disks from Season Three, several continue the trend of humorous or ironic titles. "Leggo My Eko" and "Eko of the Past" indicate how Eko dies but also play on words, whether from the popular Eggo commercial or a clichéd phrase. "Naomi Phone Home" plays on the classic *E.T.* line but helps listeners remember Naomi checking her phone to see when she could receive or send a signal to her friends on the freighter. Season Four's "Locke-ing Horns" describes the confrontation between Jack and Locke over the castaways' leadership, and "Keamy Away From Him" refers to the difficult-to-kill mercenary Martin Keamy. The song titles indicate what happens in the highlighted scene, but they sometimes are a bit too cute for critics.

Whatever the tracks are called or how much fans and critics like/dislike the titles, Giacchino's musical prowess is undisputed. His ability to create music that shifts emotional gears within a scene creates a memorable, unique soundtrack for this on-the-edge series. Audiences "feel" as well as hear the music; it supports but never overshadows what happens visually. *Lost*'s soundtrack captures the essence of what it means to be lost within oneself or from the world; it aurally illustrates what it means to be human.

CHAPTER THREE

BETWEEN THE LINES: LOST AND POPULAR CULTURE

BETWEEN THE LINES

Lost has captured the public's imagination so much so that when, tragically, a real Air France Airbus disappeared on a transatlantic flight from Rio de Janeiro to Paris, the first reports compared the tragedy to *Lost*'s fictitious flight Oceanic 815. One popular press site posted the following news blog shortly after the announcement of the plane's disappearance:

An airplane full of people disappears near a deserted tropical island. No, it's not a description of the hit TV show Lost, *it is real life. An Air France flight from Rio de Janeiro, Brazil, to Paris disappeared overnight last night without a trace. An hour after takeoff, the plane encountered heavy turbulence. Ten minutes after that turbulence, the Airbus A330 disappeared from radar screens near the Island of Fernando de Noronha. I hate to be flippant, but the first thing I thought when I read the story was, "Hey, that's like* Lost!"[36]

The article even showed a cast photo beneath the heading. This site wasn't the only one to publicly make the connection between a real event and the pop culture phenomenon; *Lost* has become ingrained in global culture to the extent that when real life mirrors television fiction, the connection is too potent to ignore. For good or bad, *Lost* is a cultural touchstone for millions around the world—not just hardcore fans but anyone familiar with what's been "hot" in entertainment for more than the past five years.

Within a two-week span in June 2009, *USA Today* also referred to *Lost* and another current event, this one a much more lighthearted comparison with debut-film-of-the-week *Land of the Lost.*[37] On Bravo, the "Lost Supper" became the elimination challenge for *Top Chef Masters.*[38] Selecting from among sea urchins, boar, coconuts, bananas, mangoes, and other island staples, plus DHARMA Initiative canned goods, the chefs served *Lost*'s cocreators Damon Lindelof and Carlton Cuse, who are fans of *Top Chef*. "There's been a big dip in quality since *Top Chef*," Lindelof joked, and Cuse admitted that they talk about *Top Chef*'s results on Thursday mornings. *Top Chef*'s presenter and at least some guest chefs expressed their admiration for *Lost*, and when DHARMA Initiative–clad servers presented the judges with two wild boar main dishes (Locke would be so proud), everyone was in on the joke.

Talk show host Jimmy Kimmel is such a fan that he regularly invites *Lost* cast members onto the program and immediately after many first-run broadcasts digitally inserts himself into a scene from the latest episode. Joel McHale, E!'s host of *The Soup*, also seems to be a fan, bringing former *Lost* actor Dominic Monaghan to the show, presumably to discuss his role in *Wolverine*, only to have him besieged by a Claire look-alike[39]; the death of Monaghan's character, Charlie Pace, also generated *Soup* commentary, as did the bunny Ben uses to threaten Sawyer during "Every Man for Himself" (3.4). Especially during sweeps ratings periods, talk show hosts and entertainment news shows regularly feature *Lost* actors or speculate on season-ending twists and possible theories about what's going to happen next.

When ABC began promoting new and returning series for the 2009–2010 season, both at the "up fronts" held in May for media representatives and, shortly after, on broadcast promotional spots, *Lost* again generated lots of controversy. ABC piqued fans' interest by parodying *Lost*'s back-from-the-dead plots. First, Dominic Monaghan's face briefly flashes on screen among the head shots of other ABC actors, prompting speculation that "Charlie" might be returning to *Lost* sometime during its final season. A later promo shows Monaghan playing football with *Grey's Anatomy*'s Patrick Dempsey, who asks about "Charlie" being dead. Monaghan shrugs; "Actually I was," he replies.[40]

Twitter quickly provided "insider" information that Monaghan had been signed for four *Lost* episodes, and Maggie (Shannon) Grace also would return to the series for six episodes. This information seemed real, following the theory that the Season Five finale would result in Oceanic 815 never crashing in the first place, and all who died as a result of the crash or their stay on the Island would be alive (and returning during Season Six). However, further tweets disputed this message, and Monaghan's representatives coyly told fans to stay tuned to see if Charlie would indeed reappear on *Lost*.[41]

The ABC promo primarily introduces Monaghan as a cast member on the series being touted as *Lost*'s pop culture successor, *FlashForward*. ABC's marketing carefully plays on *Lost*'s popularity and fans' rabid interest in every little casting development, especially as the series gears up for its final episodes. ABC undoubtedly also hopes to develop another pop culture phenomenon in *FlashForward*, with Monaghan's appearance in the promos being one way to lure his *Lost* fan base to the new series. Within the span of about a week, speculation about *Lost* generated plenty of blogs, E! news breaks, and Twitter comments, which prompted later news stories to cover the speculation.

As *Lost* enters its final season, its significance in popular culture, like the Island itself, time shifts yet again. It has moved from the "it" series of the 2004–2005 season to more of an internationally prominent cult favorite to a classic, even before its sixth and final season is broadcast. *Lost* has boldly gone where no other TV series (not even one created by J. J. Abrams) has gone before...and none other is likely to capture the same magic, fan frustration levels, or just plain intriguing storytelling. Scriptwriters, journalists, talk show hosts, and marketing execs assume that anyone watching TV has at least heard of *Lost* or, quite likely, is a regular viewer. Even those who haven't kept up with the series at least know about major plot developments and key cast members, which ensures a *Lost* reference to be easily understood.

WHY IS POPULAR CULTURE SO IMPORTANT?

The Popular Culture Association, a scholarly organization devoted to its study, defines popular culture as "the life and culture of real people,"[42] including all the things that interest them: material culture, comics, music, movies, television, fashion, games, books, magazines—in short, what we like to do and how we like to do it. Most simply, popular culture identifies us with and binds us to others with similar interests and behaviors. It provides the code by which members of the group "in the know" understand each other. It gives us a way to interpret and make meaning of our lives.

No nation is more obsessed with popular culture than the United States, and because American TV series and movies are exported globally, what's "common knowledge" in the United States rapidly is becoming known everywhere else. *Lost*'s writers understand that and make the series "real" by showing us that Hurley, for example, likes comic books just as much as we might, or that Locke, just like some of us, reads *The Brothers Karamazov* but also keeps up with rock music. Ben may share Locke's fondness for *VALIS* and play classical music on the piano, but he also keeps a copy of Olivia Newton John's *Xanadu* around the house. Even the mysterious Jacob spends time between off-island encounters with future castaways reading Flannery O'Connor's *Everything That Rises Must Converge*. Understanding a reference to a book, movie, TV character, or scene adds depth to our understanding of *Lost* and the background of key characters, and so far, international audiences seem to understand the many references to popular culture sprinkled throughout episodes.

Like the majority of *Lost* viewers, the series' characters grew up with television. Younger castaways don't remember a (pre-crash) time when television, movies, music, video games, and computers weren't part of their everyday experience. They are likely to identify with pop culture icons. Even children in the DHARMA Initiative follow popular trends; time-addled Charlotte Staples reverts to childhood memories and pleads with Dan Faraday to let her stay up past her bedtime. She wants to listen to Geronimo Jackson (a fictitious band who continues to pop up frequently in *Lost* culture) ("This Place Is Death," 5.5). Just like off-islanders, DHARMA Initiative recruits in the 1970s boogie to "Ride Captain Ride" ("Namaste," 5.9). Back in LA, before her return to the Island, Kate's home is littered with Aaron's media-related toys, and the youngster happily is babysat by TV cartoons during a visit with Sun ("The Little Prince," 5.4).

A running pop culture theme is based on *Star Wars*, the iconic films of Hurley's youth. Hugo first invokes *Star Wars* when he reveals he was something of a warrior back home ("Confidence Man," 1.8). When Hurley says that Jack creates a "Jedi moment" by talking Shannon through an asthma attack ("Confidence Man," 1.8), we understand Hurley's level of respect or even reverence for what Jack has done. Like Obi-Wan Kenobi with his ability to make others think and then do what he wants (e.g., "These are not the droids you are looking for"), Jack seems capable of great focus and mental persuasion; he can do what ordinary people can't. Pop culture icons, whether real people or fictitious characters, have become the heroes that people like Hurley not only revere but want to become.

During Season Five, Hurley spends his off time from working in the DHARMA Initiative's kitchen to write a better script for *The Empire Strikes Back*. Hurley knows that in 1977 Lucas is looking for the follow-up to the first *Star Wars* film, and Hurley hopes to help the filmmaker avoid characters and plot traps that fans would come to hate. As Hurley succinctly tells Miles Straume, "Ewoks suck, dude" ("Some Like It Hoth," 5.13).

Hugo also warns Miles that he should talk with the father he grew up without, the Island's own DHARMA Initiative filmmaker, Pierre Chang, to avoid a possible Luke Vader confrontation now that returned-to-the-island Miles is an adult. According to Hurley's *Star Wars*–based philosophy of life, many problems in the Empire could've been avoided by better communication. Stories like the *Star Wars* saga go way beyond entertainment; they help audiences develop their own philosophies based on the adventures of fictional characters.

Comic books also must have played a big role in Hurley's childhood. He reads a comic book on ill-fated Oceanic Flight 815 ("Exodus," 1.24) and again on his return-to-the-Island ride, Ajira Flight 316 ("316," 5.6). When Desmond first indicates that he knows the future, Hurley's response is to ask whether or not he is going to "Hulk out" ("Further Instructions," 3.2). The Incredible Hulk of comic books, TV, and film changes into a superhero (or monster, depending on one's point of view) when he becomes angry; this transformation of an average guy into the Hulk comes about after a lab explosion, perhaps similar to the Hatch's implosion. For Hurley, the similarity between the two explosions makes him wonder about Desmond's new "superpower."

A discussion of immense importance concerns whether the Flash or Superman is the better/faster/smarter superhero. Hurley (expounding upon the Flash's superiority) is matched by Charlie (arguing for Superman) in a passionate exchange as they hike through the jungle ("Catch-22," 3.17). Such a debate, moments before Charlie narrowly escapes death-by-arrow, seems "normal" and underscores the abnormality of the rest of their Island life.

Whether on the Island or off, in the 2000s or the 1970s, Hurley continues to relate to comic book or film heroes. He even thinks of his increasingly frequent conversations with dead friends as a superpower of sorts. When he realizes that Miles also communicates with the dead, but without seeing or hearing them as if they are still alive, Hurley feels superior. Miles explains that his knowledge of the dead's experiences comes to him differently. After hearing how Hurley's "power" works, Miles derisively tells him that communication with the dead "doesn't work that way." Hurley merely smiles: "You're just jealous that my power is better than yours" ("Some Like It Hoth," 5.13).

Science fiction and fantasy are important touchstones for many young people. On the Island, young men far more often that women use popular culture references to infuse their language with meaning. *Star Wars* is mentioned more than any other movie, and Seasons Four and Five are full of references to the film series. Just before his death, Karl tells Alex that "It's quiet...too quiet," a line used several times in *Star Wars*. Just to make sure that all viewers pick up the reference, the enhanced episode, complete with pop culture references and explanations of the plot to date, explains the *Star Wars* connection ("Meet Kevin Johnson," 4.8). When audiences see Jack briefly contented with his life as Kate's live-in lover and Aaron's surrogate dad, the camera focuses on a miniature Millennium Falcon on the kitchen floor. Jack smiles as he picks up his son's toy ("Something Nice Back Home," 4.10). Of course, the most blatant *Star Wars* references take place in the aptly named Season Five episode, "Some Like It Hoth," a play not only on the Billy Wilder film title *Some Like It Hot* but, more important, a reference to the ice planet Hoth, a major location for *The Empire Strikes Back*, the film to which Hurley refers several times in this episode.

Television, as the medium with which the male characters in their twenties and thirties grew up, provides the source of most other references. Boone explains the concept of *Star Trek*'s "Red Shirts" to Locke when they traipse through the jungle in search of Claire and Charlie ("All the Best Cowboys Have Daddy Issues," 1.11). He details Captain Kirk's typical process of leading crew on dangerous missions, which usually involve a crewman wearing a red shirt being dissolved in phaser fire or suffering some other gruesome death (a series cliché at the heart of a running joke in 1999's *Galaxy Quest*). Whereas fans of classic *Star Trek* usually revere Kirk as a fine commander, Locke isn't impressed. "Sounds like a piss-poor captain," he tells Boone, who, ironically, is carrying a red shirt and soon dies while under Locke's leadership.

Fans similarly refer to extras cast as unnamed survivors or Others as "red shirts," because these characters are most likely to die. Blogs and message boards frequently list fan comments about who is or should be a red shirt, depending on how annoyed bloggers have become with a particular character. TV terms used by later TV series and becoming popular vernacular in discussing TV shows is a perfect example of the power of popular culture.

Ironically, long after *Lost* introduced such dialogue into the series, J. J. Abrams was tapped by Paramount to relaunch their *Star Trek* series with a new film—and once again, the "red shirt" dies a fiery death when young Kirk and Sulu embark on a dangerous mission to disable a Romulan drill (*Star Trek*, 2009)

Throughout *Lost*'s first five seasons, popular culture references abound, and most characters at some time or another invoke the name of a popular icon. In Season One, Boone refers to his mother as the "Martha Stewart of matrimony" ("All the Best Cowboys Have Daddy Issues," 1.11). Locke seems to understand this reference much better; Martha Stewart as the ideal hostess, homemaker, designer, etc., indicates just what a detail-oriented perfectionist she must be and explains a lot about Boone and Shannon's family dynamic.

Charlie refers to British literature, such as author Jane Austen ("Homecoming," 1.15) or William Golding's *Lord of the Flies* ("What

Kate Did," 2.9), a novel also mentioned by Sawyer ("...In Translation," 1.17). He, too, has been influenced by U.S. imports; he angrily laments that he's not part of the *A-Team* when he's left out yet again ("Everybody Hates Hugo," 2.4) and compares Hurley, in his search for Rousseau, with crazed "Colonel bloody Kurtz" from *Apocalypse Now* (and *Heart of Darkness*, "Numbers," 1.18). (Sawyer also refers to Colonel Kurtz in Season Four.) Nevertheless, most of Charlie's popular culture-based comments provide insight into his pre-crash life in the United Kingdom: the way that afternoon tea, shared between Charlie and Claire, makes those with a British background more civilized ("Raised by Another," 1.10), banoffee pie as a favorite dessert ("Confidence Man," 1.8), documentaries about polar bears, which Charlie loved to watch "on the Beeb" (BBC) while high ("Further Instructions," 3.2).

Newer British character Charlotte Staples Lewis introduces another prominent British author whose references pepper Season Four episodes. Being familiar with the name C. S. Lewis immediately helps audiences understand a bit more about Charlotte's well-educated background and British society in general. During Season Five, references to Lewis' *Chronicles of Narnia* series, especially *Prince Caspian*, pop up in fan discussions of "316" (5.6). *Entertainment Weekly*'s Jeff Jensen, a long-time *Lost* analyst, encouraged fans to head to the bookstore in preparation for that episode:

> [T]he Oceanic Six pull a Prince Caspian and officially start their journey back to the Island. Or, put another way, "316" is the dedication page to a whole new chapter in the veritable Chronicles of Lost. And if you go to your local bookstore today and buy HarperCollins' 2001 single-volume compendium of all seven Narnia novels, you know what you'll find on page 316? That's right: The dedication page to Prince Caspian.[43]

The Island's C. S. Lewis references science fiction, however, when her ability to speak Korean surprises Dan Faraday. She teases him that she also speaks Klingon, a "made-up" language for the TV series *Star Trek* frequently spoken by SF geeks ("This Place Is Death," 5.5).

Just about everyone makes a popular reference at some point, as the list in Table 2 illustrates.

POPULAR CULTURE REFERENCES,
SEASONS ONE–FIVE

Reference	Origin	Said by	Said to	Episode
Johnny Fever	*WKRP in Cincinnati* deejay	Hurley	Jack, about feverish marshal	Tabula Rasa
Captain America	Comic book hero	Shannon	Boone	Walkabout
Jethro	*The Beverly Hillibillies'* backward young hillbilly	Hurley	Sawyer	Walkabout
White Rabbit, *Alice in Wonderland*	Lewis Carroll's *Alice in Wonderland*	Locke	Jack	White Rabbit
Adam and Eve	Biblical first couple	Locke	Jack	House of the Rising Sun
Jedi reference: "I'm known as a warrior at home."	*Star Wars*	Hurley	Himself	Confidence Man
"Jedi moment"	*Star Wars*	Hurley	Jack, after he talks Shannon through an asthma attack	Confidence Man

Reference	Origin	Said by	Said to	Episode
Red Shirts	*Star Trek*	Boone	Locke, as Boone explains who gets killed on away missions	All the Best Cowboys Have Daddy Issues
"Martha Stewart of matrimony"	Well-known homemaking expert	Boone	Locke, about Boone's mother	All the Best Cowboys Have Daddy Issues
Jane Austen	Popular British romance novelist, knowledge-able about proper Victorian manners	Charlie	Group of young women in a bar	Home-coming
Queen Mary	Luxury cruise ship	Michael	Jack, about the raft	...In Translation
"Colonel bloody Kurtz"	Officer who goes insane in *Apocalypse Now* (and Joseph Conrad's *Heart of Darkness*)	Charlie	Hurley, when he looks for Rousseau	Numbers

Reference	Origin	Said by	Said to	Episode
"Steam-rollered Harry Potter"	J. K. Rowling's *Harry Potter* books and films	Hurley	Sawyer, about his new glasses	Deus Ex Machina
Huggy Bear	*Starsky and Hutch*	Johnny	Hurley	Everybody Hates Hugo
A-Team	*The A-Team*	Charlie	Locke	Everybody Hates Hugo
Lord of the Flies	William Golding's *Lord of the Flies*	Charlie	Kate	What Kate Did
Hulk	Comic book hero, the Incredible Hulk	Hurley	Desmond	Further Instructions
Beeb	BBC	Charlie	Locke, about television docu-mentaries	Further Instructions
Eye for an eye	Biblical justice	Alex	Jack	Flashes Before Your Eyes
"I'm sorry. You were right. Those pants don't make you look fat."	What women want to hear—and all men need to be able to say	Jin	Sawyer	Tricia Tanaka Is Dead

Reference	Origin	Said by	Said to	Episode
(Slap) "Snap out of it!"	Cher's line to Nicholas Cage in *Moonstruck*	Hurley	Charlie	Tricia Tanaka Is Dead
"Victory or death!"	Many U.S. historic references: motto of 32nd Army Armored Regiment; code word for 1776 attack on Trenton, NJ; battle cry at the Alamo, etc.	Charlie	Hurley	Tricia Tanaka Is Dead
Nadia Comaneci	Famous Olympic gymnast	Mikhail	Sayid, about a cat	Enter 77
Phil Collins	Pop music star, very popular in the 1980s	Sawyer, giving her a mix tape	Kate	Catch-22
"Afternoon Delight"	Hit song by Starland Vocal Band, but more importantly, a euphemism for sex	Sawyer	Kate	Catch-22
The Flash	Comic book character	Hurley	Charlie	Catch-22

Reference	Origin	Said by	Said to	Episode
Superman	Comic book character	Hurley	Charlie	Catch-22
AWOL	Absent Without Leave, a military term	Sawyer		Catch-22
"Bridge on the River Kwai" theme	Song prominently used in World War II movies	Charlie and Jin whistle it as they march along the beach, a scene made ironically humorous because a Brit and an Asian (although Korean instead of Japanese) are friends, instead of enemies portrayed in the movie, and because both Jin and Charlie know the same song.		Catch-22

Reference	Origin	Said by	Said to	Episode
Catch-22	Episode title; Joseph Heller's novel, which Naomi carries; more importantly, a popular reference to a no-win situation, like the one in which Desmond finds himself			Catch-22
The Man Behind the Curtain	Episode title; a *Wizard of Oz* reference applied to Ben Linus, the Island's apparent "wizard" or "man behind the curtain"			The Man Behind the Curtain
Rambo	Fierce jungle played in the movies by Sylvester Stallone	Bernard says he's not Rambo	Rose	Through the Looking Glass
Rambo	Sylvester Stallone action hero (see above)	Rose	Bernard	The Beginning of the End

Reference	Origin	Said by	Said to	Episode
Ho Hos	Cupcake treat found in a convenience store	Hurley first sees the now-dead Charlie standing by the Ho Hos; *H* is the eighth letter of the alphabet and *O* is the fifteenth, as in 815	Charlie	The Beginning of the End
H-O-R-S-E	Basketball hoop–shooting game played and discussed by Jack and Hurley	Jack quits the game after reaching H-O (an 815 reference; see above)	Hurley	The Beginning of the End
"It's quiet… too quiet"	Han Solo in every *Star Wars* movie he was in	Karl	Alex	Meet Kevin Johnson
"They're here."	Prescient child's line in *Poltergeist*, just before the spirits revealed themselves	Ben	Locke and Sawyer	The Shape of Things to Come

Reference	Origin	Said by	Said to	Episode
Dean Moriarty	Seeker character in Jack Kerouac's *On the Road*; secondary reference to "Moriarty," Sherlock Holmes' nemesis	Ben, using this as his alias	Tunisian hotel clerk	The Shape of Things to Come
Millennium Falcon toy	Toy based on Han Solo's ship, the Millennium Falcon, in *Star Wars*	Not said, but Jack picks up the toy in his kitchen		Something Nice Back Home
Ghost of Christmas Future	Another Charles Dickens' reference, this time to *A Christmas Carol*, in which Scrooge is visited by an apparition from the future, much like "future" Sawyer seeing the Hatch from his "past"	Sawyer. Accompanied by Locke, he bangs on the Hatch in time before Locke "officially" finds it in Season One.	Locke, Desmond (although at the time he would hear the knocking, he wouldn't have been known to the other castaways)	Because You Left

Reference	Origin	Said by	Said to	Episode
Jughead	WWII bomb names (historic reference); Jughead in the Archie comics	N/A. The bomb was already named by the U.S. government, a tradition in World War II. Daniel goes to see the Jughead bomb and, once he recognizes what it is, tells Ellie how to prevent its leaking or detonation.		Jughead
Klingon	The language Charlotte tells Dan she speaks; a *Star Trek* reference to a fictitious alien race	Charlotte	Dan	This Place Is Death
Thomas the Apostle painting in the church where Mrs. Hawking shows them the Lamppost station below it	"The Incredulity of St. Thomas," by Caravaggio	Jack is a doubting Thomas. "We're all convinced sooner or later, Jack," Ben says.	Jack	316

Reference	Origin	Said by	Said to	Episode
Nostrada-mus	Nostradamus' prophecies of the future, published in the 1500s, have been surprisingly accurate.	Sawyer says they're "not here to play Nostradamus" when Hurley wants to warn the DI of the Purge.	Hurley	Namaste
Back to the Future	In the Michael J. Fox film from 1985, Marty McFly travels to the past but changes the relationship between his parents-to-be. The result: Marty begins to fade out of existence.	Hurley worries about a time-travel paradox. If Ben dies, the castaways disappear. Miles replies that "what happened, happened." Their trip to the past doesn't create a paradox because it occurred later in the linear way that they are living their lives. Hurley keeps looking at his hand to see if he's disappearing.	Miles	What Happened, Happened

Reference	Origin	Said by	Said to	Episode
Hoth	This planet in *Star Wars* is appropriate for Hurley's story line, in which he is writing a better script (no Ewoks) for George Lucas' *The Empire Strikes Back*.			Some Like It Hoth
Some Like It Hoth	The episode's title plays on the title of Billy Wilder's popular 1959 film *Some Like it Hot*.			Some Like It Hoth

Reference	Origin	Said by	Said to	Episode
Ewoks	The cuddly comedic characters from *The Empire Strikes Back* are, like the later Jar Jar Binks, controversial characters among fans, many who despise them.	Hurley knows the *Star Wars* timeline so well that he knows when George Lucas is working on a sequel. As a true fanboy, Hurley wants to make the mythology better by revising the film's story. After all, according to Hurley, "Ewoks suck."	Miles	Some Like It Hoth
Sports Illustrated	This popular men's magazine not only features sports but is perhaps best known for its infamous "swimsuit issue" each year.	Miles is reading the magazine when Sawyer tells him to erase the security tapes.		Some Like It Hoth

Reference	Origin	Said by	Said to	Episode
Miles Davis	Revered jazz musician at the forefront of musical change from World War II through the 1990s	Dr. Chang explains that his son Miles was named for his wife's favorite jazz artist.	Hurley, Miles	Some Like It Hoth
Luke Skywalker, Darth Vader	The main protagonist and antagonist, respectively, in the *Star Wars* movie franchise.	Hurley compares Miles to Luke Skywalker and suggest that all the evils of the Empire could've been avoided with better communication, especially between father and son.	Miles	Some Like It Hoth
Microsoft	Computer corporation just beginning when Sawyer wants to invest in what will become a worldwide software phenomenon	Sawyer proposes that once he and Juliet get off the Island (via the sub), they'll buy Microsoft and get rich.	Juliet	Follow the Leader

Reference	Origin	Said by	Said to	Episode
1978 Cowboys	The Dallas Cowboys football team boasted one of the finest rosters in history. They won the NFC champion-ship, after a slow start to the regular season, and became the first team to play in five Super Bowls.	Sawyer explains that, in his post-island life in the 1970s, he plans to bet on the '78 Cowboys.	Juliet	Follow the Leader

THE HURLEY-SAWYER CONNECTION

Not surprisingly, the character with whom most of us identify, "every-person" Hurley, is one of two characters referring to popular culture most often. He recalls popular TV characters (probably seen on reruns while he was growing up), including Jethro from *The Beverly Hillbillies* and Johnny Fever from *WKRP in Cincinnati*. In backstories, Hurley's pal Johnny mentions Huggy Bear (*Starsky and Hutch*) and Pony Boy (*The Outsiders*) ("Everybody Hates Hugo," 2.4). Hurley's movie prefer-ences run to science fiction (*Star Wars*) and fantasy (*Harry Potter*). It's not surprising that Sawyer's dark, taped glasses remind Hurley of a "steam-rollered Harry Potter" ("Deus Ex Machina," 1.19).

From what we know from Hurley's backstories, he was a slim boy who became traumatized by his father's abandonment ("Tricia Tanaka Is Dead," 3.10); perhaps his feelings of rejection caused him to retreat to food and fantasy as a way to escape a troubled home life. Adult mil-lionaire Hurley also feels rejected and cursed—his beloved grandfather dies suddenly ("Numbers," 1.18); his father reappears when Hurley becomes a millionaire; his mother eagerly, and to Hurley's disgust, rather passionately, welcomes her estranged husband home; his best friend Johnny abandons him and steals the one woman Hurley feels he has a chance to date ("Tricia Tanaka Is Dead," 3.10). On the Island, Hurley is belittled by Sawyer and alternately befriended and manipulated by Charlie (whose death further reduces Hurley's number of close pals). His one chance at true love seems to be a budding relationship with Libby, who dies before Hurley can even finish their first date ("Two for the Road," 2.20).

Hurley, out of all the castaways, actively seeks ways to break the monotony of Island life and make people forget for a few minutes the dangers surrounding them. He wants to be liked and goes out of his way to create a happy fantasy of a normal life (just like on a TV sitcom or in a superhero comic book with a happy ending), even if the illusion is temporary. He distributes goodies from the Hatch so that everyone can indulge their culinary vices, from coffee to chocolate to peanut butter ("Everyone Hates Hugo," 2.4). He builds a golf course ("Solitary," 1.9). He finds a VW van in the jungle and invites a depressed, marked-for-death Charlie to ride along ("Tricia Tanaka Is Dead," 3.10). He cons Sawyer into doing nice things for the castaways, including sponsoring a barbecue ("Left Behind," 3.15). He travels halfway around the world to meet baby Ji Yeon and remind lonely new-mother Sun that she's not alone ("Ji Yeon," 4.7). He introduces Sayid, who has no one to meet him at the plane, to his family ("There's No Place Like Home," 4.13).

Hurley's penchant for making others feel at ease may stem from his familial upbringing and need to please people. When his reunited parents throw their son a surprise birthday bash, they invite the Oceanic Sixers. Presumably to make them feel "at home" back in Los Angeles, the Reyes create an island-themed party, complete with drinks with little umbrellas. Their idea of life stranded on a tropical island is more *Gilligan's Island* fantasy than *Lost*'s Island reality ("There's No Place Like Home," 4.12). Hurley provides the bridge between his eager-to-please but misinformed parents and his Island comrades.

Back on the Island in 1977, Hurley finds contentment with his new job as the DHARMA Initiative's chef and enjoys offering tempting meals to his fellow castaways trapped in the past ("He's Our You," 5.10). Wherever he lands, Hurley works to "socialize" others into their new reality and to make their lives a little more enjoyable. Although Hurley may enjoy living in a fantasy world and clearly understands the importance of popular culture in the life of a social outsider, his ability to see what's special or unique about his real friends or his imaginary ones allows him to make other outsiders feel more at ease.

What might be surprising is that, for all their differences in background, life experiences, and outlook on life, Hurley and Sawyer have some things in common: a love of popular culture and a desire to fit in, despite their usual roles as social outsiders. Both men probably share feelings of abandonment and betrayal from childhood through adulthood, but they've developed different ways of coping.

Before his DHARMA Initiative life (1974–1977) Sawyer prefers to stay outside society and maintain an "outlaw" façade so that he seems tougher and meaner than anyone else. He shows moments of softness, however, and at times defends the quieter moments of his childhood. During Season Three, when he mentions *Little House* to Kate, she scoffs at his familiarity with the family TV series. Sawyer defensively explains that he had mononucleosis as a child, which required him to stay in bed at home. The family TV picked up only one channel, so *Little House on the Prairie* became his companion during the afternoons ("Tricia Tanaka Is Dead," 3.10). Justifying his obvious enjoyment of this childhood memory reveals a hidden softer side to the killer con man.

Sawyer's concept of frontier justice, as well as his need to protect (at least some) women and children, may stem from his early identification with TV characters. After Charlie's death, Sawyer looks after Claire, risking his life to rescue her from the attack on New Otherton ("The Shape of Things to Come," 4.9) and taking care of baby Aaron after Claire's surprising trek into the jungle with her dead father ("Something Nice Back Home," 4.10). Perhaps most surprising, Sawyer, self-renamed LaFleur to secure a place in the DHARMA Initiative, becomes the community's head of security. He settles down with Juliet for three years of blissful togetherness and fiercely protects his "conformist" life when the Oceanic Sixers arrive ("LaFleur," 5.8). His role as protector extends to his friends from the future, but he is most devoted to Juliet and willing to sacrifice himself in order to keep her from harm ("The Variable," 5.14; "Follow the Leader," 5.15; "The Incident," 5.16).

Sawyer's self-education and at least some of his socialization seem based on popular culture. In prison and on the Island, even when he has become one of the DHARMA Initiative's most respected citizens, he often reads books. Because he started his career as a con man at seventeen, Sawyer must have made up for what he felt he lacked by reading as much as possible. On the Island, he voraciously reads everything—from children's (*Watership Down*) and teen literature (*Are You There God, It's Me, Margaret*) to women's magazines (*Cosmopolitan*) to "shocking amounts of pornography" ("Flashes Before Your Eyes," 3.8). He even sports new glasses to help him read. He kills time reading at home while waiting for Horace to wake up from a drunken spree ("LaFleur," 4.8). Even when LaFleur is a valued part of society, an apparently committed partner, and a leader in a job that could take up as much of his spare time as he'd likely want to give, "me time" with a book is an important part of his life.

Our knowledge of literature helps us get the jokes involving Sawyer's reading list. When he explains that he's reading *Watership Down* because it's a nice little book about bunnies, we know better; this is a deceptively dark tale. Sawyer's complaint about *Are You There God, It's Me, Margaret* is that it doesn't have enough sex. Of course, the title alone indicates that this might not be a steamy novel, but understanding the subject matter gives us a better sense of Sawyer's sense of humor, best illustrated when Sawyer uses what he's learned from the women's magazine *Cosmo*. Notorious for being a magazine written by women for women, *Cosmopolitan*'s infamous love/sex quizzes and how-to's for getting a man obviously create a lasting impression. Sawyer's pre-Juliet poor track record for long-term relationships makes his "expert" advice to Jin even more humorous. He teaches his friend all the English that he'll ever need to speak to Sun: "I'm sorry. You were right. Those pants don't make you look fat" ("Tricia Tanaka Is Dead," 3.10). His knowledge of books also provides him with some popular nicknames that he's fond of bestowing. He derisively refers to the DHARMA Initiative's sub captain as Nemo, a reference to Jules Verne's *20,000 Leagues Under the Sea*, a fitting metaphor as the sub slips beneath the ocean ("The Incident," 5.16). Captain Nemo helmed the submarine *Nautilus* in the book and subsequent movies.

More than any other character, Sawyer peppers his conversation with nicknames and frequent sarcastic references to movies and television. (A fun feature of the Season Two DVD set is a rapid-fire montage of Sawyerisms, mostly nicknames.) He may not have a college education, but he keeps up with what's going on in the world, which to him is more readily accessed through popular media. Knowledge of pop culture is one way for Sawyer to feel "equal" with the richer, better educated people he loves to con.

His word choices, however, sometimes reflect his lack of under-standing. He scathingly calls Sayid "Al-Jazeera" ("Tabula Rasa," 1.3)—Charlie derisively tells him that's a news agency, not a person. Calling Hurley "Barbar" is meant to refer to his large size; Hurley cor-rects Sawyer by reminding him the elephant's name is Babar ("One of Them," 2.14). In the face of criticism, Sawyer shuts up, but he quickly comes back with more. Other nicknames for Hurley include Stay-Puff ("Raised by Another," 1.10), Pillsbury ("The 23rd Psalm," 2.10), Jabba ("Fire + Water," 2.12), Hoss ("Fire + Water," 2.12), Rerun ("One of Them," 2.14), Mongo ("Lockdown," 2.17), Avalanche ("Enter 77," 3.11), and Jumbotron ("Tricia Tanaka Is Dead," 3.10). Renaming oth-ers happens so often that Sawyer becomes annoyed when he loses a ping pong bet and is forbidden to call anyone by a nickname for a week ("Enter 77," 3.11).

During the first three seasons of *Lost*, Sawyer primarily uses his word choice to feel superior to those he considers weaker. On the Island (during the first half of the series), his most likely targets are Hurley and Charlie, each vulnerable in his own way. Because Hurley is self-conscious about his girth, Sawyer usually chooses nicknames referring to large, soft, or round characters: a huge wrestler (Avalanche), large, stupid cowboy (Mongo), cartoon gorilla (Grape Ape), soft doughboy (Pillsbury), or round, soft (and, in *Ghostbusters*, huge and out of control) Stay-Puff Marshmallow Man.

Sawyer's other favored target during the first half of *Lost*, Charlie, may believe he stands tall in the music industry, but his height is much less than Sawyer's or that of most men on the Island. Sawyer's nick-names for him cut him down to size: Munchkin (a short person in *The Wizard of Oz*, as well as a name given to diminutive children), Jiminy Cricket (a tiny singing Disney cartoon character), Chucky (not only a childish variation of Charles, but a demonic blond toy brought to life in the *Child's Play* series). Although Sawyer most often uses these nicknames in front of Hurley, Charlie is frequently discussed in these terms when he's not around or just as he arrives on scene—he's being talked about, rather than talked with.

With the increasing danger and impending annihilation of the Island and its inhabitants during *Lost*'s Season Four, Sawyer has fewer chances for lighthearted nicknames or scathing comments. The few he bestows on Hurley show a shift in their relationship. With Charlie gone and Hurley mourning his loss, Sawyer appoints himself as Hurley's protector; perhaps he understands how difficult it is to be vulnerable and admires Hurley's determination to go with Locke, look after Claire and Aaron, and follow Charlie's last message that the Freighter Folk aren't who they say they are and thus might be dangerous. When Hurley and Sawyer are reunited during Season Five, the nicknames resume.

When Sawyer first sees Hurley after a three-year absence, his initial response is to call Hurley "Kong," although he fondly tempers this "insult" by adding, "It's good to see you, Hugo" ("Namaste," 5.9). Hurley and Sawyer's friendship evolves, by Season Five, to the point where once hurtful nicknames no longer sting and have become terms of endearment—or as endearing as Sawyer will allow. Using Hurley's given first name and fiercely hugging his friend illustrate how nicknames take on different contexts throughout the course of their relationship.

Although Sawyer's relationship with Sayid also changes substantially throughout the series, to Sawyer, Sayid probably will always be first an Iraqi or a torturer and then a man or even a friend. Nicknames for Sayid always refer to his nationality or Middle Eastern culture (e.g., Al Jazeera, falafel). Even when he refers to Sayid with what Sawyer would probably term respect for his special interrogational "talent," Sayid is called "our resident Iraqi" ("One of Us," 3.16). To Sawyer, Iraqi = torturer, a comparison he sometimes resents but finds useful as a weapon against the Others. A mellower, more in-charge LaFleur continues this equation once Sayid returns to the Island but is captured as a "hostile." While awaiting interrogation, Sayid accepts the fact that he likely will be tortured for information. LaFleur, as head of security, wants to try a "civilized" method of discussion first, a tactic Sayid didn't take when he interrogated Sawyer in Season One. "Let's discuss this like gentlemen," he pointedly tells his captive. When Sayid eventually is turned over to the DHARMA Initiative's resident torturer, LaFleur explains to Sayid that "he's our you" ("He's Our You," 5.10).

Sawyer's choice of nicknames indicates the way he identifies the people around him: Hurley = fat, Charlie = small or boyish, Sayid = Iraqi or torturer. The trend continues when he is annoyed with those who don't do as he wants or whom he fails to understand. In Season Five, physicist Dan Faraday is nicknamed Dilbert ("Jughead," 5.3), Plato ("LaFleur," 5.8), and H. G. Wells ("The Variable," 5.14), depending on the level of eggheadedness he wants to convey. Security deputy Miles often receives the *Dukes of Hazzard* moniker Enos, referring to the astute but wide-eyed bumpkin sheriff's deputy ("LaFleur," 5.8), as well as the less flattering slur on his Asian heritage, Bonsai ("LaFleur," 5.8). The labels aren't always negative, however. Sawyer's choices for Jack might be sarcastic, but they indicate his acknowledgment of Jack's skills: famed poker player Amarillo Slim or frontier miracle worker Dr. Quinn.

Like Hurley, Sawyer often refers to television or movies in his choice of nicknames or references. Although Sawyer's repertoire is much greater than Hurley's, the most common references are to science fiction (sometimes horror) and fantasy movies and television series: *Ghostbusters, Indiana Jones and the Temple of Doom, Star Wars, The Wizard of Oz, Child's Play, Pinocchio, The Green Hornet, Star Trek, Fantasy Island.* The sheer number of references (see Table 3) indicates just how much time Sawyer has spent reading, watching TV or movies, and listening to the news.

SAWYERISMS

Reference	Origin	Said to	Episode
Al-Jazeera	Iraqi media outlet	Sayid, to refer to his being Iraqi (Charlie corrects Sawyer's usage).	Tabula Rasa
Playboys	*Playboy* magazine	Jack	Tabula Rasa

Reference	Origin	Said to	Episode
Pork Pie	Food reference; also a round hat	Hurley	Walkabout
Mr. Miyagi	*The Karate Kid* series of films	Kate, about Jin	White Rabbit
Omar	Sarcastic appropriation of Middle Eastern name	Sayid	House of the Rising Sun
Dr. Quinn	*Dr. Quinn, Medicine Woman*, about a frontier doctor	Jack	Solitary
Stay-Puff	Brand of marshmallows; Stay-Puff Marshmallow Man attack in *Ghostbusters*	Hurley	Raised by Another
Tattoo	*Fantasy Island*	Walt	All the Best Cowboys Have Daddy Issues
"VH1 Has-beens"	Music network known for retrospective specials about "has-been" bands and performers	Walt, about Charlie	All the Best Cowboys Have Daddy Issues
Dr. Do-Right	Combination of medical reference and Dudley Do-Right cartoon about a strait-laced Mountie	Sayid, about Jack	All the Best Cowboys Have Daddy Issues
Hoss	Gun reference to the Western *Bonanza*	Jack	Homecoming

Reference	Origin	Said to	Episode
Mohammed	Reference to Sayid's Middle Eastern origins and being Muslim	Sayid	Outlaws
Bruce	Bruce Lee, martial arts expert	Jin	...In Translation
"*Lord of the Flies* time"	William Golding's *Lord of the Flies*	Jin, who is accused of theft	...In Translation
Betty	Asian spy's Americanized name	Sun, when he accuses her of being a "double agent" between her husband and the castaways	...In Translation
Captain Falafel	Combination of military reference (Sayid was in the Iraqi Republican Guard) and food	Sayid	...In Translation
Short Round	*Indiana Jones and the Temple of Doom*	Walt	Numbers
Kato	*The Green Hornet*	Michael, about Jin	Do No Harm
Chucky	Variant nickname of Charles; also a demonic toy in the *Child's Play* series	Charlie	The Greater Good
Baby Huey	Oversized cartoon baby	Charlie, about Aaron	The Greater Good
Chewy and Han	*Star Wars*	Jin and Michael	Exodus

Reference	Origin	Said to	Episode
Kazoo	Alien on *The Flintstones*	Walt	Exodus
Hoss	*Bonanza*	Michael, when he tries to fire a wet gun	Adrift
Bluebeard	Famous pirate	Michael, about the Other who kidnapped Walt	Adrift
Shaft	*Shaft*	Ana Lucia, about Mr. Eko	Orientation
Howdy Doody	Children's TV series	Ana Lucia	Orientation
Rambina	Feminine variation of Rambo, *Rambo* action movie series	Michael, about Ana Lucia	Everybody Hates Hugo
"Beam us up"	*Star Trek*	Michael	Everybody Hates Hugo
Hot Lips	*M*A*S*H* sexy but stuck-up nurse	Ana Lucia	Everybody Hates Hugo
Mr. Ed	*Mr. Ed*	Mr. Eko	...And Found
Chewy	*Star Wars*	Jin	...And Found
Ponce de Leon	Famous explorer	Ana Lucia	Abandoned
Chewy	*Star Wars*	Jin	Abandoned
Pillsbury	TV pitchman doughboy	Hurley	The 23rd Psalm
Mr. Clean	Bald TV pitchman	Locke	The Hunting Party

Reference	Origin	Said to	Episode
Mount Vesuvius	Tall volcanic mountain	Locke, about their path through the jungle	The Hunting Party
Daniel Boone	Historic frontiersman	Locke	The Hunting Party
Zeke	"Hillbilly" name	Tom (aka Mr. Friendly)	The Hunting Party
Jabba	*Star Wars*	Hurley	Fire + Water
Jethro	*The Beverly Hillbillies*	Hurley	Fire + Water
Hoss	*Bonanza*	Hurley	Fire + Water
Sheena	*Sheena of the Jungle* comic book and movie	Kate	The Long Con
Dewey decimal system	Book classification system for libraries	Lock, as he arranges books in the Hatch	The Long Con
Tokyo Rose	Famous spy	Locke, about Sun	The Long Con
Cowboys and Indians	Children's game	Locke	The Long Con
Hoss	*Bonanza*	Locke	The Long Con
Donkey Kong	Video game	Jack, as Sawyer input the numbers	The Long Con
Rerun	*What's Happening*	Hurley	One of Them

Reference	Origin	Said to	Episode
Barbar	Mistakenly saying that instead of Babar, the elephant in a children's story	Hurley	One of Them
Thelma	*Thelma and Louise*	Kate	Maternity Leave
Amarillo Slim	Famous poker player	Jack	Lockdown
Cool Hand	*Cool Hand Luke*	Jack	Lockdown
Mango	*Blazing Saddles*	Hurley	Lockdown
Mutton-chops	Large sideburns	Hurley	Lockdown
Deep Dish	Style of pie, usually pizza, sometimes fruit	Hurley	Dave
"I'm walking here!"	Al Pacino's famous line from *Midnight Cowboy*	Christian Shephard	Two for the Road
Grape Ape	Large cartoon character from a 1970s TV series	Hurley	Three Minutes
Pippi Long-stocking	Young female heroine of books and movies	Kate	Three Minutes
Red Beret	Iraqi Republican Guard uniform (also *not* a Green Beret, the U.S. elite unit)	Sayid	Three Minutes
Dirty Dozen	Military unit on a special mission, as in the film *The Dirty Dozen*	About cast-aways headed into the jungle to find Walt	Three Minutes

Reference	Origin	Said to	Episode
Chachi	*Happy Days, Joanie Loves Chachi*	Karl	A Tale of Two Cities
Shortcake	Food tasting like strawberries	Kate	The Glass Ballerina
Chinatown	Jack Nicholson's character, who wore a bandage across his nose, in *Chinatown*	Pickett	Every Man for Himself
Costanza	*Seinfeld*	Mr. Friendly	Every Man for Himself
George	*Of Mice and Men*	Ben	Every Man for Himself
Sheena	*Sheena, Jungle Girl*	Alex	Not in Portland
Underdog	*Underdog* animated TV series, also "dog" reference to digging	Alex	Not in Portland
Lollipop	Sweet, childlike reference	Alex	Not in Portland
Wookiee	*Star Wars*, referring to a scene in *Empire Strikes Back*	Aldo	Not in Portland
Cheech	*Cheech & Chong*; also interesting because episode coauthor Carlton Cuse once created *Nash Bridges*, which starred Cheech Marin (who played Hurley's father)	Karl	Not in Portland
Captain Bunny Killer	Creating an "official" title for a character	Kate, about Ben	Stranger in a Strange Land

Reference	Origin	Said to	Episode
Magellan	Explorer, in reference to Kate deciding which direction their boat should turn	Kate	Stranger in a Strange Land
Bobby, *Brady Bunch*	*Brady Bunch*'s middle son	Karl	Stranger in a Strange Land
Sally Slingshot	Made-up alliterative name	Karl, about Alex	Stranger in a Strange Land
Are we there yet?	Typical child's reaction to a long trip	Kate	Tricia Tanaka Is Dead
Little House	*Little House on the Prairie*	Kate	Tricia Tanaka Is Dead
Snuffy	Snuffleupagus, of *Sesame Street*, sometimes called Snuffy, is large and cuddly	Hurley, who hugs Sawyer	Tricia Tanaka Is Dead
Oliver Twist	*Oliver Twist*, referring to Charlie's British origins, possibly his height, and his ability to steal from Sawyer	Charlie, accused of taking Sawyer's stuff	Tricia Tanaka Is Dead
Munchkin	*Wizard of Oz*, referring to Charlie's short stature	Desmond, about Charlie	Tricia Tanaka Is Dead
Jin-bo	Variation of Jimbo, a Southern nickname	Jin	Tricia Tanaka Is Dead
Hooked on Phonics	A method of teaching reading and language skills	Jin	Tricia Tanaka Is Dead

Reference	Origin	Said to	Episode
Skeletor	Comic book and TV character from *Masters of the Universe*	Hurley, about Roger (dead Other)	Tricia Tanaka Is Dead
International House of Pancakes	U.S. restaurant chain	Jin, about Hurley	Tricia Tanaka Is Dead
Jumbotron	Large video screen for stadiums; also sounds like a made-up name for a transformer	Hurley	Tricia Tanaka Is Dead
Jiminy Cricket	Animated character in *Pinocchio*	Hurley, about Charlie	Tricia Tanaka Is Dead
Zorro	Legendary literary, TV, and movie character, an early Californian Hispanic "Robin Hood"	Paolo	Enter 77
Crouching Tiger, Hidden Dragon	*Crouching Tiger, Hidden Dragon*	Sun, Jin	Enter 77
Grimace	Large McDonald's mascot	Hurley	Enter 77
Scotty	Desmond's Scottish origins, plus TV's most famous excited Scotsman, "Beam Me Up" Scotty from *Star Trek*	Desmond	The Beginning of the End
Colonel Kurtz	Scary *Apocalypse Now* leader	Locke	Confirmed Dead

Reference	Origin	Said to	Episode
Chicken Little	Children's book character who warned of the sky falling	Hurley	The Shape of Things to Come
Yoda	Jedi mentor and sage in *Star Wars* saga	Ben	Something Nice Back Home
Yahoo	People that Gulliver meets on his travels, also slang for an unsophisticated person (e.g., yokel, hick)	Frank	There's No Place Like Home
Shaggy	Character in *Scooby-Do*	Frank	There's No Place Like Home
Genghis	Genghis Khan, renowned ruthless leader	Miles	There's No Place Like Home
Sundance	Outlaw buddy of Butch Cassidy, doomed partner in crime in *Butch Cassidy and the Sundance Kid*	Jack	There's No Place Like Home
Kenny Rogers	Country singer, whose beard, to Sawyer, might seem similar to Frank's scragglier salt-and-pepper facial hair	Frank	There's No Place Like Home
Ginger	*Gilligan's Island*'s resident redhead	Charlotte	Because You Left

Reference	Origin	Said to	Episode
Danny Boy	A popular song title, "Oh Danny Boy," as well as a childlike variation of Daniel	Daniel Faraday	Because You Left
Frogurt	A play on Neil's job at a frozen yogurt (frogurt) stand before he left on Oceanic 815	Neil	The Lie
Blondie	*Blondie* comic strip, a reference to Blondie with her blonde hair	Ellie	Jughead
Dilbert	Nerdy comic character	Daniel Faraday	Jughead
Enos	*Dukes of Hazzard* deputy sheriff	Miles	LaFleur
Red	Typical nickname for a redhead	Charlotte	LaFleur
Plato	Famous philosopher, a "thinker" like Dan rather than a "doer" like Sawyer	Daniel Faraday	LaFleur
Chief	Typical nickname for a leader	Horace Goodspeed	LaFleur
Bonsai	Slur on Miles' Asian heritage; a Bonsai tree associated with Asian culture; also a derogative term when associated with the "bonsai" cry of Japanese bombers during World War II	Miles	LaFleur

Reference	Origin	Said to	Episode
Kong	King Kong, a reference to Hurley's size	Hurley	Namaste
Quick Draw	Television cartoon character, Quick Draw McGraw, but also a more general term for someone who is fast on the trigger—acting first and asking questions later	Stuart Radzinsky	Namaste
Twitchy	Descriptive term for an anxious Dan, who twitches with nerves as he attempts to explain what needs to be done to get rid of a bomb	Daniel Faraday	The Variable
H. G. Wells	Author of *The Time Machine*, used just when Dan explains how he plans to change the timeline	Daniel Faraday	The Variable
Nemo	Captain Nemo, the *Nautilus'* sub captain, in Jules Verne's *20,000 Leagues Under the Sea*	The sub captain	Follow the Leader

Sawyer and Hurley likely have been socialized primarily through popular culture, more so than by family or friends. Perhaps that's why Hurley, the most likely target for Sawyer's witticisms and criticisms, is the best person to socialize Sawyer for Island life. Whereas the Others couldn't change him with torture and deprivation (in Season Three), Hurley knows how to motivate Sawyer. He understands better than

Sawyer realizes that they both may not fit in with the "popular kids" but can't survive on their own.

Two prime examples of Hurley's influence over Sawyer occur in Season Three. When Hurley finds a broken-down van in the jungle, he coerces Sawyer to help get it running by offering him beer from the back of the van. Although Sawyer grouses about its quality, he nevertheless sticks around to bond with Jin and join Hurley and Charlie on a joyride ("Tricia Tanaka Is Dead," 3.10). A few days later, Hurley cons Sawyer into thinking that the castaways' little society will banish him if he doesn't "play nicely." Hurley also realizes that Sawyer may need to step in as the group's leader, if Jack, Sayid, and Locke fail to return to camp (which they later do). By forcing Sawyer to realize that he can't live well on his own (evident after a disastrous attempt at fishing), Hurley supervises while Sawyer "plays politician": praising baby Aaron, hunting boar, and making a special barbecue sauce for the community barbecue ("Left Behind," 3.15).

The Hurley-Sawyer connection grows even stronger in Season Four. When Hurley seems to have a tough time keeping up with the group meeting with Jack at the fuselage, Sawyer lags behind to make sure his companion is all right. He even offers to listen if Hurley wants to talk about Charlie ("Confirmed Dead," 4.2). Whereas Hurley could cry with Claire as they mutually mourned Charlie, Sawyer never befriended the musician, and Hurley seems reluctant to share that part of himself with Sawyer—perhaps because the former con man usually attacks when he finds a vulnerable spot. Sawyer's concern continues when Hurley is separated from the group, only to rejoin the rest of the castaways with Locke in tow.

In New Otherton, Sawyer and Hurley become domestic. They play horseshoes ("The Other Woman," 4.6) and Risk ("The Shape of Things to Come," 4.9), and only Kate's timely arrival prevents Sawyer from watching *Xanadu* with Hurley ("Eggtown," 4.4).

Hurley, however, still has the same type of control over Sawyer evident in Season Three. When Sawyer likely would've killed Ben on the trek back to the Others' compound ("Confirmed Dead," 4.2), Hurley quickly shakes his head, a subtle "no" that speaks louder than Locke's many reasoning words why Ben's life should be spared. Ben recognizes that Hurley, like Locke, is "special" and may be useful in future dealings with the elusive Jacob. When Ben commands that Locke and Hurley accompany him to Jacob's cabin, Hurley agrees—perhaps out of curiosity or a sense of duty. Only he can "call off" guard dog Sawyer, who fails to understand why Hurley would go anywhere with Ben. Retaining his threatening stance, Sawyer vows to kill Ben if "so much as one hair on [Hurley's] curly head is hurt" ("Something Nice Back Home," 4.10). Sawyer even convinces Jack to hike to the guarded and heavily fortified Orchid station because that's where Hurley was headed with Locke and Ben ("There's No Place Like Home," 4.13). After more than one hundred days on the Island, Sawyer is clearly loyal to Hurley.

Loyalty and love for others culminates in Sawyer sacrificing his spot on the helicopter headed for the freighter and, presumably, rescue. When the damaged helicopter needs to lighten its load to conserve fuel, Hurley looks distinctly worried, but Sawyer comes up with a better solution. After whispering to Kate and sealing the deal with a prolonged kiss, Sawyer leaps from the helicopter ("There's No Place Like Home," 4.14). The Sawyer who crashed on the Island three months previously more likely would've pushed Hurley out the door; after his "socialization" on the Island, largely through Hurley's friendship, Sawyer reveals a nobler personality. (Sawyer's baby mama, Cassidy, convincingly tells Kate that Sawyer was only trying to get away from her in a last desperate escape from commitment ["The Little Prince," 5.4]. However, LaFleur's commitment to live-in lover Juliet seems real and may negate Cassidy's cynicism about Sawyer's plunge from the helicopter.)

Sawyer's success 1974–1977 with the DHARMA Initiative owes as much to Hurley's prior socialization attempts as the con man's ease in coming up with a convincing cover story that allows him, along with Juliet, Miles, and Dan, to be allowed to join. Pre-Hurley Sawyer couldn't have been happy or successful as LaFleur.

THE POWER OF POPULAR CULTURE

Popular culture is more than a retreat or an escape, although it sometimes serves that purpose for die-hard fans (and *Lost* characters) who find television, film, or literary characters more understanding or desirable than the real people around them. Popular culture helps us draw comparisons of our very personal, unique experiences with common public experiences and knowledge. We know exactly the shade of meaning provided by a common cultural reference.

Season Four's episode title to Juliet's backstory, "The Other Woman" (4.6), takes on a double meaning, one cultural, one purely *Lost*-related. Juliet is (or was) one of the Others, and this backstory clearly indicates her place within and history with this group. She also is "the other woman" via her affair with the adulterous Goodwin, whose wife is introduced in this episode. Juliet's duplicitous nature takes on another dimension when viewers see that she often has led a double life: as the other woman in a love triangle, as a secret saboteur within Ben's "family," as Ben's spy on Jack and his friends. Juliet's continuing ability to convincingly live a double life makes her seem even more dangerous and less trustworthy. Throughout her adult life but especially on the Island, Juliet lives comfortably as "other" from accepted social norms.

A similar association with another episode title occurs between "Some Like It Hoth" (5.13), a dual reference to two very different but popular movies. We understand both plays on words.

Pop culture references and a preference for inserting them in everyday conversations mark Hurley and Sawyer as Americans; the TV series and movies on which "Sawyerisms" are based are clearly stamped "Made in the U.S." With the exception of Charlie's or Charlotte's comments, influenced not only by British traditions and television but also U.S. imports, brief glimpses of Dan's Oxford life, and the occasional offhand references by Claire (e.g., her love of peanut butter, unusual for an Australian) and Kate (e.g., Patsy Cline is popular everywhere, not just in the United States), the culture being referenced is mainstream Hollywood. Count the number of references to U.S. television programs broadcast between the mid-1960s and 1990s, when Hurley and Sawyer, in particular, would've been watching U.S. TV in first-run or syndicated rerun episodes (see Tables 2 and 3). During the first five seasons of *Lost*, Sawyer alone mentions *Dr. Quinn, Medicine Woman*; *Bonanza*; *Fantasy Island*; *The Flintstones*; *M*A*S*H*; *Mr. Ed*; *Star Trek*; *The Beverly Hillbillies*; *Happy Days*; *Seinfeld*; *Underdog*; *The Brady Bunch*; *Little House on the Prairie*; and *The Dukes of Hazzard*, among others. That's quite a range!

Better educated characters, including Jack, and older characters, such as Locke, don't use popular culture references themselves. Locke prefers nature-based metaphors or stories, such as his comparison of the moth's journey to Charlie's ("The Moth," 1.7); what's most important to Locke is the Island (nature). He also discusses literature with the ease of someone who's read classic books. Jack understands what Sawyer means when the con man calls him Amarillo Slim ("Lockdown," 2.17) or Dr. Quinn ("Solitary," 1.9), but he doesn't use the same vocabulary. Physicist Dan Faraday doesn't comment on Sawyer's nicknames, and his strict adherence to a science-based education may have left him unsure (or unaware and unconcerned) with the basis of Sawyer's jibes. Popular culture (especially film and TV) seems to be the province of the younger, less highly educated, male, and multimedia-friendly castaways—the "common men" among the group, which is appropriate, because popular culture is "of the people."

Even the Others use popular culture to bridge the gap between themselves and the castaways. Ben knows that baseball is an important metaphor for life, especially to Jack. Christian Shephard repeatedly said that the unlikely would happen "when the Red Sox win the Series" ("Exodus," 1.24), a phrase akin to "when hell freezes over." Ben wants to impress upon Jack the fact that the Others access current technology and can truly send him home; to convince him, he shows Jack the latest televised World Series game, the night when the Red Sox finally win ("The Glass Ballerina," 3.3). Later in the series, but earlier in time, the 1970s DHARMA Initiative enjoys popular music in everyday life and during group orientations. They choose film as the medium by which to impart the most important information to new recruits. Even on the Island, music, TV, films, and books are prized elements to share culture.

LOST AS REFLECTOR AND CREATOR OF POPULAR CULTURE

But what about the rest of the world in which popular culture isn't so heavily reliant on television or film? During Season Four, a few non-U.S. cultural references have come into play, but with few exceptions, mostly U.S. cultural references have become part of *Lost*'s dialogue.

In a flashback sequence ("Ji Yeon," 4.7), Jin buys a huge plush panda to present to a business client shortly after the birth of his grandson; the baby gift, carefully tied with a blue ribbon, helps seal future deals between the businessman and Jin's employer, Mr. Paik. Even this symbol of friendship between two parties is understood outside Chinese culture. Especially since the early 1970s, when Ling-Ling and Hsing-Hsing were given as a goodwill gift from China to the United States, Americans have linked China to the image of giant pandas. The idea of blue as a "boy" color is common in many countries, too, and Jin's careful selection of the proper bow doesn't seem specific either to Korean or Chinese culture.

Similarly, our brief glance at the funeral of Sayid's wife, Nadia, provides minimal insight into Iraqi funeral traditions. Sayid is one of several male pallbearers carrying a simple casket bedecked with flowers, but this sight seems as appropriate to Nadia and Sayid's Westernized lives as to their Middle Eastern upbringing ("The Shape of Things to Come," 4.9). The funeral differs from a similar "casket" scene in (5.15) "The Incident." At the funeral of young James Ford's parents, a hearse carries the bodies to the cemetery; Sayid and close friends or family carry Nadia's body through the streets.

"Other" Mikhail Bakunin shares the name of a father of anarchism and Russian revolutionary, a reference perhaps lost on many U.S. viewers, but this nod to Russian history doesn't occur often. Hermann Minkowski may be the Lithuanian-born father of space-time theory, but *Lost*'s namesake George Minkowski, the hapless victim of yo-yoing between the past and present, is definitely American. (U.S. audiences are more likely to recognize famous names in French or British politics, science, or philosophy, such as Rousseau, Locke, Burke, or Faraday.) *Lost* is, of course, a U.S. TV series made primarily for those at home, although with the series' huge international following, it may seem surprising that a series boasting international characters with widely divergent views on religion and politics offers few "insider" references from other cultures.

The reasoning behind this decision may be twofold. From a pragmatic perspective, *Lost* is popular culture, promoting the United States just like any other product exported internationally, no different from Levi's, Coca Cola, or McDonald's. *Lost* exports knowledge of U.S. products, past and current, as well as the American way of life. From a story perspective, the castaways would be even more "lost" without their understanding of U.S. popular culture. A glimpse into the 1970s DHARMA Initiative reveals a Westernized, heavily "white" culture complete with music and clothing reflecting a post-hippies' Ann Arbor–influenced society; Ann Arbor, Michigan, home to the DeGrootes who began the DHARMA Initiative, also is the site of a university well-known for its free-thinking students during this time period.

Almost everyone on the Island(s) seems to understand Sawyer-speak; few references need to be explained. With the exception of Karl, who's never seen *The Brady Bunch* and doesn't know why Sawyer calls him "Bobby" ("Stranger in a Strange Land," 3.9), no one seems "lost" in their understanding of U.S. popular culture—a political statement itself. Everyone in the world has been exposed to U.S. television and movies, at least as much as and usually more than critically acclaimed literature from the past thousand years.

Lost doesn't limit its references to only the best-known television series or movies. Only *Lost*'s literary references truly span the globe (see Chapter One for a rundown of the most important ancestor texts). Many characters seem to have read and reference the same books: Locke and Henry/Ben analyze Dostoyevsky's *The Brothers Karamazov*; Ben and Sawyer discuss *Of Mice and Men*; Desmond adores the works of Charles Dickens but also reads Irish author Flann O'Brien's *The Third Policeman*; Locke remembers *Gilgamesh* when filling out a crossword; the Others seem to read everything from Stephen King's *Carrie* to Stephen Hawking's *A Brief History of Time*; Jack reads *Alice in Wonderland* to toddler Aaron, just as his father read the book to him as a favorite bedtime story.

More than most entertainment series, *Lost* brings previously obscure works to the public's attention; it makes some usually overlooked books popular, simply because *Lost* fans go out of their way to find (and often buy) any possible source of clues to the series' mysteries. Fans who may never have heard of, much less read, "An Occurrence at Owl Creek Bridge" expand their literary knowledge once the story is shown on *Lost*. Dickens is a well-known author, but *Our Mutual Friend* is hardly as commonly read as *Oliver Twist* (which Sawyer calls Charlie, "Tricia Tanaka Is Dead," 3.10) or *A Christmas Carol*. H. G. Wells' lesser-known *The Shape of Things to Come* (4.9) serves as an episode title as well as a clue to the castaways' post-Island future. In the same episode, Ben uses "Dean

Moriarty" as his alias during a trip to Tunisia; although "Moriarty" is commonly associated with Sherlock Holmes, Dean Moriarty is a principal character in Beat novelist Jack Kerouac's *On the Road*. *The Little Prince* provides another dual reference to privileged Aaron's upbringing with surrogate mother Kate as well as veiled references to the plot of Antoine de Saint-Exupéry's novel. Although the book has been translated from French and is a global bestseller, it probably isn't as well known in the United States as other ostensibly children's books. *Lost* not only references pop culture but makes lesser-known works more popular among the series' fans—and with an audience in the multimillions internationally, previously unknown artists or works gain quite a bit of notoriety. (The same process occurs, if more subtly, with music. See Chapter Two for a discussion of artists and songs used in episodes.)

Television audiences around the world not only are "bonding" over the widely syndicated and highly successful *Lost*, but they also are learning even more about Western popular culture by investigating the meanings behind *Lost*'s many references. *Lost* is socializing fans to the pervasive, now international culture promulgated by television and film, but it also pays a great deal of attention to the literary tradition; it's helping to bring everyone up to speed on cultural touchstones that the series' creators (and thus their characters) believe are important.

Although *Lost* remains trendsetting, and many critics and fans believe Seasons Four and Five's episodes are the best ever—or at least as good as those in groundbreaking Season One—the series' instant first-season success couldn't be sustained indefinitely. *Lost* made an amazing comeback after a largely disappointing third season, but its ever-denser mythology has increasingly limited its core audience each week. As well, popular culture changes rapidly, and audiences eagerly anticipate the next big trend. In 2005, it was serials and more science fiction, based in large part on *Lost*'s success, which almost every producer wanted to copy. The trend in 2007 was to move away from complex serials and back toward shorter story arcs and easy-to-understand plotlines. Although 2007–2008 saw the arrival of more quirky fantasies (e.g., ABC's *Pushing Daisies* or *Eli Stone*), devilish supernatural comedies (e.g., *Reaper*), or vampiric romances (e.g., *Moonlight*), nothing in the strike-plagued shortened TV season captured audience's attention as much as *Lost* did during its first season. Notably, all these series new in

2007–2008 lasted two or fewer seasons. Most series new in 2008–2009 suffered a similar sudden death. The time-tripping adventures in *Lost*'s Season Five provided many answers to fan questions (e.g., What happened to Rose and Bernard? and Vincent? What about that four-toed statue? Will Charlie's DS ring ever be found?). However, a faster plot and multiple time/location shifts also kept fans and critics hooked. Even if *Lost* is no longer the shiny new series people "have" to see, it continues to grab the attention of clue-seeking, mystery-loving, detail-obsessed fans and critics. *Lost* has forever changed the landscape of popular culture.

Chapter Four

WAKING THE DEAD

The cliché says, "You can't keep a good man down." On *Lost*, that's very true, but not only for good men—or women. Even the questionably good, downright bad, as yet unknown, or simply mysterious have the chance for a cosmic "do-over." One of the best "buried" treasures, and one that resurfaces far more often than might be expected, is the "dead," who have quite an active afterlife on *Lost*.

Given the number of "dead" characters who seem to inhabit the Island and make trips to the mainland to visit loved ones, almost any character may be dug up for further adventures. After seeing firsthand all the Island can do, Ben may have anticipated Alex as his judge when Locke (or "Not Locke," an impostor taking dead Locke's form) guides him into the temple to confront his past. Whatever Ben expects when he returns to the Island to receive his punishment, he likely never believes that Smoky/Alex will allow him to live. Ben may have gone into the temple to face death, but instead he is forced to live, not as a leader, but as Locke's follower ("Dead Is Dead," 5.12). Perhaps only Jacob truly knows who lives, who dies, who gains immortality, who returns (and how and why), but even he apparently dies in the Season Five finale. Whether he stays dead for long is debatable.

Those who died in the first half of *Lost* began to return more frequently beginning in Season Four; even characters who might not seem as important in the overall story, such as Ben's gunned-down daughter Alex, returned in Season Five, with more comebacks promised for

Season Six. Before Season Five, Tania (Alex) Raymonde confided to *TV Guide* that she'd been asked if she'd be willing to come back to the series. She agreed that the possibility of turning up again "would be *so* cool."[44] And cool it was to see avenging Alex make her father relive his fondest moments with her, as well as her death.

As the cast began filming Season Five episodes in August 2008, one of the hottest news items was the return of Ana Lucia, but her role was carefully kept secret.[45] Indeed, Ana Lucia is the traffic cop who pulls over a fleeing-from-the-law Hurley. Although Ana Lucia was a character fans either vehemently hated or loved during Season Two, her reappearance generated plenty of smiles. She warns Hurley how to act so that he won't appear suspicious to police, and her parting "Libby says hello" is a shout-out to another deceased character apparently alive in some type of after-death ("The Lie," 5.2). With this track record in mind, fans expect more of the same for *Lost*'s final season.

The following death roll (Table 4) for Seasons One–Five illustrates many possibilities for the "undead" to return during Season Six:

LOST'S BODY COUNT

Dead	Killed/Death Caused by	Cause of Death	Episode
Matthew Abaddon	Ben	Gunshot	The Life and Death of Jeremy Bentham
Alex	Martin Keamy	Gunshot	The Shape of Things to Come
Alvarez	The Island	Filling pulled through his brain by electromagnetism	Some Like it Hoth
Andropov	Sayid	Gunshot	He's Our You

Dead	Killed/Death Caused by	Cause of Death	Episode
Leslie Arzt	Accident	Dynamite explosion	Exodus
Peter Avellino	Sayid	Gunshot	The Economist
Ishmael Bakir	Sayid	Gunshot	The Shape of Things to Come
Mikhail (Patchy) Bukunin	Desmond, his own hand	Spear-gun; grenade	Through the Looking Glass
Ben's opera-tive in the videotape	Charles Widmore (?)	?	The Other Woman
Bonnie	Mikhail Bakunin	Gunshot	Through the Looking Glass
Brennan (member of Rousseau's party)	Danielle Rousseau	Gunshot	This Place is Death
Tom Brennan	Kate	Gunshot (accidental)	Born to Run
Edmond Burke (Juliet's husband)	Juliet's wish	Hit by a bus	Not in Portland
Juliet Burke		Dragged into the Swan drill site and (most likely) killed in a nuclear blast	The Incident

Dead	Killed/Death Caused by	Cause of Death	Episode
Caesar	Ben	Gunshot	Dead Is Dead
Boone Carlyle	Locke	The crash of the drug plane	Do No Harm
Christian Shephard's patient	Christian Shephard	Malpractice	All the Best Cowboys Have Daddy Issues
Copilot of Ajira 316	Plane crash landing	Impaled by a tree branch	Pilot
Anthony Cooper	Sawyer	Garroted	The Brig
Ana Lucia Cortez	Michael	Gunshot	Two for the Road
Cunning-ham	Charles Widmore	Neck snapped	Jughead
Michael Dawson	Mercenaries	Explosion of the freighter	There's No Place Like Home
DHARMA Initiative	Ben	Poison gas (aka the Purge)	The Man Behind the Curtain
Naomi Dorritt	Locke	Knife in the back	Through the Looking Glass
Mister Eko	Smokezilla	Crushed by Smokezilla	The Cost of Living
Elsa	Sayid	Gunshot	The Economist
Daniel Faraday	Eloise Hawking	Gunshot	The Variable
Nikki Fernandez	Castaways	Buried alive	Exposé

Dead	Killed/Death Caused by	Cause of Death	Episode
Tom Friendly	Sawyer	Gunshot	Through the Looking Glass
Frogurt (Neil)	The Hostiles	Flaming arrow	Jughead
Captain Gault	Martin Keamy	Gunshot	Cabin Fever
Horace Goodspeed	The Purge (initiated by Ben)	Poison gas	The Man Behind the Curtain
Greta	Mikhail Bakunin	Gunshot	Through the Looking Glass
Hostile (about to shoot Kate)	Sayid	Gunshot	Follow the Leader
Hostile (attacking Amy and Paul)	Sawyer	Gunshot	LaFleur
Hostile (attacking Amy and Paul)	Sawyer	Gunshot	LaFleur
Kelvin Inman	Desmond	A fall, a blow to the head	Live Together, Die Alone
Jacob (possibly)	Ben (at Not Locke's bidding)	Stabbed	The Incident
Wayne Janssen (Kate's father)	Kate	Gas explosion	What Kate Did

Dead	Killed/Death Caused by	Cause of Death	Episode
Noor Abed Jazeem (Nadia)	Ishmael Bakir (possibly at Widmore's orders) or at Jacob's bidding or an accident	Hit by a car	The Shape of Things to Come; The Incident
Kahana crew	Martin Keamy	C4 explosion triggered by Keamy's death	There's No Place Like Home
Karl	Mercenaries	Gunshot	Meet Kevin Johnson
Martin Keamy	Ben	Stabbed	There's No Place Like Home
Beatrice Klugh	Mikhail Bakunin	Gunshot	Enter 77
Kocol	An anonymous Other	Neck snapped	There's No Place Like Home
Lacombe (member of Rousseau's party)	Danielle Rousseau	Gunshot	This Place Is Death
Lacour	The Others	Unknown	There's No Place Like Home
Jae Lee	Suicide	Jumped from a hotel window	The Glass Ballerina
Charlotte Staples Lewis	The Island	Time sickness	This Place Is Death

Dead	Killed/Death Caused by	Cause of Death	Episode
Libby	Michael	Gunshot	Two for the Road
Roger Linus	Ben	Poison gas	The Man Behind the Curtain
John Locke	Ben	Strangulation	The Life and Death of Jeremy Bentham
Edward Mars	Oceanic 815 crash, Sawyer, Jack	Injuries, gunshot, euthanasia	Tabula Rasa
Mattingly	Locke	Knife wound	Jughead
Jason McCormick	Ana Lucia	Gunshot	Two for the Road
George Minkowski	The Island	Time sickness	The Constant
Montand (member of Rousseau's party)	Smoky	Ripped off arm, dragged into Smokezilla's lair	This Place Is Death
Nadine (member of Rousseau's party)	Smoky	"Eaten" by Smoky	This Place Is Death
Nathan	Goodwin	Broken neck	The Other 48 Days
Seth Norris, (the pilot of Oceanic 815)	Smoky	Smokezilla-ed	The Pilot

Dead	Killed/Death Caused by	Cause of Death	Episode
Omar	Martin Keamy	Redirected grenade	There's No Place Like Home
Charlie Pace	Mikhail Bakunin	Grenade explosion, drowning	Through the Looking Glass
Paolo	Castaways	Buried alive	Expose
Passengers of Oceanic 815	Accident (likely caused by Desmond's failure to push the button)	Plane crash	The Pilot
Paul	The Hostiles	Gunshot	LaFleur
Phil	The Incident	Impaled by rebars	The Incident
Colleen Pickett	Sun	Gunshot	The Glass Ballerina
Danny Pickett	Juliet	Gunshot	Not in Portland
Ryan Pryce	Hurley	Run over by the DHARMA van	Through the Looking Glass
Stuart Radzinsky	Suicide	Gunshot	Live Together, Die Alone
Ray (doctor on freighter)	Martin Keamy	Gunshot	Cabin Fever
Redfern	The Others	Stun dart, electrocution	There's No Place Like Home
Regina	Suicide	Jumped off freighter	Ji Yeon
Ethan Rom	Charlie Pace	Gunshot	Homecoming

Dead	Killed/Death Caused by	Cause of Death	Episode
Danielle Rousseau	Mercenaries	Gunshot	Meet Kevin Johnson
Robert Rousseau	Danielle Rousseau	Gunshot	This Place Is Death
Shannon Rutherford	Ana Lucia	Gunshot	The Other 48 Days
Christian Shephard	Natural causes	Heart attack	White Rabbit
Goodwin Stanhope	Ana Lucia	Impaled on a spear	The Other 48 Days
Talbot, Peter	Anthony Cooper	Unknown	The Man from Tallahassee
Widmore (?) operative in Miles' audition	Unknown	Unknown	Some Like It Hoth
Widmore Operative 1 at Sayid's Safe House	Sayid	Pushed over a railing and fell to his death	Because You Left
Widmore Operative 2 at Sayid's Safe House	Sayid	Impaled by kitchen knives in a dishwasher	Because You Left
Widmore Operative outside Hurley's mental hospital	Sayid	Gunshot	There's No Place Like Home

Dead	Killed/Death Caused by	Cause of Death	Episode
Widmore Operatives (numerous)	Sayid	Gunshot	Various
Yemi	Drug Dealers	Gunshot	The 23rd Psalm

Lost's lifespan of six seasons allows, even encourages, more characters to die and possibly return, in some form, to finish what they feel they need to complete. After all, redemption is another big theme on *Lost*.

THE MEANING OF DEATH

By Season Four, fans had become so accustomed to seeing the dead return to the series, either in flashbacks or current time, that when John Locke (or Jeremy Bentham) was revealed to be the man in the coffin, they didn't worry too much about the loss of a favorite character. Ben's instruction to Jack to bring Locke's body along with the Oceanic Sixers on a return to the Island ("There's No Place Like Home," 4.17) indicated Locke's continuing importance, both to the Island and *Lost*'s plot.

At the end of Season Five, Locke's body again is revealed as part of the finale's cliffhanger ("The Incident," 5.17). The man fans see as "Locke" is not be the man they thought he was. Is "Not Locke" the revitalized island protector in a new version of his dead body? Is he Jacob's nemesis in shape-shifter disguise (in summer 2009 the most likely possibility)? Is he another Smoky illusion, like that of Yemi, who fools Mr. Eko into thinking he is the real deal ("The Cost of Living," 3.5), or who, like the image of Alex, makes Ben promise to do exactly what Locke says ("Dead Is Dead," 5.12)? All of the above? In whatever form, "Locke" continues to be an intriguing character, before, during, and after death.

Locke's apparent resurrection seems to stump Ben, who has seen enough death on the Island to know when something strange(r) is going on. Although the Island's healing powers are well documented, according to Ben, "Dead is dead," and the Island hasn't ever truly resurrected anyone ("Dead Is Dead," 5.12).

According to Terry (Locke) O'Quinn, Ben is right—Locke is really, truly, unalterably (even in the *Lost*verse) dead. Soon after the Season Five finale was broadcast, O'Quinn stated that "[U]nfortunately, I think it's ended for Locke. But I'm still there, as far as I know. I don't know how it's going to end for this other guy [a new character he'll play in Season Six]. I'm sad. I miss John Locke, poor guy. He was a pawn."[46] Instead, during Season Six, O'Quinn may play "Not Locke," the impostor revealed during the Season Five finale—Jacob's nemesis, who some fans have dubbed Esau.[47] If that is indeed the case, O'Quinn may end his long *Lost* days playing an immortal or a very long-lived character who may have the ability to look like anyone else, including the John Locke of the series' first four and a half seasons.

Nevertheless, Locke's importance as a character continues into the final season. As O'Quinn commented, the shift may be leading to a confrontation among characters, a way of "setting up good and evil. It's the way Locke said in the very beginning of the show: One is light, and one is dark. Two sides. I think that's what we've got."[48] Matthew Fox seems to concur; a June 2009 interview revealed that "like the recent clash between Jack (Fox) and Sawyer (Josh Holloway), Locke (Terry O'Quinn) and the doctor 'will come head to head.'" Furthermore, Fox hinted, the series will end in "an incredibly powerful, very sad and beautiful way," with the denoument "very satisfying and cathartic and redemptive and beautiful."[49]

According to some fans' speculation, Jack soon will join Locke among *Lost*'s dead.[50] One of the many theories popular in summer 2009 was that dealing with the finality of death is *the* important theme of *Lost*. All possibilities of cheating death are simply ways for the audience, like the characters, to come to terms with the meaning of their life and the understanding that it one day will end. With so much emphasis on life and death, the dead and "undead" among the living, *Lost*'s whole purpose thus would be to provide "a narrative to explore Big Themes, maybe the biggest theme of all: Our acceptance—and denial—of death."[51]

The conflict between good and evil, the nature of life or death, the need to face past actions and either seek redemption or face judgment—*Lost*'s long story embodies these themes and forces fans to consider such weighty issues at least in light of their favorite characters' development. With so much emphasis on the ramifications of the choices now-dead characters made and how they affect those still living, it's no wonder that most characters need more time to grapple with all their unresolved issues and damaged relationships. After all, the series is called *Lost*. Coming to terms with the past—their own and that of the deceased—is an important part of (Island) life.

SEASON SIX: THE ZOMBIE SEASON

True to form, the hottest early rumors circulating about Season Six are which formerly dead characters may gain new life in *Lost*'s final episodes. Emilie (Claire) de Ravin signed a contract for the full season; Carlton Cuse verified this news by telling the press "Damon (Lindelof) and I are very excited to bring Claire back to the show…[a]nd even more excited for people to experience just how she will return."[52]

Of course, a comment like this prompts *Lost* fans, including TV critics, to begin speculating on just what Cuse means. Doc Jensen, one of the most respected *Lost* theorists, responded in this way:

Any scenario that brings Claire back to Lost must address the mysterious circumstances of her disappearance at the end of Season Four, in which many of us were led to believe that she was as dead—or rather, undead—as the Ghost Christian that's been haunting The Island since Season One. So here's one thought: Juliet changed time in the season finale by detonating Jughead, and Season Six will tell the story of the new timeline, one in which Claire is alive. Another thought: In light of the revelation that John Locke was actually a supernatural impostor for half of Season Five, perhaps in Season Six, we'll get a storyline in which Claire just emerges out of the jungle…this the real Claire or another impostor…? Heck, maybe that's going to be the major idea of next season: Who's really alive and who's really (un)dead? It really will be the fabled zombie season of Lost!

Whether playing a zombie or a still-alive Juliet in an altered timeline, Elizabeth Mitchell, signed for another ABC series, *V*, reportedly will be in at least a few Season Six *Lost* episodes.[53] Fan sites along with entertainment news outlets initially took the bait that both Dominic (Charlie) Monaghan and Maggie (Shannon) Grace would be back for a few episodes. After the feeding frenzy died down, neither Grace's nor Monaghan's representatives would confirm the rumors,[54] although fans clearly hoped for the return of Charlie and Shannon. Nevertheless, fans expect more surprises in casting news and character returns during Season Six.

Even characters who so far have escaped the ax (or bomb, Smoky, flaming arrows, etc.) may not live to see the series' finale; many fans speculate if Jack Shephard, the first character seen in the pilot episode, lives to be the last man standing. On the other hand, perhaps Jacob somehow saves those he touched or met with off-Island (e.g., Jack, Kate, Sawyer, Hurley, Locke, Sun, Jin, Sayid) to survive longer than anyone else. After all, Richard Alpert thinks that his long life is directly attributable to Jacob. Whether or not these characters survive as what most mortals would consider "dead" has yet to be determined.

The beauty of *Lost* is that many characters may be added or deleted to a cast list each season, which increases the pool of potential characters to be reinserted into the story anywhere or when. Not all characters, however, may return in the flesh, so to speak. After all, when Hurley mentions that Mr. Eko plays chess with him or Charlie sends yet another message, the actors who played those roles may not actually be seen on screen. Although M. Night Shamayalan taught us in *The Sixth Sense* that we "see dead people," on *Lost* we may hear from or about them as often as we see them.

The dead are always with us—and in full view of at least some characters—throughout *Lost*'s first five seasons, with some characters making multiple guest appearances. In fact, all we know of Jack's father, Christian Shephard, comes from flashbacks and his often mute visits to the Island. Only in a webisode shortly before Season Three began does Christian voice a line on the Island; he instructs Vincent to awaken Jack, who has just survived a plane crash, because "he has work to do."[55] Once Christian makes himself at home in Jacob's cabin, he apparently becomes much more talkative. The dead seem to know much more than their living friends or relatives; because they seem more at peace after death than they ever were while alive, the living castaways and audience want to know just how they came by that peace. The living are lost; the dead seem to have found everything they needed but lacked in life.

Lost so far has offered no definitive answers but presents many possibilities, which can be interpreted scientifically, metaphysically, or science fictionally, depending upon the viewer's life experiences and belief system. In the *Lost*verse, the following types of "metaphysical human entities" regularly show up to offer advice or give direction to the castaways or Oceanic Six: supernatural spirits who may take corporeal form, possibly by occasionally shape shifting[56] (e.g., Jacob, "Esau"), illusions presumably created by Smoky (e.g., Yemi, Alex),[57] apparitions (e.g., Christian, Charlie, Libby, Ana Lucia), and dream-visions (e.g., Charlie's dream of his mother, Eko's dream of Yemi, Locke's vision of Boone).

Table 5 lists some of *Lost*'s strange encounters with characters known or presumed to be dead. Some characters, such as Dave—who may be one of Esau's forms, just like "Not Locke"—hasn't been included in the list for lack of a definitive category; Hurley may have really seen Dave, or he may, uniquely, be one of Hurley's hallucinations. Jacob receives his own section after the list instead of a mere mention in the following table. Richard Alpert also lacks a definitive category. He reminds Horace about his other-than-mortal status when he says that the sonic fence can't stop him ("LaFleur," 5.8). Although Alpert seems as "real" as other living characters, he apparently is kept living; we don't know if he's ever died or is another one of the "undead." He so far defies easy categorization.

MESSAGES FROM THE LIVING DEAD

Episode	Character	Sighting	By	Type of Encounter	Message from Beyond
Walk-about	Christian Shephard	On the Island	Jack	Vision/Hallucination	None. Seen but not heard
White Rabbit	Christian Shephard	On the Island	Jack	Vision/Hallucination	None. Seen but not heard

Episode	Character	Sighting	By	Type of Encounter	Message from Beyond
?	Ana Lucia	On the Island	Mr. Eko	Vision/ Hallucination	Presence makes Eko aware of her death
?	Yemi	On the Island	Mr. Eko	Dream	"Help John."
Further Instructions	Boone Carlyle (showing Locke still-living castaways' future)	On the Island (in Locke's sweat lodge)	Locke	Vision/ Hallucination	Clean up your mess, among others.
The Cost of Living	Yemi	On the Island (in Eko's tent)	Mr. Eko	Dream	Warning of danger
The Cost of Living	Yemi	On the Island (close to his plane's crash site)	Mr. Eko	Vision/ Possible encounter with Smoky	Eko forced to justify his actions
The Beginning of the End	Charlie Pace	In a convenience store (California)	Hurley	Apparition	None. Seen but not heard.
The Beginning of the End	Charlie Pace	In a police interrogation room (California)	Hurley	Apparition	"They need you," written on Charlie's hand.

Episode	Character	Sighting	By	Type of Encounter	Message from Beyond
The Beginning of the End	Charlie Pace	At Santa Rosa mental institution (California)	Hurley and another mental patient	Apparition	"They need you," among others.
Meet Kevin Johnson	Libby	In a New York City hospital	Michael	Possible hallucination	None. Seen but not heard.
Meet Kevin Johnson	Libby	On the freighter	Michael/Kevin	Apparition	"Don't, Michael."
Something Nice Back Home	Christian Shephard	In the jungle	Claire	Apparition	None. Seen but not heard, as he happily holds Aaron and then leads Claire into the jungle.
Cabin Fever	Horace Goodspeed	On the Island	Locke	Dream	Directions for finding a map to Jacob's cabin.
Cabin Fever	Christian Shephard and (possibly dead) Claire	In Jacob's cabin	Locke	Apparition	Claiming to speak for Jacob, Christian reveals the message: "Move the Island."

Episode	Character	Sighting	By	Type of Encounter	Message from Beyond
There's No Place Like Home	(possibly dead) Claire	In Aaron's bedroom in Kate's house, Los Angeles	Kate	Dream	Hovering near her child, Claire warns Kate not to let "him" take Aaron back to the Island.
Because You Left	Dan Faraday (although still alive at the time)	At the Swan Hatch	Desmond	Dream/ Induced memory	Trapped in the past, Dan tells Desmond to find his mother at Oxford.
The Lie	Ana Lucia (Libby implied)	On the streets of LA	Hurley	Apparition	Ana Lucia instructs Hurley on how to stay away from the law; she also says Libby says hello.

Episode	Character	Sighting	By	Type of Encounter	Message from Beyond
This Place Is Death	Christian Shephard	In the tunnel at the bottom of the well, leading to the Donkey Wheel	Locke	Apparition	Christian guides Locke to the wheel so that he can get time back on track and leave the Island to solve the greater problem. He says the journey may cost Locke his life. "That's why they call it sacrifice."
The Life and Death of Jeremy Bentham	Christian Shephard (via Locke)	None—message delivered by Locke	Jack	Locke delivers the message.	Locke tells Jack that his father says hello.

Episode	Character	Sighting	By	Type of Encounter	Message from Beyond
Namaste	Christian Shephard	In the ruins of New Otherton	Sun and Frank Lapidis	Apparition	When Sun asks to see Jin, who is in the DHARMA Initiative photo Christian shows her, he tells them, "You have a bit of a journey ahead of you."
Dead Is Dead	Alex	In Smoky's underground lair	Ben	Illusion created by Smoky	She tells him to follow Locke's instructions and not try to kill him.

Notice how the number of messages from the dead and the number of people who have such experiences increase as the plot thickens. Although the "undead" have the mysterious island and death in common, their experiences in life and their purpose in the story vary. In this chapter, we'll look at some interesting and different roles the dead play in this series.

JACOB

On *Lost*, many people die but still live on in the story and return as messengers to the living, but one of the most enigmatic characters, Jacob, most often brings instructions. Lindelof and Cuse's build up to Jacob's first in-the-flesh appearance during the finale of Season Five helped create the mystery so essential to the mastermind behind the Island—and perhaps all the Island's mysteries. After all, the Hawking-Widmore connections to the Island revealed during Season Five only explain what the DHARMA Initiative and its former followers have learned from Richard Alpert and by living on the Island—the mystery as to how it all began may depend on our further understanding of who, or what, Jacob is. Along the way, we've had some tantalizing clues and multiple potential red herrings:

- Is Jacob's eye peering back at Hurley through the cabin window ("The Beginning of the End," 4.1)?

- Is Jacob the one in the rocking chair—or is the glimpse really of Christian Shephard, who seems very familiar with Jacob's cabin and later tells Locke that he speaks on Jacob's behalf ("Cabin Fever," 4.11)?

- Is Jacob responsible for making the Island "work"? Who else could command "move the Island" and have master game-player Ben and faithful Locke rush to the Orchid Station to make the seemingly impossible come true ("Cabin Fever," 4.11; "There's No Place Like Home," 4.12)? With the revelation that the Island can move in space and time came questions whether or not Jacob is timeless and truly godlike.

During Season Five's latter episodes, the revelations about Jacob increase, leading to his appearance at the beginning of the finale. Richard Alpert, who never seems to age, no matter when *Lost*'s time-traveling characters turn up on the Island, eventually explains to returned-from-the-dead Locke that he thinks Jacob wanted him to be ageless ("The Incident," 5.15). If this is true, Jacob has the power of life and death. He can stave off aging and manipulate the destinies of Richard and the Oceanic Six, at least, although his inference at the beginning of "The Incident" that the *Black Rock* would be arriving soon indicates prescience of its imminent wreck. Jacob thus seems as godlike as fans long have speculated he may be.

Richard's role has been revealed as an advisor to the many shorter-lived humans living on the Island and as a messenger on behalf of Jacob. Thus, Alpert's immortality seems pragmatic for Jacob, not Richard, who simply accepts what Jacob has given him and plays his role in the Island's history, neither relishing his longevity nor decrying it. He simply does his job, decade after decade.

In the Season Five finale ("The Incident," 5.15–16), Jacob not only seems godlike but may indeed be the Egyptian god Anubis, under whose statue he lives. If Jacob is Anubis and has been on the Island since ancient Egyptian times—or before—that explains the many references to Egyptian culture, such as hieroglyphics and Richard's penchant for guyliner.[58] Amy, Horace's wife and Ethan's mother, prominently wears or clutches an ankh in "LaFleur" (5.8). The full statue of Anubis holds an ankh, typically regarded as symbolizing eternal life. Jacob certainly seems to have that capability (despite his apparent murder in the Season Five finale), and Amy may want that for her soon-to-be-born child. In fact, Horace becomes concerned about Amy's love for him because she insists on keeping the ankh of her first husband, who was killed by "hostiles." Perhaps Horace (a spelling variant on another Egyptian deity, Horus, who most often is depicted as a protector of his people) really worries that Amy's first husband may return from the dead.

After all, Anubis judges the dead and guides them toward the underworld, rather like Christian Shephard as Locke's guide through the tunnels leading to the Donkey Wheel of Time; even Smoky as lie detector and bringer of life or death bears an uncanny similarity to Anubis' role.

In "The Incident" (5.15–16), funerals and funeral rites become the focus of key scenes. Anubis is also in charge of funerals and funeral rites. Locke's embalmed body is carried through the jungle to be presented to Jacob but is intercepted by Richard and revealed to the audience as being the "mystery" inside the casket. In flashback, Jacob talks with James Ford as he begins his fateful "Dear Mr. Sawyer" letter at his parents' funeral. Soon after Jacob's meeting with Sawyer, the caskets heading for burial are placed in the waiting hearse.

The presence of "Esau" increases the number of questions about Jacob's role, his intercession with the Oceanic Six, and his ability truly to bring the dead back to life. If "Esau" is a shape-shifter currently taking the appearance of John Locke, then is he also connected to (or the same as) Smoky, who changes shape and at least heralds the arrival of the familiar dead to talk to their living relatives? In other words, does Smoky create the image of Alex or Yemi, or does it merely meet out judgment? Does another entity ("Esau"? Jacob?) shift into the appropriate form?

Fans have previously assumed that Christian, Charlie, Ana Lucia, et al. are the dead brought back to life. Are the "living dead" from previous episodes really the dead somehow brought back, or are they merely "costumes" that a shape-shifter wears to infiltrate the lives of the living? Is Ben right, and "dead is dead?" Or can Anubis keep some souls from entering the underworld yet so that they become messengers on his behalf? The symbolism surrounding Anubis and the conflicting symbolism of the biblical Jacob-Esau story present fans with plenty of ways to interpret the roles of the dead, as well as Jacob and his counterpart.

Although the Jacob-Anubis connection may be fan speculation at this point, Jacob certainly influences, if not controls, the lives of those who are mysteriously brought to the Island. During "The Incident"'s first scenes, Jacob alludes to the social evolution of humans, wondering if they will surpass their propensity to destroy each other before the end of the world. Jacob and his counterpart, possibly representing the extremes of Good and Evil, seem immortal.

Jacob wears white on the Island; his counterbalance, or "Esau," for lack of a better name, in the opening scene wears black. However, off the Island, Jacob wears dark clothes. The change from light to dark seems like a deliberate costuming choice, and black and white are potent symbols on *Lost*. Many fans question whether Jacob works for good or evil, based on his off-Island interactions with those who will one day live on the Island.

Although Jacob permits, and sometimes even encourages, those he visits to choose their own course of action, his influence may instead turn characters away from good choices and toward those that will eventually prove their undoing. Each time Jacob is shown interacting with a character off the Island, sometimes many years in advance of Oceanic 815's crash, his ambiguous statements or actions can be interpreted either as good or bad:

- Does Jacob save Sayid from being killed by a hit-and-run driver? Or does Jacob distract Sayid so that he can't push Nadia out of the way of a car he, but not she, would see in time?

- Does Jacob save little Katie from the police when she is caught shoplifting, or does he show her that she may get away with crime because he pays the clerk for her lunch box?

- Does Jacob convince Hurley that seeing the dead is a blessing (one that Anubis could understand) or merely con him into doing his bidding because he understands Hurley's "gift?"

- Is Jacob's pronouncement to newlyweds Jin and Sun to "never take your love for granted" a reminder to save them future grief or a curse indicating what he hopes will take place?

- Does Jacob really support Jack emotionally against his father's tutelage in and out of the operating room, or does he merely want to provide a counterargument in order to manipulate Jack more effectively? After all, Christian Shephard will become an important force for "controlling" Jack on the Island, and Jacob might be up for a game of "good cop, bad cop." Is Jacob subtly luring Jack to the Island by handing over an Apollo bar that Jack couldn't get from the vending machine himself?

- Is Jacob waiting for Locke's inevitable fall before going to comfort him and give him hope for his eventual healing, or does he refuse to intercede so that Locke will suffer the fall?

Jacob seems to be "good" from his reminders to Hurley and Ben that they can choose what to do—even if his demeanor and words slyly coerce them onto a particular path. Is Jacob "good," a reminder that humans have free will and can choose their action, free of fate? Or is he "evil," showing up at pivotal emotional points in a character's development to sow those seeds of doubt or to make one path seem imminently more attractive than another? Furthermore, Jacob seems to weave time, just like the mythologized Fates wove the destinies of people. Jacob seems to be taking that role off Island and on. Despite reminding characters that they have a choice, the Island life of many later castaways does seem to be preordained.

For all the Egyptian symbolism or even Greek mythology, there is also a heavily Christian element, well noted by fans who named Jacob's nemesis "Esau" in reference to the biblical story of feuding brothers Jacob and Esau. Jacob steals Esau's birthright, proving to be a crafty opportunist, just as Island Jacob seems to be. Island "Esau" also seems all too eager to vent his hatred on Jacob and eventually finds a way to kill him, although suspicion runs high that Jacob isn't so easily dispatched.

Then there's Ben's comment that "Locke" is allowed to enter Jacob's home like Moses coming up the path. Moses asked the Egyptians to let his people go free, and who's more Egyptian than Anubis? Is the foreshadowing of "Locke"'s promise to Ben that, after Jacob dies, "things will change once he's gone," an indication of change for the better or worse ("The Incident," 5.16)? Jacob may not look Egyptian to the audience, but he does seem to have a great deal of godlike control over who comes and goes on the Island.

Yet one more way to analyze Jacob's relationship with "Locke" involves *Lost*'s continuing debate between the Man of Faith (Locke) and the Man of Science (Jack). During Season Five, Jack increasingly comes to believe that the Island is his destiny—a Man of Faith argument previously espoused by Locke. Even the "suicide" note that Locke leaves for Jack encourages the surgeon to open his mind: "I wish you had believed me" are Locke's final words to Jack ("316," 5.6). Although the good doctor does understand Dan Faraday's scientific explanation why Jughead might be used to blast the past and keep Oceanic 815 from crashing in the future, Jack relies more on his newfound faith that his course of action is right than empirical evidence that such a drastic action will result in the outcome he so desires. In contrast, the man who appears to be John Locke, Man of Faith, manipulates Ben to stab

Jacob. In effect, "Locke" kills his "god." Of course, when "Locke" is revealed to be "Not Locke," that imagery loses significance, but at the time fans hear "Locke" coercing Ben to kill Jacob, they have no reason to believe that this character is anyone other than the John Locke, Man of Faith, they've watched follow Jacob's orders.

Whether fans subscribe to any or all of these symbol-laden theories—or develop their own—Season Five's revelations about Jacob unearth the answers to many questions while still burying the complete truth somewhere on the Island.

APPARITIONS

Apparitions primarily are messengers to the living. During Seasons Three and Four, Boone Carlyle, Charlie Pace, and Libby all appear to still-living characters; in Season Five, Ana Lucia returns for a chat with Hurley, and Christian Shephard is busy guiding Locke, Sun, and Frank Lapidis, among others. Season Six promises the return of Claire, who seemed ghostly when fans last saw her visiting Aaron and Kate in LA. The audience, like *Lost*'s many apparition-seeing characters, must determine whether these encounters are real or imaginary. Although these characters lived, however briefly, in "real time" in the story and return later to haunt their friends, one character—who increasingly seems key to these buried treasures—has "lived" only in flashbacks. When the pilot episode introduces *Lost* via a horrendous plane crash on a mysterious island, Christian Shephard already is dead, his corpse part of Oceanic 815's cargo that lands on the Island.

Christian Shephard

"Those who are dead aren't dead / They just live inside my head"[59] may be a popular *Coldplay* lyric in the aptly symbolic "42" (not only one of Hurley's infamous Numbers but also Douglas Adam's meaning of life), but Jack (as well as Hurley) could sing this song with equal conviction. In an early Season One episode ("Walkabout," 1.4), Jack first sees an apparition of his father. He doesn't speak; he simply appears, looks at his son, and then wanders into the jungle. After another sighting ("White Rabbit," 1.5), Jack follows his father, eventually finding water in the caves, something the newly appointed Island leader needed to do. Jack is initially afraid to follow his vision, because he fears he may be going crazy. Locke counsels him that it doesn't matter whether Jack's vision is real or not, as long as he believes in it (a philosophy foreshadowing Locke's upcoming visions and dreams that guide him throughout much of the series). That advice seems to be a recurring theme concerning the living dead in the *Lost*verse.

Throughout the following seasons, Christian Shephard gained a more prominent role in the series, especially in flashbacks. Through flashback episodes, we learn more about his and Jack's troubled relationship, as well as his fathering an out-of-wedlock child, Claire. Whenever Christian Shephard appears in flashbacks as a living man, he seems emotionally isolated from his children. Jack feels he can never live up to his father's expectations but also judges his father's actions harshly when Christian increasingly turns to alcohol to relieve stress (e.g., "All the Best Cowboys Have Daddy Issues," 1.11; "Do No Harm," 1.20; "Man of Science, Man of Faith," 2.1). A Season Five flashback shows Jack berating his father for forcing him to take, in effect, a "time out" during surgery to regain his composure ("The Incident," 5.16). Claire only meets her father when he visits Sydney after her mother's car crash; when Christian suggests that Claire pull the plug on her comatose mother, she tells him she doesn't want to have anything to do with him ("Par Avion," 3.12). After death, however, the returned Christian Shephard acts more fatherly, for better or worse. The mere sight of him prompts Jack to feel guilt over what he has or hasn't done; when Claire sees her father on the Island, he is joyfully cradling grandson Aaron. Christian talks most to John Locke, however, explaining Jacob's message to him and claiming to speak on Jacob's behalf.

Dear old dad may not need words to convey messages to his children. His larger than life presence ensures that, dead or alive, he can unnerve his son. In Season Four, for example, he appears in present time to Jack at the hospital where father and son once worked together ("Something Nice Back Home," 4.10). He doesn't say anything, but his presence rattles Jack. It probably doesn't help that this encounter begins with a nagging beep-beep-beep of a fire alarm, which Jack investigates. When he finds the apparently malfunctioning smoke detector in a dark, quiet hospital lounge, he sees his father comfortably sitting on a couch, watching as Jack turns off the alarm. Jack probably wishes he could so easily turn off the alarm bells going off in his life—and his father's presence reminds him that no matter how long he may choose to ignore the warning signs, or sounds, sooner or later he'll have to deal with recurring Island issues.

Christian Shephard also makes a sudden surprise visit to Claire and, for the first time, sees his grandson Aaron ("Cabin Fever," 4.11). Awakened one night during her trek back to the beach, Claire sees her father kneeling by the campfire. Perhaps her last word as a living being is "Dad?" which may be a fitting introduction to a new (after)life. Claire then serves as a messenger to the living when, via a dream, she tells Kate not to let "him" take Aaron back to the Island ("There's No Place Like Home," 4.14). In this way, Claire, like Charlie, mysteriously looks after the baby even though she isn't physically part of his present life.

Miles later tells Sawyer that he watched Claire follow her father into the jungle, but whether both are dead (as many fans suspect) or whether Claire simply can see her dead father hasn't yet been confirmed. Her changed demeanor in Jacob's cabin and simply the act of leaving her baby behind—when she has been so protective of him to this point—indicate that the "new" Claire is vastly different from the character we've come to know.

In Season Five, Christian relies not on the past but on the present in his more active role as an Island guide. He shows Locke the light, quite literally, by arriving soon after a well cave-in. Locke seeks a way to get his friends out of their time-leaping mess; Christian shows him the way. He refuses to help Locke, who breaks his leg falling into the well, to walk (in effect making Locke stand on his own two feet), but he does show him to the Donkey Wheel so that Locke can push the off-kilter wheel back on track. Also, Christian sends another message for Locke to deliver: "Say hello to my son." Locke delivers this message to a skeptical Jack when the two are reunited in an LA hospital ("The Life and Death of Jeremy Bentham," 5.7). Although Christian is less available to his son during Season Five, at least he manages to say hello.

Christian also guides Sun and Frank when they follow Locke into the ruins of New Otherton in 2007. Spookily enticing the new arrivals into one of the cabins, Christian shows Sun a DHARMA Initiative orientation photo. Jin is in the photo, and Sun naturally wants to find him. She doesn't yet know that thirty years separate them. Christian's cryptic words convince her that he knows how she can reach him, although he warns her that she has to travel a long way ("The Life and Death of Jeremy Bentham," 5.7).

Because of his wider role and appearance to more people, Christian seems more integral to the Island's purpose and more closely associated than ever with Jacob, although the two aren't seen together. With the promised return of Claire in what Cuse and Lindelof hint will be an unusual reintroduction, Christian's role may be further enhanced in Season Six.

Boone Carlyle

Another one of the early dead characters coming back to life is Boone Carlyle. He appears to Locke during a vision quest ("Further Instructions," 3.3), and he seems to know what's going on with other characters on the Island. During that vision quest, Boone shows Locke that Kate and Sawyer will flirt and for a time be together. The dream/vision also features Desmond as a pilot surrounded by beautiful flight attendants; perhaps it is no surprise that Desmond flies off to become reunited with true love Penny ("There's No Place Like Home," 4.14). Boone also tells Locke that Claire, Charlie, and Aaron will be "Okay—for now," but his tone and word choice foreshadow troubled times for the little family. The information Boone provides helps Locke decide what to do next. Boone, like Christian Shephard and Claire, seems to be working on behalf of the Island to ensure the reality it wants/knows to come true will turn out as planned.

Locke's vision helps him deal with his guilt over Boone's death. Although he comes to accept that Boone needed to be "sacrificed" for the Island, he probably also feels guilt over the young man's death. When Boone becomes Locke's spirit guide in the dream/vision, Locke trades roles with his former mentee, who followed Locke's commands even to his death. When Boone appears as his guide, Locke gets a chance to apologize for his actions, as well as to honor the young man by following his counsel.

Charlie Pace

Another active dead character is Charlie Pace. In the Season Four opener ("The Beginning of the End," 4.1), Charlie fans were relieved to see their favorite character reappear in the present. When his pleas for understanding and his multiple appearances don't seem to get the message across to Hurley that he's returned from the dead, Charlie slaps his friend, a very physical metaphysical wake-up call. During these initial encounters, he consistently reminds Hurley that "they need you." Seeing Charlie convinces Hurley that he is indeed crazy, and he willingly returns to the Santa Rosa Mental Health Facility.

Charlie must visit his friend there regularly, because Hurley later tells Jack that Charlie has left a message for him ("Something Nice Back Home," 4.10). In fact, Charlie tells Hurley to write down the message—Jack shouldn't raise Aaron—so that he won't forget it. At that time, Jack is playing "daddy" to Aaron and living with Aaron's new "mommy," Kate. Charlie, who in life loved Aaron and looked after the baby, would certainly seem to have a vested interest in the child's welfare. After all, he sacrificed his life in order to pave the way for his "family's" rescue.

Seeing Charlie as one of the living dead not only helps Hurley come to grips with his friend's death, but it allows Charlie fans closure. By giving him a further role in the story, as well as showing him as a sexier, more confident man in the afterlife, the writers help fans get on with the story, just as Charlie gets on with his new (after)life.

Hurley also visits with Mr. Eko and tells Sayid he regularly sees dead people ("There's No Place Like Home," 4.14). In fact, his chess game with Eko is in progress when Sayid arrives. Chess, like backgammon, is an important game on Lost. Not only is it a game of strategy, but black and white symbolism has been important since the early episodes. For Hurley to be playing chess with the dead suggests his greater role in the story. If Lost represents the "game" of life, black-and-white symbols, such as backgammon or chess pieces, indicate the importance of opposites but, more importantly, that life can't be reduced to absolutes. Everyman Hurley may be the best character to come to understand that such apparent oppositions (e.g., black/white, life/death) may not be as opposite as we would like to think. Hurley's journey to this understanding may be "crazy," but it may turn out to be our journey as well. By identifying with lovable, average Hurley, audiences may see just how strange or extraordinary "reality" can be.

The link between Charlie and Hurley continues in Season Five, although Charlie doesn't make an appearance or send a new message via Hurley. Instead, Hurley arrives for his flight on Ajira Air carrying a guitar case ("316," 5.6). It arrives with him on the Island. Because the Oceanic Six are encouraged to make their Ajira 316 flight as similar to their original experience on Oceanic 815, fans assume that Hurley brings the guitar case to represent Charlie. How Hurley comes by the case is answered in the Season Five finale, when Jacob shares a taxi with Hurley, the case already inside. As Jacob exits the taxi, he leaves it behind. Ever helpful Hurley alerts him, but Jacob says that the case isn't his. Of course, that comment leads fans to wonder if the guitar case somehow is really Charlie's. Although speculation ran high in summer 2009 that Charlie would return during Season Six, how or even if he returns may indicate his "permanent" status as one of the dead, undead, or somehow still living. In any case, this character has had an enduring role in the story, which is surprising because he died about halfway through *Lost*'s six-year run.

Libby

In addition to Charlie and Boone, Libby also makes several appearances as one of the living dead in Season Four. She has unfinished business with Michael, who accidentally shot and killed her in Season Two ("Two for the Road," 2.20). When Michael is grievously injured in an aborted suicide attempt, Libby appears to him in the hospital ("Meet Kevin Johnson," 4.8). She also visits Michael when he is moments away from detonating a bomb on the freighter and tells him not to do so. When he disregards Libby's plea, he discovers that the bomb isn't real but merely a test from Ben Linus. Michael apparently needs to learn to listen to the dead. He becomes grateful for Christian Shephard's message shortly before a real bomb explodes on the freighter, killing him. Christian tells Michael that his work is finished and, in essence, gives him permission to move on to death. He had told his former friends from the Island he expected to die on the freighter as part of his penance for killing Ana Lucia and Libby, as well as leaving the Island behind. Although Michael didn't seem to be a highly spiritual character, his ability to receive "supernatural" messages may not require belief in an afterlife. The dead who need to talk with him about his actions may have been sent by the Island, and who better to get his attention, especially at first, than a woman he killed?

Although Libby isn't seen again on screen, her after-death presence still haunts Hurley. Ana Lucia makes sure to tell Hurley that his would-have-been girlfriend says hello when she, also an apparition, advises Hurley during Season Five.

DEATH BECOMES THEM

A not-so-great film's title noted that *Death Becomes Her*, a theme taken to heart on *Lost*, where the dead gain new gravitas once freed of their earthly challenges. Perhaps Jacob, or the Island, changes characters after they die, once their earthly troubles are behind them. Christian Shephard seems more decisive and confident in his role as messenger and an "insider" to Jacob's plan; as Claire lounges in the cabin, she, too, seems less concerned with her duties as Aaron's mother and acts as if she understands a grander plan, one in which she accepts that Aaron is exactly where he should be ("Cabin Fever," 4.11). Only in Kate's dream ("There's No Place Like Home," 4.14) does Claire seem agitated, adamantly telling Kate to keep Aaron away from "him"—whether Jacob, Locke, Ben, or another character is unclear.

Charlie also seems more confident and even tempered during his visits with Hurley. He relays messages to his friend as well as helps him understand the circumstances surrounding his drowning; he may not understand exactly how he can visit as a corporeal being, but he confidently explains that he's dead but also here in Hurley's present ("The Beginning of the End," 4.1).

Ana Lucia is much more relaxed and playful in her return to LA. She gives Hurley some good advice on ways to avoid the police. Post-death Ana Lucia should know; she arrives dressed as an officer, complete with pad of traffic tickets ("The Lie," 5.2). All her worries have vanished, and she seems to enjoy her conversation with Hurley.

Life after death imbues these characters with greater authority and self-assurance, not only about what they need to do but who they are. Whether their roles and images are produced by another entity or whether they really are the living dead has not yet been revealed, but the sheer number of characters whose personalities generally are improved by death indicates that whatever afterlife awaits helps characters find themselves so that they can help their friends and family. Through death, these characters may have found themselves, making them more likely to want to help the still-lost living.

Surprisingly, because conventional ghost wisdom indicates otherwise, the dead aren't bound to the place where they died or even to the Island. Christian died in a Sydney alley but first appears on the Island and later in Los Angeles; Charlie died in the Looking Glass station but visits Hurley in California; Libby died in the Hatch but travels to a New York hospital and a South Pacific freighter to visit Michael. Even Claire turns up in Kate's dream in Los Angeles. Although each appearance might be logically explained as a character's hallucination due to stress, medication, or mental illness, the number of otherworldly visitations suggests many other possible interpretations.

PROPHETIC DREAMS AND VISIONS

Many characters who return after death also received "supernatural" messages in life. In a dream, Yemi alerts Eko to danger in his tent and saves his life ("The Cost of Living," 3.5). Ana Lucia appears to Eko on the beach hours before he learns of her death, and Yemi directs his brother and Locke to a new hatch ("?"2.21). This hatch provides Locke with more information about the Others and leads Eko to a new mission. Although Locke begins to question the spiritual nature of the Island at this point, he must prove to himself that the Island does indeed have the type of power he originally attributed to it. Locke's crisis of faith, initially instigated by interpreting a vision, is later resolved by more dream-vision guidance that he believes comes from the Island. Mr. Eko, however, isn't as fortunate in the outcome of his "visions." What he thinks is a waking vision of dead Yemi ("The Cost of Living," 3.5) turns out to be a manifestation of Smoky, which evaluates and later kills him.

It likely isn't a coincidence that Charlie's dream/vision includes Hurley, who seem linked in life and death. Catholic Charlie's dreams involve the most important people in his life—Claire, his mother,

Hurley—telling him to save his surrogate son Aaron; these characters appear in the dream wearing biblical dress ("Fire + Water," 2.12), which would be an important way of getting Charlie's attention by playing into his belief system.

Just who has visions in service of Jacob or the Island is questionable, because many characters see things they can't believe are real. Some "messages" or "visits" don't seem to carry much weight beyond being strange encounters. Charlie, Hurley, Locke, Eko, and Jack have had more meaningful dream-visions or supernatural visits, but even skeptical Kate has seen a black horse from her past ("What Kate Did," 2.9), and Sayid and Sawyer, among others, can attest that the Island "whispers" (e.g., "Solitary," 1.9; "Outlaws," 1.16).

When Ben wistfully confides to Locke that he "used to have dreams" ("Cabin Fever," 4.11), he indicates that those chosen by Jacob to help the Island may be "given" insightful dreams, such as the one from which Locke has just awakened. In that dream, Horace Goodspeed—forever chopping down a tree to make a getaway cabin—tells Locke that the location of Jacob's cabin can be found in a map in the dead man's pocket. Locke remembers the pit where the bodies of the DHARMA Initiates, killed in the Purge, are decomposing, and he finds Horace's body—and the map—there. Perhaps, as many fans have speculated over the years, the Island (or Jacob or "Esau") does indeed provide the dreams or visions that people need to see in order for the Island's grand plan to be furthered.

THOSE WHO SEEK THE DEAD

In addition to characters who have waking dreams or visions, there are those who seek the dead and wholeheartedly believe in their existence. Charlotte Malkin, for example, claims to see the dead. (She also had connections with Libby and Mr. Eko shortly before Oceanic 815's departure.) Eko argues with Charlotte when she tells him she bears a message from Yemi ("The 23rd Psalm," 2.10). He believes the girl is trying to entrap him and wants nothing to do with her. Libby, who watches this encounter, intercedes, possibly believing that young Charlotte might be in danger from the angry Eko. Charlotte seems to have a psychic gift, although her father, a "professional" psychic, confesses to Eko that he is a fraud who conducts research on his clients, rather than reveals information from supernatural sources. Whether the senior Malkin has the gift of foresight or simply milks clients is unclear, but Charlotte seems a sincere young woman.

She, like other characters, including Charlie, cheat death at least once. Before Charlie's death by drowning, he suffers several near misses, the most important being hanging. When Jack brings back Charlie from the dead ("All the Best Cowboys Have Daddy Issues," 1.11), the young man seems inexplicably well for someone who was clinically dead for several minutes. That Charlie survives seems a miracle, but perhaps he was merely being prepared to be a messenger from the afterlife to the live. Unlike Charlie, Charlotte Malkin survives her drowning and comes back to life on an autopsy table ("The 23rd Psalm," 2.10). Life and death, for many of these characters, are indelibly intertwined.

Another "seer" is Desmond. He also survives a near-death experience during the Hatch's implosion. Conversely, he might've died but been brought back by the Island. It seems strange that an implosion making such a large crater—and destroying Desmond's clothing—would leave the man unscathed except for a newfound ability to see "flashes" of the future. However, his ability to see the future may be part of a larger plan set in motion by Mrs. Hawking or even Charles Widmore. Because Desmond is a time traveler who can't control his back-and-forth trips and glimpses of potential futures, his visions seem less spiritual or supernatural than the result of a scientific breakthrough in time-travel experimentation.

Desmond's primary role in Season Five results from a dream/memory Dan Faraday implants in his Constant's mind. Dan visits Desmond in his past, telling him to travel to Oxford and to find Dan's mother. When Des awakens, he perceives his vivid dream as prophetic. Following his dream, his travels eventually lead him not only to Oxford but to Charles Widmore and, in California, to Mrs. Hawking and Ben Linus. Desmond's belief in the dream message almost leads to his family's destruction, but he simply can't resist the urgency of such a dream message ("Because You Left," 5.1).

One more seer/seeker of the dead, Miles Straume, talks with the dead as part of his profession. Before coming to the Island, he makes his living by "exorcising" spirits that the living no longer want in their lives ("Confirmed Dead," 4.2) and uses information from the dead to his financial advantage. On the Island, we see him talking with Naomi's body. Although we can't hear their conversation, dead Naomi obviously tells him the truth about the way she died. That revelation convinces Miles that Kate has been telling him the truth about events leading to Naomi's death.

Miles also looks at Claire strangely during the long walk toward the beach after New Otherton is attacked ("Something Nice Back Home," 4.10). Miles "feels" something wrong and finds the shallow graves where Karl and Rousseau were hastily buried. He stares so intently at Claire that her new protector, Sawyer, warns him not to look at her again. Only after Claire abandons Aaron and follows her father to Jacob's cabin do we wonder if Miles saw Claire as one of the dead.

In a flashback to Miles' off-island childhood, he first is able to hear a dead man within a nearby apartment. Of course, the man's pleas for help go unheard by everyone else, and Miles' mother and their new landlord act less than pleased when a body is indeed found where young Miles indicates. The episode further shows Miles exploiting his ability to hear the dead in order to make as much money as possible. His special ability leads Naomi to recruit him for Charles Widmore's research trip to find the Island ("Some Like It Hoth," 5.13). Miles actively seeks the dead, although his motivation is usually money.

SPECIAL OR INSANE?

Each character who "sees" someone who, to other people, isn't there is often deemed "insane" or "crazy," a term which Hurley in particular despises. *Lost* posits that these encounters might be real or they might be induced by an altered mental state. Locke talks with Boone, who shows him glimpses of the future, only after he takes a hallucinogenic drug during a vision quest ("Further Instructions," 3.3). Jack takes clonazepam to quell his anxiety and soon after sees his dad ("Something Nice Back Home," 4.10). Religious Charlie, according to the consensus of his fellow castaways, may be saying Hail Mary's to heroin once again; at the time of his dream, he maintains a convenient stash of Virgin Mary statues full of heroin, even though he swears he's sober. During this time, his "dream" of biblically garbed Hurley, Claire, and his (likely) deceased mother tell him to save Aaron ("Fire + Water," 2.12). Mr. Eko suffers the aftereffects of a polar bear attack and the Hatch's implosion when he begins to talk with Yemi ("The Cost of Living," 3.5). When stressed out, Hurley often sees people no one else (or only other "crazy" people) can see: Dave, identified as Hurley's "imaginary" friend from the mental institution, shows up on the Island when the big man tries to give up junk food ("Dave," 2.18); now-dead Charlie shows up when Hurley has trouble coping with his return home as one of the Oceanic Six ("The Beginning of the End," 4.1).

Nevertheless, these characters often are some of the most "special" (or "chosen") people on the Island. Locke becomes important to the Others as Ben's potential rival, and even Ben worries that Locke hears, and later sees, Jacob ("The Man Behind the Curtain," 3.20). Without any intention, or even knowledge, of Jacob's cabin, Hurley seems to be summoned; no matter where he turns, he sees the cabin in front of him ("The Beginning of the End," 4.1). Ben recognizes that only Hurley may be able to find the cabin again; even Locke doesn't know where it is and may be losing his special connection with the Island ("The Shape of Things to Come," 4.9).

In Season Five, Miles and Hurley seem more confident of their respective communication skills in conversing with the dead, and the number of potentially dead characters interacting with those still alive makes such communication seem commonplace. Instead of being a novel or frightening experience, seeing or hearing the "undead" has become a regular occurrence.

Lost makes us wonder if we're the ones truly lost from the "reality" of the time-space continuum. After all, Walt's special psychic abilities have been scientifically tested by the Others; he learns how to use their equipment in order to project himself into another place in order to give his friends secret messages to help them survive, often against the Others' wishes. Knowing that Miles Straume is the son of Dr. Pierre Change (aka Marvin Candle) increases the speculation that Miles may have been affected by DHARMA Initiative research; his "ability" may have been scientifically engineered. If, as *Lost* posits, time travel is real and an important variable in the plot, then seeing the dead and sharing psychic messages are equally plausible.

Instead of focusing on which characters have died, the game going into Season Six is figuring out which characters are really alive. With Jughead's apparent detonation leading to a fade to white at the end of Season Five, perhaps *Lost*'s final episodes will be even more heavenly.

CHAPTER FIVE

THE SIGNIFICANCE OF PLACE

Lost takes us anywhere, as well as any-when, in the world. In Season Five, we sailed with Desmond, Penny, and Charlie to the United Kingdom and United States and saw where Charlie was born offshore in the Philippines. We flew Ajira Airways but, like the crew and passengers, didn't make it to Guam. Once more we traveled to NYC, this time with Locke, to see how Walt is doing, and to Oxford, past and present. A typical itinerary may not have us completely "lost," but we bounce around the globe as much as the Left Behinds bounce along the Island's timeline.

Some Hawaiian locations have stood in for distant places so often that they have widely separate geographic identities to *Lost* fans. Downtown Honolulu's Parke Chapel, with its distinctive walkways, has been cast as Queen's College, Oxford University ("The Variable," 5.14; "Jughead," 5.3; "The Constant," 4.5), a Scottish monastery and vineyard ("Catch-22," 3.17), and a Manchester parish ("The Moth," 1.7). The landmarks of the Kualoa valley and nearby fish pond represent "the Island" to most viewers, who can explore for themselves the lush landscapes—without Ben's or Smoky's interference or a sonic fence to disable.

Although filming scenes most often on Oahu, *Lost* prides itself on its global locations, and the "feel" of events and situations changes with the location. In addition to *Lost*'s chameleon quality, the series also benefits from tropical scenery and the many beautiful beach and jungle locales. Although *Lost* as a series is native to Hawaii, the international cast of characters and increasingly international intrigue make it one of the most "multinational" series ever filmed in one area. Unlike other dramas that span the globe, like *24*, *Lost* must accurately replicate dozens of very different real locations, from the past or in the present, during a single season. In Season Four, for example, *Lost* took us to Iraq, Tunisia, Scotland and England (the United Kingdom), Germany, South Korea, China, Bali, the Bahamas, and the United States. Season Five added the Dominican Republic, the Philippines, and Russia to the list—quite a feat for filming taking place on one small island in the Pacific.

Places help make people who they are, and audiences and characters often have preconceptions about others, depending on where they're from. When Juliet reminds Sayid that he doesn't need more blood on his hands, she cryptically refers to what he did in Basra ("One of Us," 3.16). The Others' vast files on the castaways, plus Ben's own visits to the region, help them understand exactly what Sayid did. Once one of the most populous cities in Iraq, the powerful port became reduced to rubble during a series of wars, including the Gulf and Iraqi Wars. Located on the "Highway of Death," the region suffered multiple bombings during the end of the 1990s; atrocities became common-place. Whatever Sayid did during the Gulf War (after being coerced by the U.S. Military to become an "interrogator") probably wasn't pleasant and most likely is something he tries to bury in his past. As Sayid's backstory is further filled in, we see Nadia's funeral in Iraq ("The Shape of Things to Come," 4.9), which provides a few more cultural details and contrasts Sayid's past with his future as Ben's assassin.

Ben apparently is a frequent visitor in the Middle East. Under the guise of "Dean Moriarty," he checks into a Tunisian hotel on October 24, 2006, between a visit (via time portal) into the Sahara Desert and Nadia's funeral in Tikrit, Iraq.[60] Basra as a location also resonates with that episode's title, "The Shape of Things to Come" (4.9), which shares the title with H. G. Wells' "future history" that features world conferences held in Basra.

During Season Five, Locke also takes an interesting route from the Island to Tunisia ("The Life and Death of Jeremy Bentham," 5.7). When he arrives, his leg broken, Charles Widmore's men retrieve him and provide medical assistance. Although we don't see much scenery beyond sand and the building where Widmore has a heart-to-heart chat with Locke, we still believe Locke has traveled far from his Island home.

Perhaps Jacob earns the most frequent flier miles. Visiting the Oceanic Six throughout their lives requires trips to Iowa and California, as well as South Korea and Russia. Each unique setting helps us realize that the world may be smaller than we first imagined, and that—although difficult to navigate—ways to and from the Island are possible. Being geographically lost from the watchful eyes of Ben Linus, Charles Widmore, or Jacob seems more difficult than we first imagined.

Any metropolis contains many distinct neighborhoods and districts, and narrowing the audience's focus to one small area provides a greater sense of place than simply showing a generic alley or apartment. Turning large cities into familiar spaces adds yet another layer of detail to *Lost* and makes it more plausible that characters might run into each other within a neighborhood or near a well-known landmark. In London, Charlie and Liam share a flat in Brixton, an interesting but (once) seedy area. During the late 1990s or early 2000s, when Charlie would have lived there, the area hadn't yet seen a resurgence of clubs and nightlife. In contrast to the Brixton Underground station close to the flat, a station in a more affluent area becomes the meeting point for Desmond and Charlie ("Flashes Before Your Eyes," 3.8). More affluent still, Charlie's girlfriend Lucy and her father live in Knightsbridge ("Homecoming," 1.15), a fashionable area with upscale shops and museums; Knightsbridge also is home to Desmond's love Penny Widmore during his incarceration ("Live Together, Die Alone," 2.23). When she agrees to answer Desmond's phone call on Christmas Eve 2004 (a strange promise made years in advance), Penny lives at 423 Cheyne Walk in London, a historic Chelsea street also favored by pre-Raphaelite painter and poet Dante Gabriel Rossetti, novelist George Eliot, Prime Minister David Lloyd George, and Rolling Stone Mick Jagger ("The Constant," 4.5). Her father likes to shop Sotheby's auctions for special items like a *Black Rock* journal, and his London home isn't a secret from Ben, who likes making a late-night visit to threaten his nemesis ("The Shape of Things to Come," 4.9).

Within Los Angeles, the Oceanic Six continue to cross paths, too. Jack returns to work at St. Sebastian Hospital but sometimes visits Hurley at the Santa Rosa Mental Health Facility. Hurley agrees to be institutionalized again after a harrowing car chase with police that begins in the La Brea district ("The Beginning of the End," 4.1). Sayid later tells Ben that Nadia died as a result of a hit-and-run at the corner of La Brea and Santa Monica ("The Shape of Things to Come," 4.9), an event we see in "The Incident" (5.17). According to Ben, Ishmael Baki, supposedly one of Widmore's operatives, was seen shortly before the accident only three blocks away, but Jacob actually is directly involved. Sayid, Kate, Jack, Aaron, Ben, Locke, Hurley, Sun, Desmond, and Penny have post-island connections in Southern California, and it turns out that even Eloise Hawking guards the Lamp Post station there ("316," 5.6). Linking so many characters within a vast urban sprawl further emphasizes that these people are inextricably bound to each other.

What makes a city special or unique also adds to a sense of place, not only for the characters but for the audience taking a virtual tour during different characters' back stories. From the very beginning, *Lost* slips in clues to local culture in culturally diverse locations like New York, London, Manchester, Glasgow, and Phuket:

- Michael wants to show Walt great architecture, including New York's Flat Iron Building ("...In Translation," 1.17), which inspired him to become an artist. This triangular landmark was an engineering feat in 1902; its steel skeleton, unusual at the time, allowed it to become one of the city's tallest buildings. Although Michael returns to New York City, he confesses his murderous ways to Walt, who refuses to have anything to do with him ("Meet Kevin Johnson," 4.8). Instead of showing Walt the sights, Michael has an enlightening conversation in the Hotel Earle's penthouse with Tom Friendly, who loves the perks (including a handsome young lover) of off-Island living. (The renamed Washington Square Hotel in the West Village once was home to Bob Dylan in the 1960s.)

- When Charlie and Naomi share Mancunian memories, he explains that DriveShaft's first gig took place in the Night and Day Bar ("Greatest Hits," 3.21). The real Night and Day Café on Oldham Street features a variety of bands. (Its current schedule is posted at www.nightnday.org.)

- Desmond's former fiancé doesn't believe that he experienced a spiritual epiphany, which causes him to leave her at the altar; his only "religious experience," she claims, was when "Celtic won the Cup" ("Catch-22," 3.17). This detail establishes Desmond in Glasgow, when previous backstories only referred in general to his Scottish past and refers to the Celtics' 1995 Scottish Cup. By 1996, Des trains with the Royal Scots Regiment at Camp Millar, north of Glasgow. Scenes of basic training in the pouring rain reinforce the stereotype of Scotland as a very wet nation ("The Constant," 4.5).

- Jack's visit to Phuket showcases diversity of place: a beach hut, a city restaurant, a street festival, and a tattoo parlor. Each setting shows a different side of the area, from tranquil beachside to colorful, pulsing streetscape. These little details bring place and character into clearer focus.

Language also helps audiences understand place. Jack doesn't understand the Thai boy selling him drinks on the beach; a U.S. audience, like Jack, probably won't understand the language without subtitles (not provided in this scene) ("Stranger in a Strange Land," 3.9). Throughout this episode Jack seems very much out of place, truly a stranger in what to him is a strange land. The customs of the people he encounters underscore his and locals' different expectations of each other and, ultimately, their inability to reconcile these differences.

Desmond also encounters a language barrier when Penny goes into labor while their boat is moored off shore a Filipino island. Apparently he doesn't speak the local dialect, because he only shouts a doctor's name as he frantically summons help ("Jughead," 5.3).

A sense of place is incredibly important to *Lost*'s characters on a very personal level, too. One of the castaways' most important early questions is "Where are we?" quickly followed by "How do we go home?" The answers have shifted during five seasons, and "home" proves not to be an ideal destination for the Oceanic Six. When Jack and Kate's flash-forwards to Los Angeles take us off-island, the juxtaposition of the Southern California metropolis with the previous scene's remote tropical island make the city seem strange and foreign ("Through the Looking Glass," 3.22–23). The modern "jungle" provides more heartaches than happy reunions, making the Island potentially the "better" home and leading us to consider the irony of the Season Four finale's title, "There's No Place Like Home" (4.13–14). "LaFleur" certainly thinks of the Island as "home." After conning women (and probably himself) around the United States and never staying in one place for long, Sawyer creates a home with Juliet in 1970s DHARMAville. As the DHARMA Initiative's chief of security, he feels secure enough with his role in the community and in Juliet's life to build a real home. No wonder he is so protective of his "turf" when the Oceanic Sixers return to disrupt his life ("LaFleur," 5.8).

Marking boundaries and establishing "home turf" are important even on an uncharted island. Identifying their territory helps the castaways establish what they deem is theirs, who they are, where they need to go—or avoid, or where other people might be. Sayid first leaves the group not only to ostracize himself from their society but to map the perimeter of the Island ("Solitary," 1.9). Rousseau hides from the Others and creates deadly boundaries to mark her territory (e.g., "Solitary," 1.9; "Everybody Hates Hugo," 2.4; "One of Them," 2.14; "Catch-22," 3.17). Everyone seems to want or have a map—Sayid finds Rousseau's and, with Shannon's help, tries to decode it ("Whatever the Case May Be," 1.12); Locke discovers the map on the Hatch blast door and tries to re-create it ("Lockdown," 2.17; "?," 2.21); the Nigerian drug runners' plane contains maps ("Deus ex Machina," 2.19); Sayid, Locke, and Kate take Mikhail Bakunin hostage and follow his map to the Others' encampment ("Enter 77," 3.11). During Season Four, Ben provides a map so Rousseau can take Alex to safety in the Temple ("Meet Kevin Johnson," 4.8). Directed by a dream in which long-dead DHARMA devotee Horace Goodspeed tells Locke to find him, John locates the body in a mass grave and removes a map stored in Goodspeed's pocket; it conveniently shows Locke how to find Jacob's cabin ("Cabin Fever," 4.11).

Compasses and instructions, sometimes from mystical sources, also play a prominent role: Locke gives Sayid his compass, but North isn't where it should be ("Whatever the Case May Be," 1.12); Locke believes that words carved on Mr. Eko's "Jesus stick" will guide him where the Others hold Jack, Kate, and Sawyer ("I Do," 3.6); Desmond leads Hurley, Charlie, and Jin on a "camping trip" guided by images of the future he sees flashing before his eyes ("Catch-22," 3.17). Most cryptically, the elusive Jacob tells Locke to "move the Island" ("Cabin Fever, 4.11), a command that Ben fortuitously knows how to obey. He turns the "Frozen Donkey Wheel" (Lindelof and Cuse's nickname for the top-secret finale script and the episode's time-and-space shifter) to alter the Island's location ("There's No Place Like Home," 4.14).

During Season Five, Mrs. Hawking finally explains how and when to return to the Island, but her "map" involves a room-size Foucault pendulum and dozens of equations to calculate exactly which flights provide the most likely travel opportunities ("316," 5.6). The Lamp Post station apparently created by the DHARMA Initiative, tracks data to determine how and where the "portal" to the Island will appear. The fact that this station exists beneath a church magnifies the mystical nature of these special calculations.

Being lost from one place, as well as oneself, and discovering how to travel to another location, literally or metaphorically, are key elements to understanding *Lost*. People gain peace of mind by knowing where they are and how they "belong" physically with the rest of the world. Culturally, too, they establish expectations of how to behave and what is "normal" based on where they are.

Other characters—and the audience—are surprised when a character exceeds cultural expectations. Jin gradually overcomes a language barrier to become a more integral part of the English-speaking community; speaking Korean is the most obvious sign of his coming from a different culture and frames the way he interacts with others. When Michael meets Jin on the freighter, he seems shocked to learn that Jin has become remarkably fluent in English during the brief time since Michael left the Island ("Meet Kevin Johnson," 4.8). As a member of the DHARMA Initiative in the 1970s, Jin develops more colloquial language skills; he becomes just another worker acclimated to the community's daily routine—listening to the van's tape deck, hauling supplies, rounding up Hostiles—as much as anyone else ("LaFleur," 5.8).

Charlotte, born in Essex, brought up in Bransgrove, and university-educated at Kent and Oxford ("Confirmed Dead," 4.2), adheres to many viewers' preconceptions of a reserved British woman. Even her interest in archeological digs in Tunisia can be explained in light of a long history of British archeologists excavating their empire. What is more surprising is Charlotte's "outside the box" ability to speak Korean ("Something Nice Back Home," 4.10). Where people come from often sets up their expectations about other people and their homelands.

HOMETOWNS AND SPECIAL PLACES

Through flashbacks, we learn a great deal about where the castaways live during crucial moments in their lives. Hometowns and native countries give audiences a better idea of the cultural expectations and experiences that made the castaways who they are today. Some places are not hometowns but gain personal significance, because they are associated with a pivotal moment or special event in a character's life. Sometimes a character may lie about her or his origins (as when Kate or Ethan Rom claims Canadian citizenship, although they are later revealed to have been born in Iowa or on the Island); the places a character may wish is a hometown or country says a lot, too. As well, the number of important places that characters have in common establishes the idea that we all must live together in the world, and the actions of one person may have unexpected ramifications for others. The following table summarizes places important to current or former island dwellers.

SPECIAL PLACES

Place	Character	Event	Episode
Jasper, AL	Sawyer	Sawyer was born there and lived there at least through the time his mother had an affair with "Tom Sawyer."	The Brig

Place	Character	Event	Episode
Englewood, CA	Miles	Miles "exorcises" the spirit of Mrs. Gardner's grandson from her home.	Confirmed Dead
Long Beach Marina, CA	Oceanic Six and Ben	They plan to meet there to leave together for the Island.	The Little Prince
	Desmond	After being shot by Ben, Desmond undergoes surgery and recovers at the Marina Medical Center.	The Variable
Los Angeles, CA	Kate	She lives there with Aaron and agrees to remain in California in lieu of incarceration. She later leaves Aaron with his grandmother there.	Through the Looking Glass; Eggtown; What Happened, Happened
	Ana Lucia	She works as a police officer.	The Other 48 Days
	Nikki	She stars in the TV series *Exposé*.	Exposé
	Jin	He plans to escape Mr. Paik's influence and start a new life with Sun.	Exodus
	Claire	She plans to give up her baby for adoption there.	Raised by Another
	Charlie	He plans to restart his musical career there.	Born to Run

Place	Character	Event	Episode
	Hurley	He lives there throughout his young adulthood. When he becomes a millionaire, he opens a Mr. Cluck's franchise and buys his mother a mansion.	Numbers; Tricia Tanaka Is Dead; The Beginning of the End; There's No Place Like Home
	Shannon	She lives there with her father and stepmother until her father's death.	Abandoned
	Jack	He grows up in LA and later becomes a surgeon, a career to which he attempts to return once he leaves the Island. For awhile, he lives with Kate and Aaron.	The Hunting Party; Through the Looking Glass; Eggtown; There's No Place Like Home
	Desmond	He takes his family there in the search for Mrs. Hawking.	Jughead
	Locke	He visits Helen Norwood's grave. Later, he attempts suicide, but he's murdered by Ben.	The Life and Death of Jeremy Bentham
	Paulo	He plans to relocate there with Nikki.	Exposé
Newport Beach, CA	Libby	Her boat, the Elizabeth, is registered out of Newport Beach.	Live Together, Die Alone
Santa Monica, CA	Hurley	He fishes with his grandfather off the pier.	Numbers

Place	Character	Event	Episode
Santa Rosa, CA	Hurley	He sometimes is a patient at the Santa Rosa Mental Health Facility.	Dave; The Beginning of the End; There's No Place Like Home; The Life and Death of Jeremy Bentham
	Jack	He visits Hurley to make sure that he'll keep his silence about the Island.	The Beginning of the End
	Locke	He visits Hurley and attempts to get him to return to the Island.	The Life and Death of Jeremy Bentham
	Sayid	He breaks Hurley out of the mental health facility.	Because You Left
Tustin, CA	Locke	He works as a regional manager for a box company.	Walkabout
	Hurley	He owns a box company there.	Everybody Hates Hugo
Miami, FL	Kate	She marries Kevin.	I Do
	Juliet	She researches genetics and fertility at Miami Central University; sister Rachel lives in Miami.	Not in Portland
	Ethan	He lives down the hall from Juliet's sister, Rachel.	Not in Portland

Place	Character	Event	Episode
Tallahassee, FL	Kate	She is trying to buy a bus ticket when she's captured by the marshal.	What Kate Did
	Sawyer	He receives a bad case of "sunburn."	Lockdown
	Anthony Cooper	He is "taken" from I-10 outside the city and transported to the Island.	The Man from Tallahassee
Tampa, FL	Sawyer	He grouses about the "Tampa job."	Confidence Man
Honolulu, HI	Oceanic Six	They meet the press at a military facility west of Honolulu.	There's No Place Like Home
Cedar Rap-ids, IA	Kate	It's her birthplace, where she periodically returns.	What Kate Did
Sioux City, IA	Sawyer	He tells Cassidy to meet him at the Sage Flower Motel there.	The Long Con
Possibly Iowa	Locke	He briefly lives in a commune.	Further Instructions
Essex, MA	Dan Faraday	He and his caretaker watch news reports of the discovery of Oce-anic 815. His parents visit him and convince him to go to the Island.	Confirmed Dead; The Variable
Ann Arbor, MI	Dan Faraday	He joins the DHARMA Initiative and becomes one of their recruits sent to the Island.	He's Our You; Some Like It Hoth

Place	Character	Event	Episode
	Stuart Radzinsky	He calls the DeGroots in Ann Arbor to make the final decision of what to do with LaFleur.	He's Our You
Las Vegas, NV	David Reyes	He lives there after abandoning his family.	Tricia Tanaka Is Dead
Taos, NM	Kate	She robs a bank to retrieve a model airplane.	Whatever the Case May Be
Bronx, NY	Rose	She tells the castaways that she lives there.	Pilot
New York, NY	Boone	He lives there briefly while working for his mother.	Abandoned
	Michael	He is born in the city and lives there after he returns from the Island.	Special; Meet Kevin Johnson
	Libby	"Ghost" Libby appears in Michael's hospital room.	Meet Kevin Johnson
	Walt	He is born there and returns to the city after leaving the Island. Locke finds him there a few years later.	Special; Meet Kevin Johnson; The Life and Death of Jeremy Bentham
	Bernard	He meets Rose and presumably lives in the city.	S.O.S.
	Shannon	She receives a dance scholarship and hopes to live with Boone.	Abandoned
	Jack	He attends Columbia University Medical School.	A Tale of Two Cities

Place	Character	Event	Episode
	Locke	He visits Walt but doesn't ask him to return to the Island.	The Life and Death of Jeremy Bentham
Niagara Falls, NY	Rose	She becomes engaged to Bernard.	S.O.S.
	Bernard	He proposes to Rose.	S.O.S.
(Outside or in) Portland, OR	Juliet	She begins a job with Mittelos Bioscience.	One of Us
	Ethan	Working with Richard Alpert, he brings Juliet to work for Mittelos Bioscience.	Left Behind
	Ben	His early birth during his parents' hiking trip leads to his mother's death.	The Man Behind the Curtain
	Locke	He is invited to a summer science camp operated by Mittelos Bioscience.	Cabin Fever
Harrison Valley, PA	Kate	Her mug shot is taken by the police.	Tabula Rasa
Knoxville, TN	Sawyer	The boy sends a letter to "Sawyer" about his parents' deaths.	Confidence Man
Tennessee	Sawyer	He tells a shrimp vendor that's his home state.	Outlaws
Washington	Kate	She says her father taught her to track there.	What Kate Did

Place	Character	Event	Episode
Australia	Kate	She is captured by the marshal.	Whatever the Case May Be
	Rose	Bernard brings her there to consult with the healer Isaac.	S.O.S.
	Bernard	He takes Rose there for healing.	S.O.S.
Kalgoorlie, Australia	Hurley	He visits Sam Toomey's widow to learn about the curse.	Numbers
Melbourne, Australia	Locke	He tries to go on a walkabout.	Walkabout
Sydney, Australia	Boone	He travels there to help Shannon with a problem boyfriend.	Hearts and Minds
	Ana Lucia	She travels there as Christian Shephard's companion.	Two for the Road
	Mr. Eko	He investigates the possibility of a miracle.	Two for the Road
	Sawyer	He follows a tip to find "Sawyer" but kills an innocent man.	Outlaws
	Sayid	He infiltrates a terrorist cell and betrays his college roommate to the authorities.	The Greater Good
	Jin	He delivers a package to Mr. Paik's associate.	Exodus
	Sun	She plans to disappear from the airport.	Exodus

Place	Character	Event	Episode
	Libby	She confronts Mr. Eko at the airport.	Exodus
	Claire	She is born and raised there.	Raised by Another; Par Avion
	Walt	His mother remarries, and the new family settles there.	Special
	Locke	After the failed attempt at a walkabout, the wheelchair-bound Locke boards his flight.	Exodus
	Charlie	He visits Liam to entice him to return to DriveShaft.	The Moth
	Hurley	He oversleeps on the day he's flying home to LA.	Exodus
	Shannon	She lives with her boyfriend and concocts a plan to scam Boone out of money.	Hearts and Minds
	Jack	He searches for his father, only to learn that he's died in an alley.	White Rabbit
Edenberg, Bahamas	Frank Lapidis	After seeing news reports of the discovery of Oceanic 815, he calls the airlines to disagree with the pilot's identification.	Confirmed Dead
Bali	Kate	She says she wants to travel there.	What Kate Did

Place	Character	Event	Episode
Brazil	Nikki	She becomes a guest on a TV show, where she meets future boyfriend and partner-in-crime, Paulo.	Exposé
	Paulo	He works as a chef and later hooks up with Nikki.	Exposé
Canada	Kate	She tells her employer that she's Canadian.	Tabula Rasa
Ontario, Canada	Ethan	He tells Hurley that he's from Ontario.	Raised by Another
China	Jin	On behalf of Mr. Paik, he takes a baby gift to an important client.	Ji Yeon
Santo Domingo, Dominican Republic	Locke	He visits Sayid in an attempt to get him to return to the Island.	The Life and Death of Jeremy Bentham
	Sayid	He helps build a school.	The Life and Death of Jeremy Bentham
	Ben	He visits Sayid to tell him that Locke has been murdered by Widmore's men and Hurley is in danger.	He's Our You
Cairo, Egypt	Sayid	He attends University of Cairo and meets his future "terrorist" roommate.	The Greater Good

Place	Character	Event	Episode
Fiji	Michael	He joins the Kahana's crew, under the name Kevin Johnson.	Meet Kevin Johnson
	Charles Widmore	His freighter Kahana sails from Fiji in an attempt to locate the Island.	Meet Kevin Johnson
Finland	Charlie	DriveShaft completes two tours of Finland.	The Moth
Paris, France	Sayid	He works as a chef but is captured by the husband of a woman he tortured in Iraq.	Enter 77
	Shannon	She works as a nanny while studying in France for a year.	Whatever the Case May Be; Abandoned
Berlin, Germany	Sayid	He briefly enjoys a romantic relationship with Elsa, initially to gather information about her employer in order to kill him.	The Economist
Dresden, Germany	Charlie	During DriveShaft's tour there, his niece Megan was born.	The Moth; Fire + Water
Guam	Ajira 316 passengers and crew	The flight is headed to Guam but fails to land there.	The Little Prince
Basra, Iraq	Sayid	He may have committed atrocities, to which Juliet alludes.	One of Us

Place	Character	Event	Episode
Tikrit, Iraq	Sayid	He is born there and returns home to bury his wife, Nadia. At that time, he joins forces with Ben.	Pilot; The Shape of Things to Come
	Ben	He recruits Sayid as an assassin.	The Shape of Things to Come
Rome, Italy	Walt	His mother relocates them again when he is a small child.	Adrift
Membata	Oceanic Six	Their cover story is that they paddled to this island after the plane crash.	There's No Place Like Home
Mexico	Anthony Cooper	He flees there after pushing Locke out a window.	The Man from Tallahassee
Amsterdam, Netherlands	Walt	His mother relocates them when he is a baby.	Special
Nigeria	Mr. Eko	He is born there.	The 23rd Psalm
Philippines	Penny	She gives birth to son Charlie.	Jughead
South Korea	Kate	Her "father" is stationed there when Kate is conceived.	What Kate Did
Namhae, South Korea	Jin	He is born there.	...And Found

Place	Character	Event	Episode
Seoul, South Korea	Jin	He works as a doorman, meets Sun and marries her, and works for Mr. Paik.	…And Found; …In Translation; The Glass Ballerina; The Incident
	Sun	In her hometown, she attends Seoul National University and later marries Jin. Upon her return from the Island, she buys controlling interest in her father's company and gives birth to a daughter at Choogdong Hospital.	…And Found; …In Translation; The Glass Ballerina; There's No Place Like Home; Ji Yeon; The Incident
	Ji Yeon	With her grandmother's help, she calls her mother from there.	This Place Is Death
Tahiti	Danielle Rousseau	She and her research team depart from Tahiti.	Solitary
	Sawyer (LaFleur)	He's told that he's not DHARMA Initiative material and will be sent on the next sub to Tahiti.	LaFleur
Thailand	Charles Widmore	He "buys" bodies to fill the fuselage of an airliner presumed to be Oceanic 815.	Meet Kevin Johnson
Phuket, Thailand	Jack	He gets tattoos revealing his true nature.	Stranger in a Strange Land

Place	Character	Event	Episode
Tunisia	Ben	He teleports into the Sahara Desert, but soon checks into a hotel in Tozeur.	The Shape of Things to Come
	Locke	He awakens in the desert after leaving the Island. Charles Widmore finds him and gets him medical attention for his broken leg.	The Life and Death of Jeremy Bentham
Medenine, Tunisia	Charlotte	She visits an archeological dig and finds a DHARMA Initiative tag near polar bear bones.	Confirmed Dead
Bransgrove, England (UK)	Charlotte	She grows up there.	Confirmed Dead
Clitheroe, England (UK)	Charlie	He first hears Drive-Shaft on the radio when the band's van breaks down outside this city.	Greatest Hits
Essex, England (UK)	Charlotte	She is born there.	Confirmed Dead
Kent, England (UK)	Charlotte	She completes her undergraduate degree work.	Confirmed Dead
London, England (UK)	Mr. Eko	Masquerading as a priest, he takes Yemi's place as a student.	?

Place	Character	Event	Episode
	Desmond	He briefly lives there with Penny; later, he has time-travel visits to London, such as the time in 1996 when he tells Penny to expect his call in 2004.	Flashes Before Your Eyes; The Constant
	Sayid	ASIA and CIA agents detain him at Heathrow Airport and persuade him to infiltrate a terrorist cell in Australia.	The Greater Good
	Ben	In a late-night confrontation with Charles Widmore, they up the ante in their high-stakes "game." Widmore wants the Island; Ben wants to kill Penny.	The Shape of Things to Come
	Charlie	He and Liam live there during DriveShaft's final days. Later, Charlie lives alone, making a living by stealing from the women he dates and busking on the city's streets.	Fire + Water; Homecoming; Greatest Hits
	Charles Widmore	He bids on a journal from the *Black Rock*. Later, he has a late-night chat with Ben, who breaks into his hotel residence.	The Constant; The Shape of Things to Come

Place	Character	Event	Episode
	Penny	She stays with her son while Desmond tracks down the location of Dan Faraday's mother.	Jughead
	Sun	She confronts Charles Widmore and joins forces with him. When she plans to leave England, security at Heathrow Airport detains her so that Widmore can confront her.	There's No Place Like Home; Because You Left
Manchester, England (UK)	Charlie	DriveShaft first performs at the Night and Day Bar in his hometown.	The Moth; Greatest Hits
Oxford University, Oxford, England (UK)	Dan Faraday	He teaches physics and conducts research. He meets Desmond and shows him one of his time-travel experiments.	The Constant
	Desmond	He visits Dan Faraday to learn more about time travel. He later returns to gather information about Faraday's mother.	The Constant; Jughead
	Charlotte	She completes her doctoral work.	Confirmed Dead
	Eloise Hawking	She takes her son to lunch after his graduation.	The Variable

Place	Character	Event	Episode
Camp Millar, Scotland (UK)	Desmond	He goes through basic training for the Royal Scots Regiment.	The Constant
Carlisle, Scotland (UK)	Desmond	Penny's family lives there.	Catch-22
	Charles Widmore	He meets Desmond upon his release from prison.	Flashes Before Your Eyes
Glasgow, Scotland (UK)	Desmond	He stands up his fiancé Ruth at their wedding.	Catch-22

In particular, Kate, Sawyer, and Jin seem more closely bound to their early origins. Kate says she's Canadian ("Tabula Rasa," 1.3), but her father taught her how to track in the Washington forests ("All the Best Cowboys Have Daddy Issues," 1.11). Of course, she's also created several aliases, too, so knowing exactly what is truth or fiction may be difficult. Much of Kate's early life seems to take place in Iowa, however, where Midwestern values often seem at odds with Kate's outlook on life.

Iowa has a "heartland" reputation of family values and solid rural living. Although in an increasingly urban, high-tech age the "Midwestern myth" of wholesome, God-fearing people living in harmony with nature often conflicts with reality, *Lost* strips the veneer off this lifestyle; Kate and Sawyer, as well as the people in their lives, aren't as well adjusted, happy, or family-oriented as the stereotype would suggest. Cities like Cedar Rapids, reportedly Kate's hometown ("Born to Run," 1.22; "What Kate Did," 2.9), promote events throughout the year designed to bring the family together. Burning dear old dad in the family home isn't socially acceptable behavior. Kate's Midwestern roots tie her to traditional American family values while pointing out just how off-kilter her family life has been.

After her trial ("Eggtown," 4.4), however, Kate settles into life as a financially comfortable suburban mom. When live-in love Jack proposes, Kate seems to have the "perfect family" denied to her as a child. She becomes determined to maintain a stable, loving home for "son" Aaron. Jack's increasing suspicion of Kate's activities while he's at work causes a rift in the relationship, forcing Kate to banish Jack from her and Aaron's life ("There's No Place Like Home," 4.13–14). Despite Kate's real childhood lacking wholesome, Midwestern family values, she has clear ideas of what the ideal family should be. The more she adapts to Jack's suburban lifestyle, the farther she moves from common ground with good ol' boy Sawyer.

Although, in Season Four, Kate seems determined to provide Aaron the perfect home life, Season Five illustrates how Kate's fantasy can't be maintained. Fearful that attorneys will prove she isn't Aaron's biological mom and certain Aaron will someday be taken from her—as temporarily "losing" him in a grocery reminds her—Kate finally decides to leave the toddler with Claire's mother. Her objective is to find Claire on the Island and reunite mother and child. Although Kate can't re-create the perfect family she longs for, she at least recognizes the strength of familial bond, despite her own lack of the same.

Similarly, Sawyer eventually creates a "family" with Juliet, even if they only have each other. When this relationship also seems domed to end in tragedy, Sawyer selflessly tries to save Juliet; he knows now that he can find happiness in a long-term, (relatively) honest relationship. The likelihood of losing Juliet shows Sawyer just how much he needs her. He seems ready to die instead of living without her.

Whereas Kate always calls the former con man "Sawyer," the alias he first gives on the Island, Juliet calls him by his real first name, James. She alone knows who he really is, and James can show his true persona to her instead of hiding behind the fake identities of "Sawyer" or "LaFleur." Whereas Kate discovers that her new "family" is a sham based on deceit, James learns that he can be accepted for who he really is.

It takes a long time for James Ford eventually to return to being himself (as much as LaFleur can within the DHARMA Initiative); his thirst for revenge and deceitful plans began when he was only a child. A letter to the original "Sawyer" bears a Knoxville, Tennessee, postmark from the U.S. Bicentennial in 1976 ("Confidence Man," 1.8). Although James (Sawyer) Ford may not have lived in the city, he tells others that he's from Tennessee ("Outlaws," 1.16), and that setting seems plausible when we see him writing that fateful letter after his parents' funeral ("The Incident," 5.16). He provides a glimpse of his early life in "The Brig" (3.19), when he finally confronts Locke's father, "Tom Sawyer," whom he blames for his parents' deaths; he reminds the traveling con man of the woman he seduced in Alabama. Creating a cover story to allow him and his friends into the DHARMA Initiative finds Sawyer turning into Jim LaFleur, a Louisiana native trying to find the *Black Rock*. Whether Tennessee, Alabama, or Louisiana feels more like "home" to the con man, he clearly sees himself as a Southerner who can slather on the charm and suggestively deepen his drawl when the need arises.

Sawyer's Southern gentleman persona comes forth when Claire and Aaron need a protector. He tries to warn Claire before New Otherton is attacked ("The Shape of Things to Come," 4.9) and watches over her and Aaron as long as possible, even caring for the baby after Claire disappears into the jungle ("Cabin Fever," 4.12). Like Kate, the product of a dysfunctional family, Sawyer reveals the positive side of the gold ol' boy charmer with his need to protect women and children, a side increasingly obvious when he protects Juliet from the DHARMA Initiative once their cover is blown.

Like Kate and Sawyer, Jin learns about families and the importance of community status during his youth in the fishing village of Namhae, South Korea ("...And Found," 2.5). As the son of a fisherman, he quickly returns to the once-familiar jobs of creating nets, knowing where and how to fish, and cleaning the catch. Although his desire to have a more affluent life led him into the darker side of business, on the Island, he seems content to have the type of life he once left behind.

Jin's work ethic, instilled early in life, helps him adjust to his role as a DHARMA Initiative employee. He doesn't seem to have developed any close relationships in his new community and remains loyal to Sun. He tells Locke not to bring her back to the Island ("This Place Is Death," 5.5). "Saving" Sun from Island life is his primary concern, even if it means he lives alone for the rest of his life. Even when separated from his wife and child by time and space, Jin does his best to protect and care for them.

Ironically, after the first plane crash on the Island, Sun is leading the life her mother always feared for her daughter—being the wife of a fisherman ("Catch-22," 3.17)—but this lifestyle brings her and Jin closer together. When Sun, sans Jin, reclaims her wealthy cosmopolitan life in Seoul ("There's No Place Like Home," 4.13; "Ji Yeon," 4.7), however, she becomes isolated. Of the other Oceanic survivors, only Hurley visits, and Sun quickly estranges herself from her parents. Life in a fishing village, even on a mysterious island, turns out to be the more emotionally comfortable home for Sun.

COMMON DESTINATIONS

During *Lost*'s four seasons, references have been made to every continent: Asia (Afghanistan, China, Iraq, Russia, South Korea, Thailand [Siam], Tunisia), Africa (Egypt, Mozambique, Nigeria, Uganda), Antarctica, Australia/Pacific (Australia, Bali, Fiji, Madagascar, [the fictitious] Membata, Sumba, Tahiti), Europe (Finland, France, Germany, Italy, Portugal, the United Kingdom [England, Scotland], Ukraine [former USSR]), North America and Atlantic (the United States, Canada, Mexico, Bahamas, Dominican Republic), and South America (Brazil). Almost everyone who lives or lived on the Island came from somewhere else; this is a well-traveled group.

For all the diversity on *Lost*, with characters coming from around the globe and representing different regions and cultures even within the same country of origin, the world does seem to be a very small place. Many characters lived in or visited the same cities as the people with whom they end up sharing an island. Some common destinations have included Sydney, Los Angeles, New York, Miami, Paris, and London.

Sydney, of course, is the common denominator for the survivors of Oceanic 815. Los Angeles and nearby cities Tustin, Newport Beach, Englewood, and Santa Monica also figure prominently into backstories, especially for the Oceanic Six, Ana Lucia, Boone, Shannon, Locke, and Desmond. Even Mrs. Hawking prefers the West Coast these days, and Jacob occasionally visits the region, too. Miami is another city well-populated by future island dwellers, including Kate, Juliet, and Ethan Rom. Paris is temporary home to sous chef Sayid and nanny Shannon. London becomes a popular home base for several characters: Charlie, Desmond, the Widmores (both Penny and Charles), and Mr. Eko, but Ben and Sun also travel there on business.

Lost allows the audience to travel around the globe with characters and takes care to infuse enough local culture that international viewers accept the way non-U.S. locations are presented on screen. As with other aspects of telling the story, global geography celebrates cultural diversity while reminding characters and viewers that no matter our place of origin, we are all connected.

HAWAII AS A CHARACTER

Unlike most U.S. television series, which are filmed primarily in Los Angeles and, more often than not, in a studio, *Lost* makes the most of its Hawaiian location. Oahu, masquerading as a difficult-to-find island (or two), offers just about every possibility for "global" locations—whether in a residential area, on the beach, in warehouses, on air fields, around the business district, as well in studios geared to television production. With the right location and careful set dressing, *Lost*'s crew can create the appearance of a Thai street festival, a London neighborhood, rural Iowa, a Nigerian or a Dominican Republic village, the Sahara Desert, or the Sydney airport. The red-and-white crew parking signs alert the curious that *Lost* is being filmed nearby, but locals familiar with seeing *Lost* filmed on location are almost blasé about seeing the caravan of trucks pull into their neighborhoods or close off a section of beach.

Any trip to Oahu is worthwhile for its breathtaking scenery and diversity within a very drivable distance. Mountains compete with black, white, or brown sand beaches; busy Honolulu is the opposite of smaller towns around the rest of the Island. Sections of Wailua, complete with red dirt and a hundred-year-old former sugar mill, stand in for Nigeria. Hurley's family, as well as Kate, "live" in Kahala; near the local mall, Claire crashes her car and in the mall's food court meets her biological father, Christian Shephard. The rocky shores and long stretches of beaches toward the North Shore, where *Lost* set up temporary camps, truly seem like deserted oases in a crowded world. Fans who want to "get *Lost*" on the Island really are only limited by the number of days they want to spend tracking down locations, and they'll find at least a few former film sites in almost any direction.

A good site for virtual traveling is www.lostvirtualtour.com, a fan site that gathers tips from residents about "sightings." It may not be foolproof, but it explains what to see at the location and how the scene was filmed there. Recent magazines about Hawaii also feature former shooting locations.[61]

Because space limits our photos in this chapter, we have included a tantalizing few (different from those in the book's first and second editions). These pictures might help fans decide where and what they want to visit during a Hawaiian holiday.

Close to North Shore, Police Beach, better known to residents of Oahu as Papa'iloa, is easily recognizable as the castaways' campground in Seasons Two through Four; in Season Five, the abandoned campsites are featured in "The Incident" (5.16) when Sun finds Charlie's DS ring in the ruins of Claire's beach "house." Almost every possible camera angle has been used along the beach, among the rocks and through the trees. A walk around the beach, for example, quickly leads to a lightly wooded area, where the castaways run from the Monster during its early appearances. The grove can be seen from the path near Hale'iwa Beach Park's parking lot, but the site itself is on private land.

Filming in such public spaces provides benefits for *Lost* cinematic tourists. Even in January 2009, when the camp no longer played as prominent a role in the series, fans visiting the beach could clearly see the castaways' former home. Near the encampment stands Mr. Eko's church, also the site of Locke's vision quest. Because *Lost* locations encompass just about every part of the Island, a day trip can easily include some *Lost* highlights and allow time to enjoy the beaches along the way.

Remnants of Oceanic 815 in the castaways' camp, Papa'iloa Beach, January 2009.
Photo courtesy of Lynnette Porter

Food-drop parachute adorning the castaways' "kitchen," January 2009.
Photo courtesy of Lynnette Porter

The Kualoa Ranch, a short drive outside Honolulu, has been the location of many *Lost* scenes. Because the ranch is on privately owned land, only the ranch's ATV and horseback tours, and Ed Kos' Hummer tours,[63] can travel into the *Lost* valley. Kualoa Ranch's valleys and hills, as well as the nearby Tropical Farms and Macadamia Nut Farm (also known as Moli'i Gardens) and fish pond (the perfect place to launch or sink a sub), have provided backdrops for numerous television series and films, including *Jurassic Park* and *Pearl Harbor*.

To make the series' settings seem worlds apart, the crew repaints or adds props to make buildings look vastly different. During Season Two, a building on the Moli'i Gardens' grounds served as the Nigerian bar where drug lord Mr. Eko held court. (Our second edition shows a photograph of the building as bar.) For Season Five, crew members repainted the building to become the school Sayid helps to build, as shown below. Both Locke and Ben visit Sayid in the Dominican Republic while he works on the school.

Dominican Republic school, January 2009.
Photo courtesy of Lynnette Porter

Many *Lost* scenes are filmed in the valley or around the World War II observation "bunker" at the Kualoa Ranch. Season Three scenes shot on the ranch, for example, involved the Others' submarine, the deadly sonic fence, a Korean fishing village, the castaways' graveyard, and the tree where the mysterious parachutist lands. Hurley and Charlie took their joyride in the DHARMA Initiative's van on Kualoa property. Season Four features bunkers as well as jungle locations.

One of the notable features added to the landscape during Season Five was the frame housing Jughead. The guides from Kos Hummer Tours often take fans even closer to the action. A fall 2008 tour brought fans closer to 1950s Jughead long before Juliet whacks it to death (both its and hers). Although the bomb only stayed in place during a few episodes' filming, the framework lasted much longer. The first photograph, taken during a Kos Hummer Tour in fall 2008, shows Jughead; the second Jughead-less photo, taken in January 2009, provides a more curious view, although after the explosive developments throughout Season Five, fans could easily identify what took place at this location.

Setting up Jughead.
Photo courtesy of Ed Kos, Kos Hummer Tours

After the bomb: January 2009.
Photo courtesy of Lynnette Porter

Ed Kos recalls several times when his tours passed *Lost*'s actors between scenes. One Sawyer fan spotted Josh Holloway standing on higher ground in an attempt to find better cell phone reception. As the actor talked on his phone, a woman called out from the passing hummer, "Hey, Sawyer, what are you doing tonight?" Non-plussed by the shout out, Holloway grinned as he continued his phone conversation.[63] Although such encounters don't happen on every tour, several lucky fans can say they've said hello to "Locke" or "Ben" as they waited for the next scene to be set up.

Lost's cinematic tourism is a plus for fans and tour operators alike. Kos estimates that 6,000 visitors have taken his tours, which guide fans to Honolulu-area as well as remote filming sites all around Oahu. In 2009, the tours captured several *Lost* actors and extras on location.

Filming the Season Five finale.
Photo courtesy of Ed Kos, Kos Hummer Tours

Richard Alpert's headquarters.
Photo courtesy of Ed Kos, Kos Hummer Tours

Temporary home to Charles Widmore and Ellie Hawking.
Photo courtesy of Ed Kos, Kos Hummer Tours

Kualoa Ranch properties provide a wealth of filming options within a few miles spanning coastal waters and jungle. More *Lost* locations are added to the Ranch's tour as permission is granted to let fans know exactly which scenes were shot at different locations. (See www.kualoaranch.com for more information about Ranch tours and a history of the property.)

However fans decide to divide their time or interests in finding *Lost* locations, there is something for everyone. Just a reminder: Many scenes are filmed on private property, including near-beach and residential areas or homes. Although beaches are public space, the tree line becomes the border of private property, and eager fans are requested to respect that line.

AROUND HONOLULU

Fans with limited time or those staying in Waikiki may want to visit a section of Honolulu's Chinatown and the nearby business district to check out the former filming sites there. A good place to start is Nuuanu Avenue, home to two Irish pubs: Murphy's and O'Toole's, which are across the street from each other. O'Toole's has provided the setting for several episodes, including Desmond's Season Three backstory ("Flashes Before Your Eyes," 3.8). Although he hears the jukebox playing "Make Your Own Kind of Music," O'Toole's patrons more often watch television above the bar—the *Lost* crew brought in the jukebox. However, fans can sit at Desmond's table. Charlie or Locke fans may prefer to visit Murphy's, where Locke meets his father for a drink ("Lockdown," 2.17). Charlie chats up soon-to-be-girlfriend Lucy and her friends ("Homecoming," 1.15), while putting into play his and drug-supplier Tommy's scam. The alley outside also became a focal point for scenes between Charlie and Tommy. *Lost* creatively uses geographically close sites to represent widely divergent places. Within a few blocks of these pubs, fans might recognize the bank Kate "robbed" of a miniature airplane, the gate where Desmond stopped to read a military-recruitment poster, the alley where Rose and Bernard first meet.

A nearby Honolulu landmark, the First Hawaiian Center, is the tallest building in Hawaii and home to a museum's art gallery as well as corporations' headquarters. To *Lost* fans, however, the inside is more easily recognized than the famous exterior. Pregnant Sun slowly walks up the staircase leading to her father's office (or the first floor of contemporary museum exhibits) in Season Four's "There's No Place Like Home" (4.12). The wall at the top of the staircase is part of Mr. Paik's office (also shown in "The Glass Ballerina," 3.2). The downtown area includes many other former *Lost* shooting locations within easy driving distance of the business district, Chinatown, or Aloha Tower.

Visitors with a little more time should check out the Honolulu Convention Center. The interior is often dressed to resemble different sections of the Sydney airport, and the escalators have been shown in the background of several airport-based scenes, as well as featured in Locke's vision ("Further Instructions," 3.3). Just around the corner is the Ala Wai Canal. Sun and Jin meet while walking along the canal ("...And Found," 2.5), and Michael says goodbye to toddler Walt while seated at one of the benches along the walkway ("Adrift," 2.2).

Lost frequently features Honolulu churches, and two of the most photographed are St. Andrews Priory and Parke Chapel, which stand next to each other on Queen Emma Square. In addition to the churches' interiors, the covered walkway outside the chapel has been prominently featured in several episodes.

Charlie finds Liam waiting for him in the chapel ("The Moth," 1.7), and the two continue discussing DriveShaft as they stroll through the walkway from the chapel. Crossing the courtyard in front of the arched walkway, Desmond carries cases of wine to Penny's van ("Catch-22," 3.17), although an appropriately rural backdrop is blue- or green-screened behind Penny to hide the churches' parking lot. The churches become the monastery, home to Mariah Vineyards. Also along this famous walkway, Desmond accosts Daniel Faraday after his physics class at Oxford University ("The Constant," 4.5). Next door, St. Andrew's Priory also serves as "Priest" Eko's London sanctuary ("?" 2.22). Season Five revisits the churchyard and walkways around Parke Chapel for Daniel Faraday's graduation from Oxford ("The Variable," 5.14) and Desmond's post-dream return to Faraday's former lab ("Jughead," 5.3).

These are only a few of the many city locations featured in the past five years. A tour of Honolulu, with its beautiful architecture and blend of traditional Hawaiian culture with Western and Eastern influences, should be a priority for *Lost* fans. Not only will they find locations "as seen on TV," but even a quick tour of the city leads to a deeper appreciation for the diversity and cultural history of Oahu.

THE ART OF SELECTING LOCATIONS AND DRESSING SETS

Lost does an excellent job of selecting locations and then dressing the sets and creating the right mood so that, for example, downtown Honolulu becomes London, Seoul, Los Angeles, or Sydney. What may be surprising to fans is just how many ordinary buildings—homes, churches, supermarkets, hotels, high-rise offices—can take on a very different atmosphere with the right decoration and camera angles. Honolulu's rich culture offers a wide range of architectural styles, historic and modern buildings, and restaurants of varied cuisines; the Island offers streetscapes, beaches for sunrises or sunsets, rugged peaks, and lush jungle. There are vast opportunities to transform these different styles into the location the script calls for, and when all else fails, interiors can be shot in studio.

Lost often has to capture the exotic and the quirky in order to provide audiences with a visual experience unlike most viewers' everyday reality; Hawaii, Oahu in particular, offers the ambiance and variety needed to tell such a complex story. In 2006, producer Jean Higgins emphasized that "*Lost is* Hawaii, pure and simple...You don't have these looks on the mainland."[64] *Lost*'s location, sets, and careful attention to the details within them take fans to other times and places and bring audiences into the story.

Dedication to detail is a trait of location manager Jim Triplett. Triplett's more than thirty years in Hawaii pay off for *Lost*; he knows where to find likely locations for just about any place the characters need to be. During the series' first five seasons, he scouted Hawaiian locations for at least half the episodes and is listed as an associate producer on several Season Five episodes.

Although *Lost*'s high production values and surprising plot twists have made the series a huge success, it wouldn't have the same stunning cinematography or "flavor" if it were filmed anywhere but Hawaii. Even after the series ends production and the final episode is broadcast in 2010, Oahu will be the land of the *Lost* for years to come.

CHAPTER SIX

LOST QUESTIONS WITHOUT ANSWERS

An earlier version of this table—a much longer one—was posted on one of our blogs early in Season Five. Looking at it now, after Season Five has come to an end, it is remarkable how many questions were answered within 2008–2009's seventeen episodes, for all their continuing and new enigmas.

As we await *Lost*'s final season, many, many questions remained to be answered however. Darlton have warned again and again that we cannot expect answers to all of our questions, and no doubt Season Six will open up whole new cans of WTF?

Here is a certainly incomplete list. Some of these were touched on in earlier chapters, but are presented here in a concise, useful compendium.

LOST QUESTIONS WITHOUT ANSWERS

Character/ Aspect	Questions/Mysteries
Adam and Eve	Who are Adam and Eve? (It seems more likely than ever that they are Bernard and Rose.)

Character/ Aspect	Questions/Mysteries
Agelessness	What causes it, and is anyone else (in addition to Richard Alpert) ageless? (We know that Jacob made Richard ageless, and it would appear that he—and his nemesis—might well be.)
Richard Alpert	What is his origin? How can he pass through the sonic fence without difficulty? Why does he recruit Ben as a young boy? Why did he not recognize Daniel Faraday in "The Variable"?
Birth on the Island	What caused the 100 percent infant mortality rate on the Island? When did this problem begin? It must have begun after 1977, at which time Juliet was able to successfully deliver Amy's baby.
The *Black Rock*	What happened to the crew of the *Black Rock*? Why did Widmore purchase its log at an auction?
The Cabin	What is the Cabin? Why was Horace Goodspeed its designated builder? How does it move? Who was its inhabitant? Why did Ilana and her people torch it? What is the significance of the ash outside the Cabin?
Brother Campbell	How does Brother Campbell know Mrs. Hawking? Why does he keep a framed photo of her on his desk?
Christian Shephard	Why does Christian Shephard serve as Jacob's mouthpiece? Is he alive or dead? What is his link, if any, to Smokezilla?
Claire	Is Claire alive or dead? (Kate tells her mother she is returning to the Island to find her.)
Desmond	What did Desmond do that landed him in an army prison? Was his stranding on the Island somehow purposeful? Was Libby's gift of a sailboat to him coincidental or purposeful?

Character/ Aspect	Questions/Mysteries
The DHARMA Initiative	Who ordered the extermination of the DHARMA Initiative? Why is it so secretive about the construction of the geodesic dome and the Swan Hatch?
Ethan Rom	How did Ethan Rom transfer from DHARMA to the Others?
Daniel Faraday	Why does young Ellie Hawking say to Faraday (in 1954 in "Jughead"), "You just couldn't stay away, could you?" Why does he cry when he first learns of the discovery of the Oceanic 815 wreckage? What was he doing in Ann Arbor? What was his plan in returning to the Island? Why did he tell Pierre Chang Miles was his son? Why did he tell Jack he had no destiny? Why did he seem to invite the Hostiles (i.e., his mother) to shoot him? Did he really intend to set off Jughead?
Four-Toed Statue	When/why was the statue built in the Island's history? Why does it represent an Egyptian deity? What destroyed the statue (except for the foot)?
The Frozen Donkey Wheel	How does the Frozen Donkey Wheel "move" the Island? Why does it not appear to be frozen when Locke moves it? What is the "dust" that comes out of the opening when it is turned?
Henry Gale	Who was (was there a real) Henry Gale?
Eloise Hawking	Why/how was Mrs. Hawking in the jewelry store when Desmond came to buy Penny's ring? How does she know Brother Campbell? How did she come to be in charge of "the Lamp Post"? What news disturbed her at the beginning of "The Variable" so much that she began to push her son toward a career in science? What prompted her to slap Charles Widmore in "The Variable?" Did young Eloise Hawking know she would kill her son?

Character/ Aspect	Questions/Mysteries
The Hostiles/ The Others	What is the origin of the Hostiles? How exactly do they choose their leader? Why do they believe themselves to be protectors of the Island?
Hurley Bird	What is the Hurley Bird? Is it connected in any way with Smokezilla?
Ilana	How did she know Jacob prior to their meeting in Russia in "The Incident?"
The Island 6 (Sawyer, Daniel, Charlotte, Miles, Juliet, Locke)	Who is shooting at them from a pursuing canoe? (We can now be reasonably certain it was Ilana, Bram, and their group.)
Jacob	Who/what is he? Why does he visit (and touch) Kate, Sawyer, Jack, Jin and Sun, Hurley, Locke off the Island? What is the significance of his weaving? What is his relationship with the mysterious man in black? What is the argument they are having? Is he really dead at the end of Season Five?
Sayid Jarrah	Was his gunshot wound (from Roger Linus) fatal?
Jughead	Did it explode at the end of Season Five? Did it alter the destiny of everyone?
Juliet's Husband's Death	Was the death of Juliet's husband—hit by a bus—arranged?
Frank Lapidus	Was Frank Lapidus piloting Ajira 316 on purpose?
Charlotte Staples Lewis	Why did Charlotte disappear when she died?
Libby	Why was Libby in Santa Rosa with Hurley? Was her late husband David/Dave a character we have met or will meet?

Character/Aspect	Questions/Mysteries
Benjamin Linus	Why did Ben have so many passports? Can he (how can he) control Smokezilla? Why did he change seats just before the "crash" of Ajira 316? What are the future reverberations of Sayid's attempted killing of Young Ben in the 1970s? Why will the wounded Young Ben being taken in by the Hostiles result in 1) loss of memory? 2) loss of innocence? 3) forever being an Other?
John Locke	What was the "something" Locke had to do (in "Dead Is Dead") when he disappeared for a time prior to taking Ben to find the Monster? Is it true that he is the first person brought back from the dead by the Island? Is this even John Locke—or Esau?
Locke's Father	How did Ben bring the Man from Tallahassee (Locke's father) to the Island?
The Magic Box	Is there really a "magic box" on the Island?
Charlotte Malkin	Was Charlotte Malkin's "resurrection" really a miracle?
Mind Control	What is the mind-control technique being used on a reluctant Carl in Room 23?
The Others	See The Hostiles.
Polar Bears	Why was a polar bear with a DHARMA tag in Tunisia?
The Purge	Who ordered the Purge? Did anyone other than Ben survive it.
Rousseau's Expedition	What happened when Rousseau's expedition (minus Rousseau) descended into the well to rescue Montand from Smokezilla? What was the nature of the "infection" plaguing it?

Character/ Aspect	Questions/Mysteries
Smokezilla	Why is Smokezilla's home in the well near the Temple? Why does it make a mechanical sound—like a roller coaster? How can Smokezilla "read" people's memories and incorporate them holographically into its substance? Why does the mural in the summoning room in "Dead Is Dead" show a face-off between Anubis and Smokezilla?
Miles Strohm	What is the origin/cause of Miles' ability to communicate with the dead?
The Temple	What exactly is the Temple? Why is it located adjacent to the Orchid Hatch and Frozen Donkey Wheel? Why did Ben believe the Temple is the only safe place when the attack on the Island began? Why did Richard Alpert take the wounded Young Ben there?
The Others' Lists	What was the basis for the lists the Others kept of individuals they wished to take? (We do know that Jacob prepared the lists.)
Tunisia	Why was there a polar bear in Tunisia? Why was Charlotte Staples Lewis there? What was Benjamin Linus' business there?
Walt	What is the nature of Walt's specialness? Why were the Others interested in him?
Charles Widmore	Why does Widmore consider the Island to be his? Can he be killed? (Ben implies that he cannot.) Who was his wife (Penny's mother)? Why does he have a painting of a polar bear on the wall of his office? Why does he have a painting of Thomas (Aaron's father) on the wall of his office? What is his connection with Mr. Paik? What is the coming "war" he tells John Locke about?

Character/ Aspect	Questions/Mysteries
Penelope Widmore	Was Penny's meeting of Desmond at the Eddington Monastery arranged? How did she know Desmond would be found where an electromagnetic anomaly was detected?

CHAPTER SEVEN

BEHIND THE SCENES

LOST ACTORS

Adewale Akinnuoye-Agbaje (1967–). *Lost* Character: Mister Eko. **You might recognize him as** Simon Adebisi in *Oz* and from roles in such movies as *G.I. Joe: The Rise of Cobra*, *Get Rich or Die Tryin'*, *The Bourne Identity*, *The Mummy Returns*, *Ace Ventura: When Nature Calls*, and *Congo*.

Sam Anderson (1945–). *Lost* Character: Bernard Nadler. **You might recognize him as** Holling Manners in *Angel* or from numerous roles in movies (*Critters 2*, *The Puppet Masters*, *Airplane 2*) and TV series (*CSI: NY*, *Cold Case*, *Medium*, *ER*, *Boston Legal*, *CSI*, *Boomtown*, *Everybody Loves Raymond*, *The X-Files*, *The Adventures of Brisco County, Jr.*, *L.A. Law*, *Growing Pains*, *Dallas*, *Magnum, PI*, *Hill Street Blues*).

Naveen Andrews (1969–). *Lost* character: Sayid Jarrah. **You might recognize him from** such movies as *The Brave One*, *Grindhouse*, *Bride & Prejudice*, *Rollerball*, *Mighty Joe Young*, *The English Patient*, and *London Kills Me*.

Reiko Aylesworth (1972–). *Lost* Character: Amy Goodspeed. **You might recognize her from** a recurring role on *ER* and as Michelle Dressler on Days 2, 3, and 4 of *24*.

Anthony Azizi (1973–). *Lost* character: Omar. **You might recognize him from** such television series as *Veronica Mars*, *Without a Trace*, *Sleeper Cell*, *Criminal Minds*, *Desperate Housewives*, *Commander in Chief*, *24*, *The West Wing*, *NYPD Blue*, *Threat Matrix*, *Gilmore Girls*, *The Shield*, and *JAG*.

Blake Bashoff (1981–). *Lost* character: Karl. **You might recognize him from** a recurring role on *Judging Amy*.

Sterling Beaumon (1995–). *Lost* Character: Young Ben Linus. **You might recognize the busy young actor from** appearances in *Four Christmases, Bones, ER, Scrubs, Heroes, Cold Case, House, Crossing Jordan*, and *7th Heaven*.

Zoe Bell (1978–). *Lost* character: Regina. **You might recognize her as** a busy stunt double (in *Kill Bill* and other films) and from such movies as *Grindhouse*.

Ron Bottitta (1960–). *Lost* character: Leonard Simms. **You might recognize him from** a variety of movies (*Pirates of the Caribbean: Dead Man's Chest, In Good Company*) and TV series (*Jericho, E-Ring, Alias, The Shield, Boston Public*).

Julie Bowen (1970–). *Lost* character: Sarah Shephard. **You might recognize her from** roles in such movies as *American Werewolf in Paris, Happy Gilmore, Multiplicity* and TV series like *Boston Legal, Jake in Progress, Ed, Dawson's Creek, ER*.

Michael Bowen (1953–). *Lost* character: Danny Pickett. **You might recognize him from** roles in movies like *Cabin Fever II, Walking Tall, Kill Bill II, Magnolia*, and *Jackie Brown* and such TV series as *Bones, CSI, The X-Files, Walker, Texas Ranger, Nash Bridges, JAG, NYPD Blue, ER*, and *The Adventures of Brisco County, Jr.*

Grant Bowler (1968–). *Lost* character: Captain Gault. **You might recognize the Australian actor from** such television series as *Outrageous Fortune* (a New Zealand crime family drama) and *Farscape*.

Clancy Brown (1959–). *Lost* character: Kelvin Inman. **You might recognize him as** the sadistic prison guard in *The Shawshank Redemption* and Brother Justin Crowe in HBO's *Carnivàle*. Has also done voice work in scores of films and television series.

L. Scott Caldwell (1944–). *Lost* character: Rose Henderson. **You might recognize her from** roles in such movies as *Gridiron Gang, Devil in a Blue Dress, Dutch* and on such TV series as *Ghost Whisperer, Cold Case, ER, Nip/Tuck, The Practice, Judging Amy, Chicago Hope, JAG, Murder One, Hunter, L.A. Law*, and *The Cosby Show*.

Nestor Carbonell (1967–). *Lost* character: Richard Alpert. **You might recognize him from** the TV series *Cane* and the movie *Dark*

Knight (he played the Mayor), Batmanuel on *The Tick* and Luis Rivera in *Suddenly Susan*, and from voice work on *Kim Possible.*

François Chau (1959–). Cambodian born. *Lost* character: Dr. Marvin Candle. **You might recognize him from** roles in such movies as *Lethal Weapon 4* and on such TV series as *Numb3rs*, *Grey's Anatomy*, *24*, *Alias*, *Nash Bridges*, and *The Adventures of Brisco County, Jr.*

Byron Chung. *Lost* character: Mr. Paik. **You might recognize him from** several appearances (as different characters) in *M*A*S*H.*

Tom Connolly. *Lost* Character: Young Charles Widmore. **You might recognize him as** a regular in *The Ambassador* and a role in *Veronica Mars.*

Brett Cullen (1956–). *Lost* character: Goodwin. **You might recognize him from** recurring roles in *Ugly Betty*, *The West Wing*, *Friday Night Lights*, and *Desperate Housewives.*

Henry Ian Cusick (1967–). Peruvian born. *Lost* character: Desmond David Hume. **You might recognize him from** roles in *24*, *Waking the Dead*, *The Book Group*, *Casualty*, and *Taggart.*

Guillaume Dabinpons. *Lost* Character: Robert Rousseau. **You might recognize him from** one previous role in *The Young and the Restless.*

Alan Dale (1947–). New Zealand born. *Lost* character: Mr. Widmore. **You might recognize him** as Bradford Meade on *Ugly Betty*, Caleb Nicholson on *The O.C.*, and VP James Prescott on Day 3 of *24.*

Jeremy Davies (1969–). *Lost* character: Daniel Faraday. **You might recognize him** as Charles Manson in a made-for-TV movie of *Helter Skelter*, from such television series as *Dream On*, *Melrose Place*, *The Wonder Years*, and films like *Saving Private Ryan*, *Rescue Dawn*, *Twister*, *Dogville*, *Nell*, *Solaris*, and *Spanking the Monkey.*

Emilie de Ravin (1981–). Australian born. *Lost* character: Claire Littleton. **You might recognize her from** a recurring role in *Roswell* and for playing the female lead in *The Hills Have Eyes*, as well as the TV movie *High Noon* and the Johnny Depp film *Public Enemies.*

Kim Dickens (1965–). *Lost* character: Cassidy Phillips. **You might recognize her as** Joannie Stubbs in *Deadwood.*

Andrew Divoff (1955–). Venezuelan born. *Lost* character: Mikhail Bakunin. **You might recognize him from** scores of television and film roles, usually as a villain.

Starletta DuPois (1941–). *Lost* character: Michael's mom. **You might recognize her from** such TV series as *Chicago Hope, Crossing Jordan, Doogie Howser, Falcon Crest, Hill Street Blues, Knots Landing, The Steve Harvey Show, The Jeffersons, The Equalizer, Little House on the Prairie,* and *St. Elsewhere* and movies like *A Raisin in the Sun* (for TV), *Big Momma's House, Hollywood Shuffle, Family Reunion, The Notebook, Waiting to Exhale,* and *Pee-Wee's Big Adventure.*

Kevin Durand (1974–). *Lost* character: Martin Keamy. **You might recognize the Canadian-born actor from** the TV series *CSI: Miami, Without a Trace, The Dead Zone, Kyle XY, Threshold, CSI, Dead Like Me, Dark Angel, Stargate SG-1, ER,* and *Shark* and the movies *X-Men Origins: Wolverine, 3:10 to Yuma, Wild Hogs, The Butterfly Effect, Walking Tall, Scooby Doo 2, Mystery, Alaska,* and *Austin Powers: The Spy Who Shagged Me.*

Michael Emerson (1954–). *Lost* character: Benjamin Linus. **You might recognize him from** his Emmy-winning role (for Outstanding Guest Actor in a Drama Series) as William Hinks in *The Practice* and for appearances in a wide variety of films (including a memorable part in *Saw*) and television series.

Alice Evans (1971–). British born. *Lost* Character: Young Eloise Hawking. **You might recognize her from** roles in movies and television shows like *Bruno, Curb Your Enthusiasm, The Chris Isaak Show, CSI: Miami,* and *102 Dalmatians.*

Jeff Fahey (1952–). *Lost* character: Frank Lapidus. **You might recognize him from** the TV series *Nash Bridges, Crossing Jordan, Criminal Minds, The Cleaner, American Dreams, Alfred Hitchcock Presents,* and *One Life to Live* and the movies *Grindhouse, Wyatt Earp, The Lawnmower Man, White Hunter, Black Heart,* and *Silverado.*

Melissa Farman. *Lost* character: Young Danielle Rousseau. **You might recognize her from** one previous role in *Cold Case.*

Sarah Farooqui. *Lost* character: Theresa Spencer. **You might recognize her from** a recurring role in *Mile High* and appearances in *The Bill.*

Nathan Fillion (1971–). *Lost* character: Kevin Callis. **You might recognize him** as the title character in *Castle,* Captain Hammer in *Dr. Horrible's Sing-Along Blog,* Captain Mal Reynolds in *Firefly* (and the film *Serenity*), and Caleb in *Buffy the Vampire Slayer.* Has also played a recurring role on *Desperate Housewives* and the male lead in such films as *Slither*, *Waitress*, and *White Noise 2*.

Patrick Fischler (1969–). *Lost* character: Phil. **You might recognize the busy actor as** the insult comic Jimmy Barrett in *Mad Men*, recurring roles in *Southland* and *Nash Bridges*, and many appearances on TV—*Pushing Daisies*, *Cold Case*, *Burn Notice*, *NCIS*, *Moonlight*, *Veronica Mars*, *According to Jim*, *Drive*, *E-Ring*, *Enterprise*, *CSI: NY*, *The West Wing*, *ER*, *CSI*, *Angel*, *Birds of Prey*, *Judging Amy*, and *The Adventures of Brisco County, Jr.*—and in the movies—*Ghost World*, *Mulholland Dr.*, *Twister*, and *Speed*.

Fionnula Flannigan (1941–). Irish born. *Lost* character: Mrs. Hawking. **You might recognize her as** Mrs. Bertha Mills in *The Others* and multiple roles in *James Joyce's Women*.

Matthew Fox (1966–). *Lost* character: Jack Shephard. **You might recognize him as** Charlie Salinger in *Party of Five* and from major roles in the movies *We Are Marshall*, *Vantage Point*, and *Speed Racer*.

Mira Furlan (1955–). *Lost* character: Danielle Rousseau. **You might recognize her as** Delenn in *Babylon 5*.

Andrea Gabriel (1978–). *Lost* character: Noor "Nadia" Abed Jazeem. **You might recognize her from** roles in *Law and Order*, *JAG*, and *Criminal Minds*.

M. C. Gainey (1948–). *Lost* character: Tom Friendly. **You might recognize him as** a busy character actor in both film and television, best known perhaps for his performance as inept deputy Roscoe Coltrane in the big screen version of *Dukes of Hazzard*.

Billy Ray Gallion. *Lost* character: Randy Nations. **You might recognize him from** minor roles in *The X-Files* and *Charmed*.

Jorge Garcia (1973–). *Lost* character: Hugo (Hurley) Reyes. **You might recognize him from** his recurring role as Hector Lopez on *Becker* and as a pot dealer on *Curb Your Enthusiasm*.

April Grace (1962–). *Lost* character: Bea Klugh. **You might recognize her as** Detective Toni Williams in *Joan of Arcadia* and recurring roles in *Chicago Hope* and *Star Trek: The Next Generation*.

Maggie Grace (1983–). *Lost* character: Shannon Rutherford. After *Lost* appeared in such movies as *The Fog* and *Taken* and in such TV series as *Cold Case*, *Oliver Beene*, and *CSI: Miami*.

Jon Gries (1957–). *Lost* character: Roger Linus. **You might recognize the busy character actor from** a regular role in *The Pretender*, a recurring role in *Martin*, and many appearances in such television series and films as *CSI: NY*, *Taken*, *The Astronaut Farmer*, *Carnivàle*, *Las Vegas*, *Napoleon Dynamite*, *24*, *ER*, *Twin Falls Idaho*, *Men in Black*, *Chicago Hope*, *Get Shorty*, *Beverly Hills, 90210*, *Quantum Leap*, *The Grifters*, *Jake and the Fatman*, *Cagney and Lacey*, *Falcon Crest*, *The Jeffersons*, *The White Shadow*, and *Will Penny* (when Gries was only eleven).

Evan Handler (1961–). *Lost* character: Dave. **You might recognize him from** his roles as Harry Goldenblatt in *Sex and the City* and Charlie Runkle in *Californication* and many other films and television shows.

Brad William Henke (1966–). *Lost* character: Bram. **You might recognize him as** Thor in *Nikki* and in a variety of film and television roles in *Life on Mars*, *Law & Order*, *Choke*, *Cold Case*, *Dexter*, *Hollywoodland*, *World Trade Center*, *North Country*, *The Zodiac*, *Must Love Dogs*, *CSI*, *Judging Amy*, *Providence*, *Crossing Jordan*, *Sports Night*, *The Pretender*, *Arli$$*, *Nash Bridges*, *Silk Stalkings*, *Chicago Hope*, and *The Fan*.

Josh Holloway (1969–). *Lost* character: Sawyer (James Ford). **You might recognize him from** minor roles in several movies and such TV series as *NCIS*, *CSI*, *Angel*, and *Walker, Texas Ranger*.

Neil Hopkins (1977–). *Lost* character: Liam Pace. **He has appeared in** a variety of films and television series.

Lillian Hurst (1949–). *Lost* character: Carmen Reyes. **You might recognize her from** recurring roles as Celia in *Dharma and Greg* and on *The Nine* and *The Comeback* and scores of other film and television appearances.

Doug Hutchison (1960–). *Lost* character: Horace Goodspeed. **You might recognize him as** a regular in *Kidnapped* or Eugene Victor Tooms in *The X-Files* and from roles in both film and television: *Punisher: War Zone*, *Kidnapped*, *The Guiding Light*, *Law and Order: SVU*, *CSI: Miami*, *Boomtown*, *The Practice*, *The Green Mile*, *Party of Five*, *The Lawnmower Man*, and *China Beach*.

Tom Irwin (1956–). *Lost* character: Dan Norton. **You might recognize him as** Graham Chase, the father in *My So-Called Life*, Father Hanadarko in *Saving Grace*, and Joe Sorelli in *Related*, and a variety of roles in both film and TV: *24*, *Marley & Me*, *Eli Stone*, *7th Heaven*, *Ghost Whisperer*, *The Closer*, *CSI*, *Angel*, *21 Grams*, *Frasier*, *The Haunting*, *China Beach*, *Midnight Run*, and *Crime Story*.

Nick Jameson (1935–). *Lost* character: Richard Malkin. **You might recognize him from** *24*, in which he plays Russian President Yuri Suvarov and from scores of television and movie roles.

Kimberley Joseph (1973–). Canadian born. *Lost* character: Cindy Chandler. **You might recognize her from** recurring roles on *Cold Feet* and *All Saints*.

Malcolm David Kelley (1992–). *Lost* character: Walt Lloyd. **You might recognize him as** the young *Antwone Fisher* and from several television appearances.

Daniel Dae Kim (1968–). *Lost* character: Jin Kwon. **You might recognize him as** Gavin Park in *Angel* and from recurring roles in *24* and *ER*.

Yunjin Kim (1973–). *Lost* character: Sun Kwon. Most of her previous screen roles were in her native Korea.

Alexandra Krosney (1990–). *Lost* character: Teen Eloise Hawking. **You might recognize her from** roles in such TV series as *CSI, Criminal Minds, Without a Trace, Numb3rs, Bones, NCIS, Crossing Jordan,* and *ER*.

Swoozie Kurtz (1944–). *Lost* character: Emily Locke. **You might recognize her as** a character actress in many movies, as Alexandra "Alex" Reed Halsey Barker in *Sister*, a recurring role in *Huff*, and as Lily Charles in *Pushing Daisies*.

Eric Lange (1973–). *Lost* character: Stuart Radzinsky. **You might recognize him from** a variety of television roles—*Monk, Numb3rs, Bones, Criminal Minds, Boston Legal, Journeyman, Entourage, Ghost Whisperer, My Name Is Earl, NCIS, CSI: NY, ER, The Bernie Mac Show, JAG, Judging Amy, CSI, The Shield, Angel, Firefly, The Bold and the Beautiful.*

Tony Lee. *Lost* character: Jae Lee. **You might recognize him from** numerous television and film roles.

Fredric Lehne. *Lost* character: U.S. Marshal Edward Mars. **You might recognize him from** scores of movie parts and recurring roles in such television series as *Supernatural* (as the yellow-eyed demon), *Mancuso, FBI,* and *Dallas*.

Ken Leung (1970–). *Lost* character: Miles Straume. **You might recognize him from** the TV series *The Sopranos, Law & Order,* and *Oz* and the movies *X-Men: The Last Stand, Inside Man, The Squid and* *the Whale, Saw, Red Dragon, Vanilla Sky, AI, Spy Game, Rush Hour,* and *Welcome to the Dollhouse.*

Evangeline Lilly (1979–). *Lost* character: Kate Austen. **You might recognize her from** small roles in *Smallville* and *Tru Calling* and more recent films *The Hurt Locker* and *Afterwards.*

Paula Malcolmson. *Lost* character: Colleen Pickett. **You might recognize her as** Trixie in *Deadwood* and in *John from Cincinnati.*

William Mapother (1965–). *Lost* character: Ethan Rom. **You might recognize him as** the abusive, murderous ex-husband in *In the Bedroom* and roles in *Threshold, Mission Impossible 2,* and *The Grudge.*

Cheech Marin (1946–). *Lost* character: David Reyes. **Best known as** half of the stoner comic duo of *Cheech & Chong,* as Joe Dominguez in *Nash Bridges,* in a recurring role in *Judging Amy,* and for many movie appearances.

Adetokumboh M'Cormack. *Lost* character: Yemi. **You might recognize him from** a recurring role in the final season of *Gilmore Girls.*

Elizabeth Mitchell (1970–). *Lost* character: Juliet Burke. **You might recognize her from** performances in movies like *Frequency* and recurring roles in *ER, The Lyon's Dean,* and *Time of Your Life.*

Dominic Monaghan (1976–). German born. *Lost* character: Charlie Pace. **You might recognize him as** the hobbit Merry in *The Lord of the Rings* trilogy and as Bolt in *X-Men Origins: Wolverine.*

Rebecca Mader (1979–). *Lost* character: Charlotte Lewis. **You might recognize the British actress from** the TV series *Justice, Mr. and Mrs. Smith, One Life to Live, The Guiding Light, All My Children, Third Watch* and the movies *The Devil Wears Prada* and *Hitch.*

Terry O'Quinn (1952–). *Lost* character: John Locke. **You might recognize him as** the eponymous *Stepfather* and from recurring roles in *The X-Files, Millennium, Alias,* and many other TV series.

Robert Patrick (1958–). *Lost* character: Hibbs. **You might recognize him as** the liquid metal terminator in *Terminator 2,* Agent John Doggett in the final season of *The X-Files,* and Davey Scatino in *The Sopranos.*

Mark Pellegrino (1965–). *Lost* character: Jacob. **You might recognize him as** Rita's abusive ex in *Dexter* and Dick Hickock, one of the accused killers of *In Cold Blood,* or from scores of film and TV roles over the last twenty years in such movies and series as *CSI, Prison Break, Criminal Minds, Numb3rs, Chuck, Women's Murder Club, Grey's Anatomy, National Treasure, The Practice, CSI: Miami, The X-Files, Nash Bridges, The Big Lebowski, Northern Exposure, Lethal Weapon 3,* and *L.A. Law.* He will play Lucifer in the final season of *Supernatural.*

Harold Perrineau (1963–). *Lost* character: Michael Dawson. **You might recognize him as** a regular in *The Unusuals,* recurring roles in *Oz* and *I'll Fly Away,* or from *Matrix Reloaded* and *Matrix Revolutions.*

Jeff Perry (1955–). *Lost* character: Frank Duckett. **You might recognize him from** his continuing role as Harvey Leek on *Nash Bridges,* a recurring role in *Prison Break,* and as Meredith Grey's father in *Grey's Anatomy.*

Tania Raymonde (1988–). *Lost* character: Alexandra Rousseau. **You might recognize her from** a recurring role on *Malcolm in the Middle.*

Lance Reddick. *Lost* character: Matthew Abaddon. **You might recognize him from** important roles in TV series like *Fringe* (Agent Frank Broyles) and *The Wire* (Lt. Cedric Daniels), and appearances in *Numb3rs, CSI: Miami, Law & Order, Law & Order: Criminal Intent, Law & Order: Special Victims Unit, Oz, The Corner, West Wing,* and *New York Undercover,* as well as such movies as *Dirty Work, Don't Say a Word,* and *The Siege.*

Zuleikha Robinson (1977–). British born. *Lost* character: Ilana. **You might recognize her from** significant roles in the TV series *New Amsterdam, Rome,* and *The Lone Gunmen* and a smaller part in *The X-Files* or from such films as *The Merchant of Venice, Hidalgo,* and *Timecode.*

Michelle Rodriguez (1978–). *Lost* character: Ana Lucia Cortez. **You might recognize her from** key roles in movies like *Girlfight, S.W.A.T., Resident Evil, Blue Crush,* and *The Fast and the Furious.*

Daniel Roebuck (1965–). *Lost* character: Leslie Arzt. **You might recognize him from** a recurring role as cop-gone-bad Rick Bettina in *Nash Bridges* as well as scores of movie and TV appearances.

Katey Sagal (1954–). *Lost* character: Helen. **You might recognize her from** roles as Peg Bundy in *Married With Children* and Cate Hennessy in *8 Simple Rules.*

Kiele Sanchez (1977–). *Lost* character: Nikki Fernandez. **You might recognize her from** recurring roles in the TV series *Related* and *Married to the Kellys.*

William Sanderson (1944–). *Lost* character: Oldham. **You might recognize him as** E. B. Farnum in *Deadwood*, Sheriff Dearborne in *True Blood*, the replicant designer J. F. Sebatian in *Blade Runner*, or Larry on *Newhart*, or from scores of character actor roles in both film and television since the 1970s: *Life, Monk, Without a Trace, Gods and Generals, Dharma and Greg, Walker, Texas Ranger, Babylon 5, Coach, The Pretender, The X-Files, Matlock, Married with Children, Quincey M.E., Fletch, The Dukes of Hazzard, Coal Miner's Daughter,* and *Starsky and Hutch.*

Rodrigo Santoro (1975–). Brazilian born. *Lost* character: Paolo. **You might recognize him from** parts in movies like *300, Charlie's Angels: Full Throttle,* and *Love Actually* and those Bazz Luhrman–directed Chanel No. 5 ads with Nicole Kidman. A major soap-opera star in his native land.

Ian Somerhalder (1978–). *Lost* character: Boone Carlyle. **You might recognize him from** a role in the movie *Pulse*. He plays the male lead in the Fall 2009 TV series *The Vampire Diaries*.

Saïd Taghmaoui (1973–). French born. *Lost* character: Cesar. **You might recognize him as** a busy actor, active on both the big—*G.I. Joe: The Rise of Cobra, House of Saddam, Vantage Point, The Kite Runner, I Heart Huckabees, Hidalgo, Spartan, Three Kings*—and small screen—*Sleeper Cell, West Wing.*

Tamara Taylor (1970–). *Lost* character: Susan Lloyd-Porter. **You might recognize her from** her role as Dr. Camille Saroyan in *Bones* and as the teacher in the opening sequence of *Serenity*.

John Terry (1950–). *Lost* character: Christian Shephard. **You might recognize him from** recurring roles on *24, Las Vegas,* and *ER.*

Marsha Thomason (1976–). British born. *Lost* Character: Naomi. **You might recognize her as** Nessa Holt on *Las Vegas.*

Kevin Tighe (1944–). *Lost* character: Anthony Cooper. **You might recognize him from** scores of movie performances and recurring roles in such TV series as *Murder One* and *Emergency!*

Sonya Walger (1974–). *Lost* character: Penelope Widmore. **You might recognize her from** recurring roles in *Mind of the Married Man, Sleeper Cell, CSI: NY, Coupling, Tell Me You Love Me,* and *Terminator: The Sarah Connor Chronicles.*

Cynthia Watros (1968–). *Lost* character: Libby. **You might**

recognize her from roles on the soaps *Guiding Light* and *Another World* and *The Drew Carey Show*.

Robin Weigert (1969–). *Lost* character: Rachel. **You probably know her as** Calamity Jane in *Deadwood* and the TV series *Life*.

Titus Welliver (1961–). *Lost* character: Man #2 (Loophole Man/ Jacob's Nemesis). **You might recognize him as** Silas Adams on *Deadwood* and significant roles on *Brooklyn South* and *NYPD Blue*, as well as other appearances in such TV shows as *Life, Prison Break, Monk, Shark, NCIS, Kidnapped Numb3rs, Law & Order, Star Trek: Voyager, The Practice, Nash Bridges, Murder One, Blind Justice, The X-Files, The Commish,* and *Tales from the Crypt, Matlock* and in the movies *Twisted, Assault on Precinct 13, Mulholland Falls,* and *The Doors*.

Sean Whalen (1964–). *Lost* character: Neil Frogurt. **You might recognize him from** recurring roles on *The Bold and the Beautiful, The ½ Hour News Hour, Unfabulous,* and *My Wife and Kids,* and many appearances in both films—*Employee of the Month, Charlie's Angels, The Cable Guy, Twister, Men in Black, Waterworld, That Thing You Do*—and television—*Cold Case, Hannah Montana, The Closer, Spin City, Enterprise, NYPD Blue, Nash Bridges, La Femme Nikita, That Thing You Do, Lois & Clark, Grace Under Fire*.

LOST WRITERS

J. J. Abrams (1966–). *Lost* **episodes written/cowritten**: "Pilot, Part 1," "Pilot, Part 2," "A Tale of Two Cities." In addition to authoring/ coauthoring such films as *Taking Care of Business, Regarding Henry, Forever Young, Gone Fishin',* and *Armageddon* **has also written episodes of** *Alias* and *Felicity*.

Carlton Cuse (1959–). *Lost* **episodes written/cowritten**: "Hearts & Minds," "Deus Ex Machina," "Exodus, Part 1," "Exodus, Part 2," "…And Found," "The Other 48 Days," "The 23rd Psalm," "One of Them," "Lockdown," "?," "Live Together, Die Alone, Part 1," "Live Together, Die Alone, Part 2," "Further Instructions," "I Do," "Not in Portland," "Enter 77," "One of Us," "The Brig," "Through the Looking Glass," "The Beginning of the End," "The Constant," "There's No Place Like Home" (Parts 1, 2, and 3), "Because You Left," "The Life and Death of Jeremy Bentham,"

"Whatever Happened, Happened," "The Incident" (Parts I and II). **Has also written episodes of** *Nash Bridges, The Adventures of Brisco County, Jr.,* and *Crime Story.*

Leonard Dick. *Lost* **episodes written/cowritten**: "...In Translation," "The Greater Good," "Adrift," "The Long Con," "S.O.S.," "Collision." **Has also written episodes of** *House, Tarzan, Relic Hunter, Sister, Sister,* and *Mad TV.*

Paul Dini (1957–). *Lost* **episodes written/cowritten**: "The Moth." **Has Also Written Episodes for such cartoon series as**: *Justice League, Batman Beyond, Tiny Toon Adventures,* and *Transformers.*

Brent Fletcher. Previously a stuntman and occasional actor. *Lost* **episodes written/cowritten**: "Numbers." **Has also coauthored an episode of** *Angel.*

David Fury (1959–). *Lost* **episodes written/cowritten**: "Walkabout," "Solitary," "Special." **Has also written episodes of** *24, Angel, Buffy the Vampire Slayer, Pinky and the Brain,* and *Dream On.*

Drew Goddard (1975–). *Lost* **episodes written/cowritten**: "Outlaws," "The Glass Ballerina," "Flashes Before Your Eyes," "The Man from Tallahassee," "One of Us," "The Man Behind the Curtain," "Meet Kevin Johnson," "The Shape of Things to Come." **Has also written episodes of** *Alias, Angel,* and *Buffy the Vampire Slayer* and the movie *Cloverfield.*

Javier Grillo-Marxuach (1969–). *Lost* **episodes written/cowritten**: "House of the Rising Sun," "All the Best Cowboys Have Daddy Issues," "...In Translation," "Born to Run," "Orientation," "Collision." **Has also written episodes of** *Medium, Jake 2.0, Boomstown, Dead Zone, Law & Order: Special Victims Unit, Charmed,* and *Pretender.*

Adam Horowitz. *Lost* **episodes written/cowritten**: "Born to Run," "Everybody Hates Hugo," "Fire + Water," "Dave," "Three Minutes," "Every Man for Himself," "Trisha Tanaka Is Dead," "Exposé," "D.O.C," "Greatest Hits," "The Economist," "Something Nice Back Home," "The Lie," "This Place is Death," "He's Our You," "The Variable." **Has also written episodes of** *One Tree Hill, Birds of Prey, Felicity,* and *Popular.*

Melinda Hsu. *Lost* **episodes written/cowritten**: "The Little Prince" and "Some Like It Hoth." **Has also written episodes of** *Vanished, Medium,* and *Women's Murder Club.*

Jennifer Johnson. *Lost* **episodes written/cowritten**: "The Moth" and "Whatever the Case May Be." **Has also written episodes of** *Cold Case*, *The Guardian*, and *Providence*.

Christina M. Kim. *Lost* **episodes written/cowritten**: "The Whole Truth," "Two for the Road," "Per Avion." Her *Lost* scripts were her first.

Edward Kitsis. *Lost* **episodes written/cowritten**: "Born to Run," "Everybody Hates Hugo," "Fire + Water," "Dave," "Three Minutes," "Every Man for Himself," "Trisha Tanaka Is Dead," "Exposé," "D.O.C," "Greatest Hits," "The Economist," "Something Nice Back Home," "The Lie," "This Place Is Death," "He's Our You," "The Variable." **Has also written episodes of** *Birds of Prey*, *Felicity*, and *Popular*.

Dawn Lambertsen-Kelly. *Lost* **episodes written/cowritten**: "Maternity Leave." Her *Lost* script was her first.

Damon Lindelof (1973–). *Lost* **episodes written/cowritten**: "Pilot, Part 1," "Pilot, Part 2," "Tabula Rasa," "Confidence Man," "Whatever the Case May Be," "Homecoming," "Deus Ex Machina," "Exodus, Part 1," "Exodus, Part 2," "Man of Science, Man of Faith," "…And Found," "The Other 48 Days," "The 23rd Psalm," "One of Them," "Lockdown," "?," "Live Together, Die Alone, Part 1," "Live Together, Die Alone, Part 2," "A Tale of Two Cities," "I Do," "Flashes Before Your Eyes," "Enter 77," "Left Behind," "The Brig," "Through the Looking Glass," "The Beginning of the End," "The Constant," "There's No Place Like Home" (Parts 1, 2, and 3), "Because You Left," "The Life and Death of Jeremy Bentham," "316," "Whatever Happened, Happened," "The Incident (Parts 1 and 2)." **Has also written episodes of** *Crossing Jordan* and *Nash Bridges* and will cowrite the second installment of the new *Star Trek* relaunch.

Lynne E. Litt. *Lost* **episodes written/cowritten**: "Raised by Another." **Has also written episodes of** *Crossing Jordan*, *Tarzan*, *The Practice*, *Gideon's Crossing*, *Law & Order*, and *Nash Bridges*.

Steven Maeda. *Lost* **episodes written/cowritten**: "Adrift," "What Kate Did," "The Long Con," "S.O.S." **Has also written episodes of** *Day Break*, *CSI: Miami*, *The X-Files*, and *Harsh Realm*.

Gregory Nations. *Lost* **episodes written/cowritten**: "Eggtown," "Some Life it Hoth." **Has also written episodes of** *The District*.

Monica Owusu-Breen. *Lost* **episodes written/cowritten**: "The Cost of Living." **Has also written episodes of** *Alias*, *Brothers & Sisters*, and *Charmed*.

Kyle Pennington. *Lost* **episodes written/cowritten**: "Cabin Fever" (his first television script) and "LaFleur."

Jeff Pinkner. *Lost* **episodes written/cowritten**: "The Glass Ballerina," "Not in Portland," "The Man from Tallahassee," "Catch-22." **Has also written episodes of** *Alias, Profiler, Ally McBeal,* and *Early Edition.*

Matt Ragghianti. *Lost* **episodes written/cowritten**: "Maternity Leave." His *Lost* script was his first.

Jordan Rosenberg. *Lost* **episodes written/cowritten**: "Per Avion." His *Lost* script was his first.

Liz Sarnoff. *Lost* **episodes written/cowritten**: "Abandoned," The Hunting Party," "Further Instructions," "Stranger in a Strange Land," "Left Behind," "The Man Behind the Curtain," "Eggtown," "Meet Kevin Johnson," Cabin Fever," "Jughead," "LaFleur," "Follow the Leader." **Has also written episodes of** *Deadwood, Crossing Jordan,* and *NYPD Blue.*

Alison Schapker. *Lost* **episodes written/cowritten**: "The Cost of Living." **Has also written episodes of** *Alias* and *Charmed.*

Janet Tamaro. *Lost* **episodes written/cowritten**: "Do No Harm." **Has also written episodes of** *Bones, Sleeper Cell, CSI NY, Law & Order: Special Victims Unit.*

Christian Taylor. *Lost* **episodes written/cowritten**: "White Rabbit." **Has also written episodes of** *Miracles* and *Six Feet Under.*

Brian K. Vaughan (1977–). Prolific graphic novelist (*Ave Maria, Doctor Strange, Ex Machina, Y: The Last Man, Pride of Baghdad, Runaways*). *Lost* **episodes written/cowritten**: "Catch-22" (his first television script), "Meet Kevin Johnson," "The Shape of Things to Come," "The Little Prince," "Namaste," "Dead Is Dead."

Craig Wright. *Lost* **episodes written/cowritten**: "Orientation" and "What Kate Did." **Has also written episodes of** *Dirty Sexy Money, Brothers & Sisters,* and *Six Feet Under.*

Paul Zbyszewski. *Lost* **episodes written/cowritten**: "Jughead," "Namaste," and "Follow the Leader." **Has also written episodes of** *Day Break,* which he also created.

LOST DIRECTORS

J. J. Abrams (1966–). *Lost* **Episodes Directed**: "Pilot, Part 1," "Pilot, Part 2," "A Tale of Two Cities." **Has also directed episodes of** *The Office, Alias, Felicity*, as well as *Mission Impossible III* and *Star Trek*.

Daniel Attias. *Lost* **Episodes Directed**: "Numbers." **Has also directed episodes of** over forty televisions series including *Big Love, House, The Wire, Deadwood, Entourage, Six Feet Under, Alias, Huff, Boston Legal, CSI Miami, The Sopranos, Buffy the Vampire Slayer, Ally McBeal, Party of Five, Northern Exposure, Beverly Hills, 90210, The Adventures of Brisco County, Jr., Miami Vice*.

Paris Barclay (1956–). *Lost* **Episodes Directed**: "Stranger in a Strange Land." **Has also directed episodes of** over thirty television series including *CSI, Cold Case, House, Numb3rs, The Shield, Law & Order, Huff, West Wing, ER, NYPD Blue, Sliders, Diagnosis Murder*.

Matt Earl Beesley. *Lost* **Episodes Directed**: "The 23rd Psalm." **Has also directed episodes of** ten television series including *Jericho, CSI: Miami, Criminal Minds, Law & Order: Special Victims Unit, Prison Break, CSI*.

Jack Bender. *Lost* **Episodes Directed**: "Tabula Rasa," "Walkabout," "The Moth," "Whatever the Case May Be," "Outlaws," "Exodus, Part 1," "Exodus, Part 2," "Man of Science, Man of Faith," "Orientation," "Fire + Water," "Maternity Leave," "Dave," "Live Together, Die Alone, Part 1," "Live Together, Die Alone, Part 2," "A Tale of Two Cities," "The Cost of Living," "Flashes Before Your Eyes," "The Man from Tallahassee," "One of Us," "Through the Looking Glass," "The Beginning of the End," "The Economist," "The Constant," "The Shape of Things to Come," "There's No Place Like Home" (Parts 1 and 3), "The Lie," "The Life and Death of Jeremy Bentham," "Namaste," "Some Like It Hoth," "The Incident" (Parts 1 and 2). **Has also directed episodes of** *The Sopranos, Carnivale, Carnivale, Joan of Arcadia, Judging Amy, Ally McBeal, Felicity, Profiler, Beverly Hills, 90210, The Paper Chase*.

Adam Davidson (1964–). *Lost* **Episodes Directed**: "Abandoned." **Has also directed episodes of** over twenty television series including *Shark, Rome, Big Love, Dexter, Criminal Minds, Grey's Anatomy, Deadwood, Six Feet Under, Jake 2.0, Monk*, and *Law & Order*.

Roxann Dawson (1958–). Formerly an actress (*Baywatch, Star Trek: Voyager, Matlock*). *Lost* **Episodes Directed**: "The Long Con."

Has also directed episodes of thirteen television series, including *Crossing Jordan, Cold Case, Enterprise*, and *Charmed*.

Paul A. Edwards. Former camera operator and cinematographer. *Lost* **Episodes Directed**: "What Kate Did," "Two for the Road," "The Glass Ballerina," "Per Avion," "Cabin Fever," "This Place Is Death," "The Variable." **Has also directed an episode of** *Heroes*.

Tucker Gates. *Lost* **Episodes Directed**: "Confidence Man," "… In Translation," "Born to Run," "I Do." **Has also directed episodes of** over forty-five televisions shows including *The Office, Weeds, Alias, Carnivàle, Huff, Boston Legal, CSI, CSI: Miami, American Dreams, Roswell, Angel, Buffy the Vampire Slayer, Providence, Nash Bridges, The X-Files, The Commish, Wiseguy*, and *21 Jump Street*.

Karen Gaviola. *Lost* **Episodes Directed**: "The Whole Truth" and "Left Behind." **Has also directed episodes of** *CSI: Miami, Prison Break, Bones, Alias, Crossing Jordan, Cold Case*, and *NYPD Blue*.

Mark Goldman. *Lost* **Episodes Directed**: "LaFleur," his rookie outing as a director after editing thirty-plus episodes of both *Angel* and *Lost*.

Marita Grabiak. *Lost* **Episodes Directed**: "Raised by Another." **Has also directed episodes of** *Eureka, Surface, One Tree Hill, Law and Order: Special Victims Unit, Alias, Battlestar Galactica, Wonderfalls, Gilmore Girls, Smallville, Angel, Buffy the Vampire Slayer, Firefly*, and *ER*.

David Grossman. *Lost* **Episodes Directed**: "The Greater Good." **Has also directed episodes of** over forty television series including *Desperate Housewives, Monk, Malcolm in the Middle, CSI, Dead Like Me, CSI: Miami, Buffy the Vampire Slayer, Angel, Ally McBeal, Timecop, Roswell, Lois and Clark, Hercules: The Legendary Journeys, Mantis*, and *Weird Science*.

Rod Holcomb. Veteran television director, at work since the 1970s. *Lost* **Episodes Directed**: "Hearts and Minds" and "Jughead." In addition to numerous made-for-television movies, **has also directed episodes of such series as** *Numb3rs, Invasion, ER, China Beach, Wiseguy, Scarecrow and Mrs. King, The A-Team, Hill Street Blue, Battlestar Galactica* (the original), *6 Million Dollar Man, Quincy*, and *M.E.*

Kevin Hooks (1958–). Son of actor Robert Hooks and an occasional actor himself (*White Shadow*, Sounder). *Lost* **Episodes Directed**: "White Rabbit" and "Homecoming." **Has also directed episodes of**

Prison Break, 24, Ghost Whisperer, Alias, Cold Case, NYPD Blue, Without a Trace, ER, Profiler, Homicide, V, and *St. Elsewhere.* Directed feature film *Passenger 57* (1992).

Eric Laneuville (1952–). *Lost* **Episodes Directed**: "The Other 48 Days," "S.O.S.," "Trisha Tanaka Is Dead," "The Brig," "The Other Woman." **Has also directed episodes of** over forty shows including *Ghost Whisperer, Prison Break, Invasion, Everybody Hates Chris, Medium, Gilmore Girls, My Wife and Kids, Monk, ER, NYPD Blue, Midnight Caller, Quantum Leap, L.A. Law, St. Elsewhere.*

Robert Mandel. *Lost* **Episodes Directed**: "Deus Ex Machina." **Has also directed episodes of** *Prison Break, The District, Nash Bridges, The Practice, The X-Files,* and several made-for-TV movies.

Bobby Roth (1950–). *Lost* **Episodes Directed**: "The Man Behind the Curtain" and "Whatever Happened, Happened." **Has also directed episodes of** *Numb3rs, Prison Break, Commander-in-Chief, Boomtown,* and many other series in a twenty-year career.

Deran Sarafian (1968–). *Lost* **Episodes Directed**: "?." **Has also directed episodes of** over twenty television series including *House, Night Stalker, CSI: NY, CSI, CSI: Miami, Cold Case, Without a Trace, Buffy the Vampire Slayer,* and several forgettable films.

Alan Taylor (1965–). *Lost* **Episodes Directed**: "Everybody Hates Hugo." **Has also directed episodes of** numerous HBO series like *The Sopranos, Big Love, Rome, Deadwoood, Carnivàle, Sex and the City, Six Feet Under,* as well as other series like *West Wing* and *Homicide.*

Frederick E. O. Toye (1967–). *Lost* **Episodes Directed**: "D.O.C." **Has also directed episodes of** *Ghost Whisperer, Alias* (twelve episodes), *4400,* and *Invasion.*

Stephen Williams. *Lost* **Episodes Directed**: "All the Best Cowboys Have Daddy Issues," "Do No Harm," "Adrift," "…And Found," "Collision," "The Hunting Party," "One of Them," "Lockdown," "Three Minutes," "Further Instructions," "Every Man for Himself," "Not in Portland," "Enter 77," "Exposé," "Catch-22," "Confirmed Dead," "Eggtown," "Ji Yeon," "Something Nice Back Home," "There's No Place Like Home, Part 1," "Because You Left," "The Little Prince," "316," "Dead Is Dead," "Follow the Leader." **Has also directed episodes of** *Crossing Jordan, Las Vegas, Ed, Dark Angel,* and *Kevin Hill.*

Greg Yaitanes (1970–). *Lost* **Episodes Directed**: "Solitary,"

"Special," "He's Our You." **Has also directed episodes of** *Grey's Anatomy*, *Prison Break*, *House*, *Bones*, *Nip/Tuck*, *The Closer*, *CSI: Miami*, *CSI: NY*, *Cold Case*, and *Nash Bridges*. Also directed the feature film *Hard Justice*.

Michael Zinberg. *Lost* **Episodes Directed**: "House of the Rising Sun." **Has also directed episodes of** over fifty television series, including *Gilmore Girls*, *The Practice*, *NCIS*, *Crossing Jordan*, *Everybody Loves Raymond*, *Boston Public*, *Charmed*, *Pretender*, *JAG*, *The Commish*, *Quantum Leap*, *L.A. Law*, *Cheers*, *Lou Grant*, *WKRP in Cincinnati*, and *The Bob Newhart Show*.

CHAPTER EIGHT

TEN BOOKS/ESSAYS TO READ ABOUT *LOST*

Card, Orson Scott, ed. *Getting Lost: Survival, Baggage and Starting Over in J. J. Abrams' Lost.* Dallas: BenBella, 2006. A very uneven collection which nevertheless contains some essential reading: for example, Joyce Millman's essay on games in *Lost*.

Carter, Bill. *Desperate Networks.* New York: Broadway Books, 2006. Tells the gripping story of how *Lost* (and other Fall 2004 series) managed to get on the air in the first place.

King, Stephen (2005). "*Lost*'s Soul." *Entertainment Weekly* 9 September: 150. *Lost*'s most famous fan's convincing and influential argument for why *Lost* should have a proscribed end. Darlton and ABC listened.

Lachonis, Jon and Amy Johnston. Lost *Ate My Life: The Inside Story of a Fandom Like No Other.* Toronto: ECW Press, 2008. A report from the trenches of *Lost*'s hyperenergized fandom.

Lavery, David. "The Island's Greatest Mystery: Is *Lost* Science Fiction?" *The Essential Science Fiction TV Reader.* Edited by J. P. Telotte. Lexington: U P of Kentucky, 2008. 283–98. A complex investigation into whether *Lost* is science fiction or not.

___. "*Lost* and Long Term Television Narrative." *Third Person.* Edited by Pat Harrigan and Noah Wardrip-Fruin. Cambridge: Massachusetts Institute of Technology Press, 2009. 313–22. Places *Lost* in the history of television narrative.

Mittell, Jason. "*Lost* in an Alternative Reality." *Flow* Volume 4, No. 7 (2006) http://jot.communication.utexas.edu/flow/?jot=view&id=1927. An observant look at *Lost* and the development of ARGs.

Pearson, Roberta, ed. *Reading* Lost: *Perspectives on a Hit TV Show*. London: I. B. Tauris, 2009. The first academic book on the series. Heady stuff.

Porter, Lynnette and David Lavery. *Unlocking the Meaning of* Lost: *An Unauthorized Guide*. Naperville, IL: Sourcebooks, 2006, 2007. A brilliant investigation into all aspects of the series.

Stafford, Nikki. *Finding* Lost: *The Unofficial Guide*. Toronto: ECW Press, 2006, 2007, 2008. The second best comprehensive *Lost* guidebook.

TOP TEN MOVIES AND TELEVISION SERIES FOR *LOST* FANS

1. *Alias* (ABC, 2001–2005)
2. *Fringe* (FOX, 2008–)
3. *Lost Horizon* (Frank Capra, 1937) or *Brigadoon* (Vincente Minnelli, 1954)
4. *Nash Bridges* (CBS, 1996–2001)
5. *The Prisoner* (ITV, 1967–68)
6. The Original *Star Wars* Trilogy: *A New Hope* (George Lucas, 1977), *The Empire Strikes Back* (Irvin Kershner, 1980), *The Return of the Jedi* (Richard Marquand, 1983)
7. *Twilight Zone* (CBS, 1959–64)
8. *Twin Peaks* (ABC, 1990–91)
9. *The Wizard of Oz* (Victor Fleming, 1939)
10. *The X-Files* (FOX, 1993–2002)

TOP 10 *LOST* WEBSITES

ABC's Official *Lost* Site—http://abc.go.com/primetime/lost/index?pn=index: Needless to say, offers access not available elsewhere. Home to, among other resources, the *Lost* Book Club—http://abc.go.com/primetime/lost/index?pn=bookclub.

Doc Arzt and Friends' *Lost* Blog—http://www.docarzt.com/: A thought-provoking and informative site with contributions by many.

The Fuselage—http://thefuselage.com/: A pioneering website where *Lost*'s creative team interacts with fans.

Lost **Media**—http://lost-media.com/: A comprehensive clearing-house for tracking and watching the many appearances of *Lost* and its makers on TV and other media.

Lostpedia—http://www.lostpedia.com/wiki/Main_Page: An extraordinarily comprehensive reference work. One of the finest examples of the value of a Wiki and of the work of the "fan-scholar."

Onion TV Club *Lost* **Recaps**—http://www.avclub.com/tvclub/tvshow/lost,38/: Excellent episode recaps and speculation on a website that describes itself as "A virtual couch for people who sit too close to the screen."

The Society for the Study of *Lost*—http://www.loststudies.com/: A site for intellectual and in-depth looks at the deeper significance of *Lost* themes in a peer-reviewed online journal.

The Tail Section—http://www.thetailsection.com/: A smart and informative all-purpose *Lost* site.

Totally Lost—http://www.ew.com/ew/package/0,,1550612,00.html: Offers all of *Entertainment Weekly*'s *Lost* coverage, including Jeff Jensen's endless but illuminating theories and amusing videos with Jensen and Dan Snierson.

TVgasm's *Lost* **Page**—http://www.tvgasm.com/shows/lost/: Ack's episode recaps are the funniest ever.

TOP 10 *LOST* EPISODES: KEEPERS AND THOSE TO THROW BACK
10 Must-See *Lost* Episodes

1. 1.1 | 9/22/2004 | **Pilot** | Written by J. J. Abrams & Damon Lindelof and directed by J. J. Abrams

   High-quality production, riveting pace. This episode hooked us immediately on the series. This is not your typical series opener. J. J. Abrams' major contribution to the series he would abandon, and at the time, the most expensive pilot ever was worth every penny.

2. 1.4 | 10/13/2004 | **Walkabout** | Written by David Fury and directed by Bender

Though we were fascinated with *Lost* from the first minute, this Locke backstory was the episode that made us true believers. Written by *Buffy* alum David Fury and directed, of course, by Jack Bender (who helmed seven of our ten "must-sees").

3. 2.7 | 11/16/2005 | **The Other 48 Days** | Written by Lindelof & Cuse and directed by Eric Laneuville

     An interesting look at the story from a different perspective, and an excellent reenactment of the crash from the Island's perspective. Although we may have tired of the Tailies as a separate group, we appreciate the tie-ins from previous episodes and yet another way to interpret events we thought we understood. A virtuoso piece of television narrative.

4. 3.8 | 2/14/2007 | **Flashes Before Your Eyes** | Written by Lindelof & Drew Goddard; 4.5 | 2/28/08 | **The Constant** | Written by Lindelof & Cuse | Both directed by Bender

     In a series known for blowing our minds, these two episodes (which we are counting as one since they both deal with the Desmond/Penny pre-Island story) might be the most boggling (especially the moment in "Flashes" where Mrs. Hawking explains to Desmond why he can't marry Penelope). "Flashes" introduces the possibility of time travel, sets up the prophecy for Charlie's story arc, is a referential episode for later episodes, and further develops Desmond as an integral character. "Constant" completes the time-travel part of Desmond's story and lets us eavesdrop on Des' fateful Christmas Eve 2004 phone call.

5. 3.22–23 | 5/23/2007 | **Through the Looking Glass, Parts 1 and 2** | Written by Lindelof & Cuse and directed by Bender

     Excellent story involving all cast members, a "game changer" for the rest of the series (the flash-forwards to LA), foreshadowing of the castaways' future rescue from the Island. This episode sets up all kinds of character interactions for future episodes (e.g., Alex and Rousseau's reunion), brings back Walt—who apparently brings back Locke from the (near)dead, kills one of the original castaways, kills several Others (indicating a future shake-up, reorganization, or dissolution of the Others' society)—it's action packed, well acted, and very cool. Directed (again) by Bender and written by Darlton, this is the episode that saved the series for many fans.

6. 4.1 | 1/31/08 | **The Beginning of the End** | Written by Lindelof & Cuse and directed by Bender

    We love Hurley, and although it pains us to see him back at Santa Rosa (after a glorious car chase), we are glad he can chat with old friends. Back on the Island, the freighter folk arrive, and the castaways have to decide if they should go or stay. This episode gives Charlie fans some closure while opening up the story in lots of new directions in two time frames. Even if the Season Four opener truly is the beginning of the end, we are eager to see where we're going.

7. 4.12, 13, 14 | 5/15/08, 5/29/09 | **There's No Place Like Home (1, 2, 3)** | Written by Lindelof & Cuse and directed by Williams (4.12) and Bender (4.13–14)

    Three hours for the price of one episode—what a deal! Great Sawyer moments (shirtless or not), the long-awaited Desmond-Penny reunion, the loss of Michael and Jin (or so we thought at the time), Sun's meeting with Charles Widmore (thus potentially setting her up as a world-class "player"), Locke in a coffin, and a disappearing island! (And those were just the previews.)

8. 5.13 | 4/22/09 | **Some Like It Hoth** | Written by Melinda Hsu & Gregory Nations and directed by Bender

    Both funny (Hurley writes his own version of *The Empire Strikes Back*) and touching (Miles wrestles with abandonment issues and his encounter in 1977 with his father), full of pop culture references and surprising revelations, this episode hoth it all.

9. 5.14 | 4/29/09 | **The Variable** | Written by Kitsis & Horowitz and directed by Paul Edwards

    Daniel Faraday returns to the Island, and all hell breaks loose in this companion to "Flashes Before Your Eyes" and "The Constant," in which the Oxford physicist decides to test his "Whatever happened, happened" hypothesis by exploding Jughead. No episode of *Lost* has had more memorable flashbacks as we witness Eloise Hawking's manipulation of her son in order to guarantee he will be on the Island in 1977 so she can kill him ?!?

10. 5.16–17 | 5/13/09 | **The Incident, Parts 1 and 2** | Written by Lindelof & Cuse and directed by Bender

Once more, with only one season to go, *Lost* blows our minds in a season finale. We finally meet Jacob and his loophole-seeking nemesis, engaged in an age-old debate/chess match in which all the series' characters may be mere pawns. Locke turns out to be actually dead. Loophole revealed, Jacob is murdered—by Ben. Ilana and her team make their way to the shadow of the statue. Oh, and did we mention that Jughead goes off?

Ten Miserable *Lost* Episodes

1. 1.13 | 1/12/2005 | **Hearts & Minds** | Written by Cuse & Javier Grillo-Marxuach and directed by Rod Holcomb

Unless Shannon and Boone turn up in Season Six with a major payoff to this backstory, we don't see the need to revisit this episode.

2. 2.11 | 1/18/2006 | **The Hunting Party** | Written by Elizabeth Sarnoff & Christine M. Kim and directed by Williams

If this is Jack as a warlord, we really don't want to see more. He's vindictive *but* ineffective. Asking Ana Lucia to help him build an army isn't one of his more endearing traits.

3. 2.15 | 3/1/2006 | **Maternity Leave** | Written by Dawn Robertson Kelly & Matt Ragghianti and directed by Bender

We like William Mapother as an actor. Ethan Rom, not so much. And what happened to the "quarantine" and "injections" subplots? Couldn't we have figured out that misdirection a little sooner?

4. 3.2 | 10/11/2006 | **The Glass Ballerina** | Written by Jeff Pinkner & Drew Goddard and directed by Edwards

Kate and Sawyer join a prison work gang. We miss Paul Newman. Young Sun shows us that she takes after daddy. This isn't a terrible episode, but in hindsight, we would've moved the story along a little faster.

5. 3.4 | 10/25/2006 | **Every Man for Himself** | Written by Kitsis & Horowitz and directed by Williams

    Sawyer torture. Possible bunny torture. No. Just no. We like *Lost* much better when the writers think outside the metal box.

6. 3.6 | 11/8/2006 | **I Do** | Written by Lindelof & Cuse and directed by Tucker Gates

    We don't. Kate's marriage to Captain Malcolm Reynolds was promoted by Darlton as a great episode, but it wasn't. That it finally put an end to the Season Three "miniseries" experiment was the best thing about it.

7. 3.9 | 2/21/2007 | **Stranger in a Strange Land** | Written by Sarnoff & Kim and directed by Paris Barclay

    Jack gets a tattoo on an exotic island. So did Lynnette, but it didn't warrant an episode. (We had some problems with the beginning of Season Three, didn't we?)

8. 3.12 | 3/14/2007 | **Per Avion** | Written by Kim & Jordan Rosenberg and directed by Edwards

    Lost's writing team never seems to know what to do with poor, dear Claire.

9. 4.10 | 5/1/08 | **Something Nice Back Home** | Written by Kitsis & Horowitz and directed by Williams

    They say doctors make the worst patients. And doctors as patients make for dull episodes.

10. 4.8 | 3/20/08 | **Meet Kevin Johnson** | Written by Sarnoff and Brian Vaughan and directed by Williams

    We liked Michael. In Season One.

Lost Episode Guide

Seq. #	Ep. #	Air Date	Title	Writer(s)	Director
1	1.1	9/22/2004	Pilot, Part 1	J. J. Abrams & Damon Lindelof	Abrams
2	1.2	9/29/2004	Pilot, Part 2	Abrams & Lindelof	Abrams
3	1.3	10/6/2004	Tabula Rasa	Lindelof	Jack Bender
4	1.4	10/13/2004	Walkabout	David Fury	Bender
5	1.5	10/20/2004	White Rabbit	Christian Taylor	Kevin Hooks
6	1.6	10/27/2004	House of the Rising Sun	Javier Grillo-Marxuach	Michael Zinberg
7	1.7	11/3/2004	The Moth	Jennifer Johnson & Paul Dini	Bender
8	1.8	11/10/2004	Confidence Man	Lindelof	Tucker Gates
9	1.9	11/17/2004	Solitary	Fury	Greg Yaitanes
10	1.10	12/1/2004	Raised by Another	Lynne E. Litt	Marita Grabiak

Seq. #	Ep. #	Air Date	Title	Writer(s)	Director
11	1.11	12/8/2004	All the Best Cowboys Have Daddy Issues	Grillo-Marxuach	Stephen Williams
12	1.12	1/5/2005	Whatever the Case May Be	Lindelof & Johnson	Bender
13	1.13	1/12/2005	Hearts & Minds	Carlton Cuse & Grillo-Marxuach	Rod Holcomb
14	1.14	1/19/2005	Special	Fury	Yaitanes
15	1.15	2/9/2005	Homecoming	Lindelof	Hooks
16	1.16	2/16/2005	Outlaws	Drew Goddard	Bender
17	1.17	2/23/2005	…In Translation	Grillo-Marxuach & Leonard Dick	Gates
18	1.18	3/2/2005	Numbers	Fury & Brent Fletcher	Daniel Attias
19	1.19	3/30/2005	Deus Ex Machina	Lindelof & Cuse	Robert Mandel
20	1.20	4/6/2005	Do No Harm	Janet Tamaro	Williams
21	1.21	5/4/2005	The Greater Good (aka Sides)	Dick	David Grossman

Seq. #	Ep. #	Air Date	Title	Writer(s)	Director
22	1.22	5/11/2005	Born to Run	Edward Kitsis, Adam Horowitz, & Grillo-Marxuach	Gates
23	1.23	5/18/2005	Exodus, Part 1	Lindelof & Cuse	Bender
24	1.24	5/25/2005	Exodus, Part 2	Lindelof & Cuse	Bender
25	2.1	9/21/2005	Man of Science, Man of Faith	Lindelof	Bender
26	2.2	9/28/2005	Adrift	Dick & Steven Maeda	Williams
27	2.3	10/5/2005	Orientation	Grillo-Marxuach & Craig Wright	Bender
28	2.4	10/12/2005	Everybody Hates Hugo	Horowitz & Kitsis	Alan Taylor
29	2.5	10/19/2005	…And Found	Lindelof & Cuse	Williams
30	2.6	11/9/2005	Abandoned	Elizabeth Sarnoff	Adam Davidson
31	2.7	11/16/2005	The Other 48 Days	Lindelof & Cuse	Eric Laneuville
32	2.8	11/23/2005	Collision	Dick & Grillo-Marxuach	Williams
33	2.9	11/30/2005	What Kate Did	Maeda & Wright	Paul Edwards

Seq. #	Ep. #	Air Date	Title	Writer(s)	Director
34	2.10	1/11/2006	The 23rd Psalm	Lindelof & Cuse	Matt Earl Beesley
35	2.11	1/18/2006	The Hunting Party	Sarnoff & Christine M. Kim	Williams
36	2.12	1/25/2006	Fire + Water	Horowitz & Kitsis	Bender
37	2.13	2/8/2006	The Long Con	Maeda & Dick	Roxann Dawson
38	2.14	2/15/2006	One of Them	Lindelof & Cuse	Williams
39	2.15	3/1/2006	Maternity Leave	Dawn Robertson Kelly & Matt Ragghianti	Bender
40	2.16	3/22/2006	The Whole Truth	Kim & Sarnoff	Karen Gaviola
41	2.17	3/29/2006	Lockdown	Lindelof & Cuse	Williams
42	2.18	4/5/2006	Dave	Kitsis & Horowitz	Bender
43	2.19	4/12/2006	S.O.S.	Maeda & Dick	Laneuville
44	2.20	5/3/2006	Two for the Road	Kim & Sarnoff	Edwards
45	2.21	5/10/2006	?	Cuse & Lindelof	Dean Sarafian
46	2.22	5/17/2006	Three Minutes	Kitsis & Horowitz	Williams

Seq. #	Ep. #	Air Date	Title	Writer(s)	Director
47	2.23	5/24/2006	Live To-gether, Die Alone, Part 1	Lindelof & Cuse	Bender
48	2.24	5/24/2006	Live To-gether, Die Alone, Part 2	Lindelof & Cuse	Bender
49	3.1	10/4/2006	A Tale of Two Cities	Abrams & Lindelof	Bender
50	3.2	10/11/2006	The Glass Ballerina	Jeff Pinkner & Goddard	Edwards
51	3.3	10/18/2006	Further Instructions	Cuse & Sarnoff	Williams
52	3.4	10/25/2006	Every Man for Himself	Kitsis & Horowitz	Williams
53	3.5	11/1/2006	The Cost of Living	Monica Owusu-Breen & Alison Schapker	Bender
54	3.6	11/8/2006	I Do	Lindelof & Cuse	Gates
55	3.7	2/7/2007	Not in Portland	Cuse & Pinkner	Williams
56	3.8	2/14/2007	Flashes Before Your Eyes	Lindelof & Goddard	Bender
57	3.9	2/21/2007	Stranger in a Strange Land	Sarnoff & Kim	Paris Barclay
58	3.10	2/28/2007	Trisha Tanaka Is Dead	Kitsis & Horowitz	Laneuville

Seq. #	Ep. #	Air Date	Title	Writer(s)	Director
59	3.11	3/7/2007	Enter 77	Lindelof & Cuse	Williams
60	3.12	3/14/2007	Per Avion	Kim & Jordan Rosenberg	Edwards
61	3.13	3/21/2007	The Man from Tallahassee	Goddard & Pinkner	Bender
62	3.14	3/28/2007	Exposé	Kitsis & Horowitz	Williams
63	3.15	3/4/2007	Left Behind	Lindelof & Sarnoff	Gaviola
64	3.16	4/11/2007	One of Us	Cuse & Goddard	Bender
65	3.17	4/18/2007	Catch-22	Pinkner & Brian K. Vaughan	Williams
66	3.18	4/25/2007	D.O.C.	Kitsis & Horowitz	Frederick E. O. Toye
67	3.19	5/2/2007	The Brig	Lindelof & Cuse	Laneuville
68	3.20	5/9/2007	The Man Behind the Curtain	Sarnoff & Goddard	Bobby Roth
69	3.21	5/16/2007	Greatest Hits	Kitsis & Horowitz	Williams
70	3.22	5/23/2007	Through the Looking Glass, Part 1	Lindelof & Cuse	Bender

Seq. #	Ep. #	Air Date	Title	Writer(s)	Director
71	3.23	5/23/2007	Through the Looking Glass, Part 2	Lindelof & Cuse	Bender
72	4.1	1/31/08	The Beginning of the End	Lindelof & Cuse	Bender
73	4.2	2/7/08	Confirmed Dead	Goddard & Vaughan	Williams
74	4.3	2/14/08	The Economist	Kitsis & Horowitz	Bender
75	4.4	2/21/08	Eggtown	Sarnoff & Gregory Nations	Williams
76	4.5	2/28/08	The Constant	Lindelof & Cuse	Bender
77	4.6	3/6/08	The Other Woman	Goddard & Kim	Laneuville
78	4.7	3/13/08	Ji Yeon	Kitsis & Horowitz	Williams
79	4.8	3/20/08	Meet Kevin Johnson	Sarnoff and Vaughan	Williams
80	4.9	4/24/08	The Shape of Things to Come	Vaughan & Goddard	Bender
81	4.10	5/1/08	Something Nice Back Home	Kitsis & Horowitz	Williams
82	4.11	5/8/08	Cabin Fever	Sarnoff & Kyle Pennington	Edwards

Seq. #	Ep. #	Air Date	Title	Writer(s)	Director
83	4.12	5/15/08	There's No Place Like Home, Part 1	Lindelof & Cuse	Williams
84-85	4.13-14	5/29/08	There's No Place Like Home, Parts 2 and 3	Lindelof & Cuse	Bender
86	5.1	1/21/09	Because You Left	Lindelof & Cuse	Williams
87	5.2	1/21/09	The Lie	Kitsis and Horowitz	Bender
88	5.3	1/28/09	Jughead	Sarnoff & Paul Zbyszewski	Holcomb
89	5.4	2/4/09	The Little Prince	Vaughan & Melinda Hsu	Williams
90	5.5	2/11/09	This Place Is Death	Kitsis & Horowitz	Edwards
91	5.6	2/18/09	316	Lindelof & Cuse	Williams
92	5.7	2/25/09	The Life and Death of Jeremy Bentham	Lindelof & Cuse	Bender
93	5.8	3/4/09	LaFleur	Sarnoff & Pennington	Mark Goldman
94	5.9	3/18/09	Namaste	Vaughan & Zbyszewski	Bender
95	5.10	3/25/09	He's Our You	Kitsis & Horowitz	Yaitanes

Seq. #	Ep. #	Air Date	Title	Writer(s)	Director
96	5.11	4/1/09	Whatever Happened, Happened	Cuse & Lindelof	Roth
97	5.12	4/8/09	Dead Is Dead	Vaughan & Sarnoff	Williams
98	5.13	4/22/09	Some Like It Hoth	Hsu & Nations	Bender
99	5.14	4/29/09	The Variable	Kitsis & Horowitz	Edwards
100	5.15	5/6/09	Follow the Leader	Zbyszewski & Sarnoff	Williams
101	5.16	5/13/09	The Incident, Part 1	Lindelof & Cuse	Bender
102	5.17	5/20/09	The Incident, Part 2	Lindelof & Cuse	Bender

INDEX

ABOUT THE AUTHORS

Lynnette Porter is an associate professor at Embry-Riddle Aeronautical University. She has collaborated with David Lavery on books about *Lost*, *Heroes*, and *Battlestar Galactica*, as well as having contributed chapters and written books about *The Lord of the Rings*. She is frequently a speaker at scholarly and fan conventions internationally. During visits to Oahu in 2009, she took the photographs for this book.

David Lavery holds a chair in film and television at Brunel University in London. The author/coauthor/editor/coeditor of scores of essays and twelve books (three with Lynnette Porter) on such television series as *Twin Peaks*, *The X-Files*, *The Sopranos*, *Buffy the Vampire Slayer*, *Deadwood*, *Seinfeld*, *My So-Called Life*, and *Heroes*, he has lectured on American television around the world.